CENTRAL
ASIA
AND THE
NEW GLOBAL
ECONOMY

Also from *M. E. Sharpe*

CENTRAL ASIA IN TRANSITION
Dilemmas of Political and Economic Development
Boris Rumer, Editor

CENTRAL ASIA
The Challenges of Independence
Boris Rumer and Stanislav Zhukov, Editors

CENTRAL
ASIA
AND THE
NEW GLOBAL
ECONOMY

EDITED BY
BORIS RUMER

M.E. Sharpe

Armonk, New York
London, England

Copyright © 2000 by M. E. Sharpe, Inc.

Library of Congress Cataloging-in-Publication Data

Central Asia and the new global economy / edited by Boris Rumer : translated by
Gregory Freeze
    p. cm.
  Includes bibliographical references and index.
  ISBN 0-7656-0629-1 (alk. paper)
   1. Asia, Central—Economic conditions—1991– 2. Asia, Central—Politics and
government—1991– 3. Post-communism—Asia, Central. 4. Asia, Central—Foreign
relations. I. Rumer, Boris Z.

HC420.3. C44 2000
338.958—dc21   00-026579

Printed in the United States of America

Contents

List of Tables

Preface

At the end of the twentieth century, the situation in post-Soviet Central Asia has become increasingly unstable. After less than a decade of independent development, the countries of this region are inexorably descending into the category of failed countries. Their economies, oriented toward the exploitation and export of natural resources, are now mired in profound and protracted crisis. To be sure, Central Asia still elicits the world's attention, primarily because of the hydrocarbon resources of the Caspian Sea. But the prospects for tapping these resources, like other natural resources in the region, depend on whether these countries are able to preserve domestic stability and the status quo in their mutual relations. The ruling regimes, to this point, have been able to maintain their control over society, but now are emitting signals that tensions—both within each state and among them—are steadily intensifying. The desperate impoverishment of the vast majority of people here directly erodes long-term social stability and weakens their resistance to the virus of aggressive Islamic fundamentalism that now threatens to engulf the region.

There are growing signs that Central Asia may indeed become the arena for geopolitical games and what Samuel Huntington has called a "clash of civilizations." At stake is a region with four million square kilometers (equal to the size of India and Pakistan), populated with sixty million inhabitants, and located at the strategic crossroads between Russia, China, Iran, Pakistan, and Afghanistan. Given the fact that the countries of Central Asia are virtually defenseless against foreign aggression, the secular regimes here curry support simultaneously in Moscow, Washington, and Beijing, all the while, of course, maneuvering between the contradictory interests of these potential benefactors. Significantly, despite all the fundamental differences in interests, neither Russia nor America nor China has reason to favor destabilization in Central Asia. Should such a breakdown occur, it would inevitably draw them into a treacherous whirlpool of conflict—with unforeseeable consequences and a high risk of direct confrontation between these great powers.

The multifaceted complexity of the Central Asian problem, together with the heightened importance of what happens here for geopolitical stability in the world, makes it essential to examine both the political and economic aspects of development in this region.

With each year, it is becoming increasingly apparent that an approach to Central Asia as an integrated region is simply irrational and groundless. In both political and economic terms, the countries of Central Asia are drifting apart from one another: pulled in the wake of various forces, they act individually and autonomously—regardless of periodic bombast about "regional solidarity." Each of them, on an entirely individual basis, plots its course in the stormy seas of world politics and seeks to find its own special niche in the global economy. Hence, while it is still important to examine the problems facing the region as a whole, the principal focus of analysis should be the development and strategies of each individual state.

The complex approach—one that takes into account both economics and politics, both regional and individual-country dynamics—lies at the basis of this volume, as indeed was the case in the two preceding works (*Central Asia in Transition* [1996] and *Central Asia: The Challenges of Independence* [1998]). The current volume explores a number of critical issues: the emergence and underlying causes of tension among the states of Central Asia; the principal foreign and domestic problems confronting the three main states in the region (Turkmenistan, Kazakhstan, and Uzbekistan); their relations with the United States, Russia, and China; the economic dynamics of the 1990s; the basic problems of market transition and adaptation to the globalization of the world economy; the question of foreign investment; the prospects for Kazakhstan and Uzbekistan to join the World Trade Organization (and the potential consequences for their domestic economies); and the development of economic ties with the countries of the Asian-Pacific region. A final chapter also analyzes the midterm economic prospects for the countries of Central Asia. A close analysis of these cardinal problems can shed considerable light on what awaits the countries of Central Asia in the foreseeable future.

It bears noting that this book seeks to elucidate the broader, long-term structural patterns, problems, and process, with less concern about the impact of short-term fluctuations in the price structure for Central Asian imports and exports. This book was written in 1999 and relied upon information on the previous decade that was then available for economic analysis. To be sure, in 1999–2000 the world witnessed sharp fluctuations in global prices (most notably, the spike in oil prices), which of course had an impact on Central Asian export earnings, but did not alter the long-term structural factors elucidated here.[1]

Note

1. For an explanation of why short-term price increases for the Central Asian exports will not have a lasting impact on the decreasing price tendency for hydrocarbons and cotton, see: Amy Myers Jaffe and Robert A. Manning, "The Shocks of a World of Cheap Oil," *Foreign Affairs*, January–February 2000, pp. 16–29; A. Koksharov, "Khlopok rastet v tsene," *Ekspert*, 2000, no. 10: 7.

Acknowledgments

The editor and contributors would like to express their gratitude to the Sasakawa Peace Foundation and especially to Messrs. Akira Iriyama, Takashi Shirasu, and Lau Sim-Yee, for the support that has made the present volume possible. The studies presented here are the product of a multi-year project sponsored by the Sasakawa Peace Foundation and devoted to the problem of transition in post-Soviet Central Asia. At various stages, the research from this project has been the focus of animated, productive discussion by scholars from the United States, Great Britain, Japan, China, Korea, Russia, and Central Asia at international conferences convened in Issyk-Kul', Tokyo, Washington, DC, Oxford, Tashkent, and Ashgabat. The authors of the present volume have profited much from commentaries and presentations at these conferences.

A great debt of gratitude is also due to Professor Gregory L. Freeze for help in preparing the final text, and to the editorial staff of M.E. Sharpe for their expert assistance in the publication of this volume. The editor would also like to recognize the support of his home institution— the Davis Center for Russian Studies at Harvard University, where it has been his good fortune to work for the last two decades.

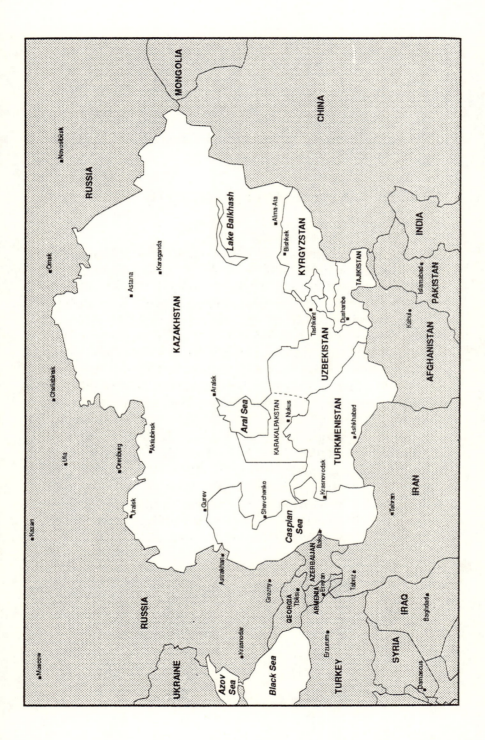

CENTRAL ASIA
AND THE
NEW GLOBAL
ECONOMY

1

Economic Crisis and Growing Intraregional Tensions

Boris Rumer

At the end of the 1990s, two distinct tendencies emerged as the dominant features of contemporary Central Asia: a degradation in the social and economic spheres (now on the path to becoming a full-blown depression), and mounting tension in the relations among states in the region. The root cause of both tendencies is profound economic crisis, which, as has become increasingly obvious, the existing regimes can neither resolve nor even contain. These two tendencies threaten not only to unleash a massive social explosion (which appears all the more likely amidst the increasing importance of the Islamic factor), but also to trigger interstate conflicts that could result in a general "Balkanization" of this vast region in the heart of Eurasia.

In the first half of the 1990s, it was generally thought that the principal dynamics of change in the Central Asian countries consisted of two key processes: (1) the transition from the Soviet command-mobilization economy to a market-based system, and (2) the establishment of institutions of political democracy. In the span of less than a decade, it has become perfectly clear (if one dispenses with ideological fantasies) that the real constellation of coordinates for Central Asia indicates neither the triumphant formation of a market economy nor an inexorable process of democratization. Rather, the primary dynamics in this region are fundamentally different: economic degradation, a precipitous decline in the standard of living, a dismantling of the social infrastructure, and the consolidation of authoritarian regimes that are based on personal rule and bear scant resemblance to democracy. In terms of their level of development, all five Central Asian states are rapidly hurtling downward and appear fated to join the ranks of the poor countries of the world—with all the attendant consequences.

I. From Regional Unity to Regional Confrontation

The Social and Economic Crisis

During the 1990s, the countries of post-Soviet Central Asia had to traverse a tortuous, twisted path—one that led them from a euphoria of unbounded hopes to a mood of profound despair and disenchantment. The exhilaration that accompanied the sudden (and unexpected) acquisition of independence at the start of the decade has given way to intense public frustration and a pervasive economic crisis.

In the years 1991–98, the level of economic activity plunged catastrophically—by 39 percent in Kazakhstan and Kyrgyzstan, 45 percent in Turkmenistan, and 66 percent in Tajikistan.[1] The main exception to this pattern was Uzbekistan, where the gross domestic product (GDP) decreased by less than 10 percent during this period. Although in 1995–96 that country even exhibited some signs of modest economic growth, those gains are highly misleading: Uzbekistan has actually been rebuilding the economic model of the former Soviet Union, a policy that can only, sooner or later, lead to stagnation and perhaps even collapse.

This general economic crisis in Central Asia has been unfolding against a background of continuous demographic growth: the economic crisis notwithstanding, the population continues to increase at exceedingly high rates. Thus, in the 1990s, the annual rate of population increase was 1.5 percent in Kyrgyzstan, approximately 2 percent in Turkmenistan, and more than 2.5 percent in Uzbekistan and even in Tajikistan (which has been rent by a decade of war and ceaseless military conflict).[2] In the next fifteen to twenty years, demographic growth in this region (with the exception of Kazakhstan) is expected to continue at a high rate.

The incessant demographic growth, given the simultaneous process of rapid economic decline (especially in the most modern spheres of production), has had the effect of concentrating an ever greater proportion of the labor force in agriculture and in the urban service sphere.

However, both sectors (and especially agriculture) were already over-burdened with a surfeit of labor, a problem already apparent back in the 1980s. It is hardly surprising therefore that, in every sector and in the economy as a whole, the productivity of labor has fallen dramatically.

The economic crisis has also seriously aggravated the intensity of social problems. By the end of the 1990s, the main mass of population in the region fell into absolute poverty. Although precise data are wanting, rough calculations indicate that up to 70 or even 80 percent of the population of Kazakhstan and Kyrgyzstan are now living in poverty. The proportion is still higher in Tajikistan, where no less than 95 percent now fall under the poverty line. Reliable data on poverty in Uzbekistan and Turkmenistan have not been published; the available figures are distorted by the fact that the national currencies are not convertible. In any case, however, the situation in these two countries is not substantially better than that reported in Kazakhstan and Kyrgyzstan.

The poorest strata of the population are concentrated primarily in rural areas. In 1998 and 1999, however, a wave of new devaluations of the national currencies in Kazakhstan and Kyrgyzstan significantly increased the level of poverty in urban areas as well. Nor is the problem limited to those two states: Turkmenistan, Tajikistan, and especially Uzbekistan may face the necessity of making an analogous devaluation of their currencies. Hence these countries share the prospect of an explosive increase in poverty among their urban populations.

The escalating impoverishment of the population, when coupled with the dismantling of state services (in education, welfare, and especially medicine), has contributed to an uncontrolled spread of diseases like tuberculosis and hepatitis. Indeed, in the past two years, Kazakhstan even reported some localized outbreaks of the bubonic plague. But the prospects for combating these negative tendencies appear even more dismal. That is because the standard prescription for macroeconomic policy, as recommended by the International Monetary Fund (IMF), still calls for the Central Asian states to reduce demand by making sharp reductions in the government's budgetary expenditures. In reality, such budget-slashing inevitably means a further reduction in spending for the social sphere, including public health and medicine.

Political Consequences

As many indicators make clear, powerful pressures are building for a social cataclysm in the region—openly in the cases of Kazakhstan,

Kyrgyzstan, and Tajikistan, and covertly in the cases of Uzbekistan and Turkmenistan. This peril cannot fail, of course, to have an impact on the political processes in these five countries. To this point, the most sensational expressions of this turmoil and tension include the series of explosions in Tashkent, the capital of Uzbekistan (February 1999), and the activity of Islamic militants in Kyrgyzstan (fall 1999). The authorities there hastened to ascribe this and similar incidents to the growing power of "Islamic fundamentalists" (or, to invoke the jargon now popular in the post-Soviet realm, Wahhabites).

However, the roots of these Uzbek explosions and the rising activism of the so-called Wahhabites in this region have little to do with Islam itself. Rather, these phenomena have their roots in the catastrophic destitution that is now overwhelming the majority of people in this region. For the general populace, at least, it is perfectly obvious that the coming decades do not offer the slightest prospect for an improvement in their living conditions. It is hardly surprising therefore that a highly politicized Islam (to be sure, one that also exploits the religious sensibilities of believers) has become a powerful force throughout Central Asia, and especially in Tajikistan, Uzbekistan, and Kyrgyzstan.

The Consolidation of "Crony Capitalism"

A complex set of processes, fraught with serious conflict, is also reconfiguring political authority and how it functions. At a superficial level, all five countries would appear to have stabilized a democratic political order. Thus, the populace regularly elects the presidents and parliaments and does so in accordance with constitutionally defined norms and in compliance with a democratic procedure based on direct, equal, and secret balloting. In fact, however, the real situation is quite different. Namely, behind this democratic facade, powerful presidents have established regimes of personal rule and have not shied away from using all the means necessary to consolidate and reinforce their power. For example, rather than hold regularly scheduled elections, they feel so uncertain of electoral support that they have resorted to special referenda to extend the presidential term beyond its prescribed limit.

How this unfolds, to be sure, varies from one republic to the next. In Turkmenistan, President Saparmurad Niiazov has firmly entrenched his personal rule, bearing the title of "Turkmenbashi" (father of all Turkmen). But the situation is not all that encouraging even in Kyrgyzstan and

Kazakhstan, which are widely regarded as the states that correspond most fully to the standard Western definition of political democracy. Here too the presidents have, in fact, significantly expanded their executive powers. Thus, in both Kyrgyzstan and Kazakhstan the head of state does not feel bound by constitutional norms and often intercedes in the political process to redirect it in ways that suit his own interests.

Still worse is the fact that, in most post-Soviet states (those in Central Asia being no exception), the attempt to separate power from property has failed. On the contrary, in the course of privatization in 1992–97, the presidents of these countries relied upon the levers of state power and conducted the redistribution of property and economic assets so as to benefit their immediate entourage (and, above all, their own relatives).

To be sure, "crony capitalism" is a virtually universal and defining characteristic of most developing countries. In this sense, the Central Asian countries correspond entirely to a "third-world" paradigm of development. However, as the experience of these same developing countries amply demonstrates, such political-economic structures to regulate power and property can claim neither longevity nor the capacity to ensure continuity in the historical process.

The Lesser of Two Evils

Thus, eight years of independence have not only failed to bring an improvement to the lives of ordinary people but, on the contrary, have caused a drastic decline in their standard of living—indeed, reducing it to a level below that of the Soviet era. Year in and year out, the authoritarian leaders of Central Asia have promised fundamental economic reform and the liberalization of civil society, but all these declarations have proven to be nothing more then empty rhetorical bombast. By now, these promissory notes are so badly overdue that the Central Asian regimes—which ensconced themselves in power during the post-Soviet era—can no longer deny their political bankruptcy.

Nevertheless, one must also concede that these regimes, for all their oppressiveness, have also played a positive role: thus far they have been able to maintain the status quo in the region, to stifle eruptions of interethnic conflict, and to prevent new explosions of popular discontent. This fact explains the West's ambivalence toward the Central Asian regimes, which range from the relatively liberal (but still fundamentally authoritarian) regime in Kyrgyzstan to the unvarnished totalitarian dictatorship in Turkmenistan. Whatever misgivings one might have toward these undemocratic regimes, it is clear that they alone prevent this region from dissolving into bloody chaos, and that they alone can counteract a host of negative dynamics—such as artificial state boundaries, ethnic enclaves, and the build-up of interethnic animosity.

Realpolitik—a choice of real outcomes, not subjective preferences— requires that the West make a calculated judgment in defining policy toward the regimes of Central Asia. To be sure, one option is to choose a compromising policy and do business with these regimes, while making periodic protests against any major excesses. In effect, that has essentially been Western policy to this point. A second option for the West is to withhold recognition and support for these regimes and, in particular, to deny them material assistance. However ideologically self-satisfying that might be, that policy runs the risk of precipitating the collapse of these regimes and thereby opening the door to massive political and social destabilization, with all the untoward and unpredictable consequences that this outcome would entail.

In choosing between these two alternatives, Western powers might well keep in mind the instructive case of Yugoslavia. It bears recalling that, with good reason, everyone in the West once roundly condemned the dictatorial regime of Marshal Tito. With the advantage of hindsight, it is now clear that only his authoritarian regime was capable of preventing the tragedies of first Bosnia, and now Kosovo. Should not the Serbs, Albanians, and others feel genuine nostalgia for the Tito era, especially its later years? And was it so onerous for the West, NATO, and Washington to deal with Tito; that is, with someone who for nearly forty years acted as a bulwark of stability in the Balkans?

The Myth of Regional Unity

At the dawn of the post-Soviet era, the union of the five newly independent states of Central Asia at first appeared to be entirely natural and realistic. Indeed, many regarded unity as the most important precondition for political stability and economic development in the region. This belief in the possibility of economic integration and political solidarity tended to emphasize several factors: a shared Islamic faith, a common Turkic language (except for Tajikistan), territorial unity, and an integrated infrastructure. These new states also had a similar leadership: namely, Russified indigenous ethnic elites, who were formerly members of the upper ranks of the republic "partocracy" and who, in principle, should serve as a unifying factor in all five states.

By the end of the 1990s, however, the hopes for any kind of unity had receded into oblivion. The notion that confessional and cultural unity could play an important role has proven to be superficial and naive. Although often lumped together by outsiders as a single entity, the five states of Central Asia are anything but homogenous. Nor even is each individual state a coherent "nation-state." Above all, their state boundaries are neither historical nor geographic, but the product of artificial map-making that began with the prerevolutionary Russian state and became positively deliberate and systematic in the Stalin era. Moscow arbitrarily redefined ethnic groups and recarved borders in a transparent attempt at *divide et impera*. These borders capriciously intersected ethnic enclaves, turning Central Asia into a patchwork quilt rent by complex disputes (ethnic, regional, and tribal) over land, water, and natural resources. The veneer of a common religion and, to some extent, Turkic language only conceals the deep divisions below—territorial conflict, interethnic tensions, clan rivalries, and social antagonism. As a result, the fault lines here run far more deeply than the putative common interests and the purported will for a united front to address their common challenges and problems.

As ethnic elites built their states and consolidated the authority of their leaders, each of the republics came to define its own special political and economic interests. The net effect of this process was to drive the general impulse for regional solidarity into the background. As centrifugal forces gained ascendancy over centripetal forces, each leader began to play his own game and pursue his own interests.

The breakup of the Soviet Union actually served to accelerate this regional disintegration. After all, it had been far easier to be friends when the "Center"—that is, Moscow—had the final say on the allocation of investments, material resources, and quotas for water usage. All these assets came from a "common pot" and, in any event, their distribution did not depend upon the will of individual republics. When disputes did arise, the sides appealed to Moscow, which quickly and conclusively resolved the matter. Things are quite different now: although the elites of each country are now their own boss, there is no superior authority to whom they can appeal. Without Moscow to serve as supreme arbitrator and judge, all the contradictions dividing these countries have burst into the open. Above all, the post-Soviet era has allowed differences in the economic potential of individual Central Asian countries to become clearly apparent.

And these differences in the economic potential of the various Central Asian states are indeed prodigious. By tapping their mineral resources, three countries—Kazakhstan, Uzbekistan, and Turkmenistan—are essentially capable of surviving on their own. Tajikistan and Kyrgyzstan, by contrast, are much poorer and have far less potential; they simply do not have sufficient natural resources to sustain independent economic development. To be sure, both these countries do possess significant reserves of mineral resources and have enormous hydroelectric capacities at their disposal; hence they do have some prospects for economic growth. Nevertheless, for the present and for the foreseeable future, neither Tajikistan nor Kyrgyzstan can survive without substantial assistance from their neighbors. And, for that very reason, these same neighbors—Kazakhstan, Uzbekistan, and Turkmenistan—have little interest in regional economic integration, since that would require them to become donors and patrons for their two less well-endowed, less prosperous neighbors.

At their frequent summits, the leaders of Kazakhstan, Uzbekistan, and Kyrgyzstan have made declarations about the creation of a Central Asian economic union. Thus, in 1994 they established an "Intergovernmental Council" consisting of the heads of state. They also agreed to create a "single economic space" of the three countries and to dismantle the customs barriers that divide them.

But what is the practical result of all this? Does anything substantial stand behind these gestures? Thus far, at least, precious little. This is entirely understandable, for Central Asia simply lacks objective preconditions for regional unity: it has neither a common export specialization (as in the Middle East), nor a shared interest in a single market (as in Western Europe), nor huge investment resources from one of its component members as in the case of the North American Free Trade Agreement (NAFTA). Nor do the states of Central Asia have mutually complementary economic structures to reinforce any centripetal tendencies.

The states of Central Asia follow economic strategies that, to a large degree, are incompatible. Whereas Kazakhstan and Kyrgyzstan carried out a policy of reducing the state's regulatory role in the economy, Uzbekistan pursued a contrary course. In Turkmenistan, the state structure and economic policy have taken the form of a voluntaristic, Eastern variant of "Leaderism." It should be painfully evident that this institutional discordance can hardly contribute to the process of drawing these five states closer together in the economic sphere.

Far from leading toward closer regional ties, 1999 became a year of unprecedented economic confrontation among the states of Central Asia. Once these countries had reoriented all production with any semblance of viability and vitality toward export, the economic dynamics of the region became totally subject to the conditions prevailing on the world markets for such commodities as hydrocarbons, cotton, and metals. Although this tendency affected all the Central Asian states, it had a lesser impact on Uzbekistan. In any event, the high level of export and import quotas (which constitute a distinctive feature of all five of the Central Asian states) has left all of them essentially defenseless in the face of economic shocks from the outside. That vulnerability to foreign conditions is further magnified by the fact that the investment process in the Central Asian economies has also come to depend increasingly upon the influx of foreign capital. The simple fact is that the states of Central Asia lack any substantial domestic potential to propel their economic development. In addition, the dismal macroeconomic situation of recent years has been aggravated by the geographic isolation of the region and its remoteness from the main developed trade centers of the modern world.

The resumption of an economic recession (itself a response to the financial crisis that gripped the Asian importer-states), together with the fall in the demand and prices for Central Asian exports, has irrevocably shattered the mirage of regional economic unity. This most recent downturn has exposed the basic contradictions in interests and unleashed a conflict over the mutual claims and grievances that have gradually accumulated over the years. The disputes erupted in those spheres where the economic interests of the different states intersected: trade, energy, transportation, and water.

Economic Collision

The Trade War

In early 1999, the states of Central Asia began to impose severe restrictions and customs duties on imports. Thus, in February 1999, Kazakhstan established limits on the import of goods (primarily foodstuffs) from Russia, Uzbekistan, and Kyrgyzstan; Kazakhstan also levied a 200 percent customs duty on imports from Uzbekistan and Kyrgyzstan (not without grounds, complaining about the need to shield domestic pro-ducers from the dumping practices of these two neighbors). In July 1999, Kazakhstan introduced an export restriction on the delivery of fuel oil to Russia and Kyrgyzstan, both of which desperately needed this fuel for the coming harvests. It bears noting that Kazakhstan and Kyrgyzstan are members of a customs union with Russia and Belarus. Uzbekistan also established analogous trade barriers against goods from Kazakhstan and Kyrgyzstan. President Askar Akaev of Kyrgyzstan has accused his neighbors of organizing a trade blockade against his small state. More-over, he attributes these actions to the fact that Kyrgyzstan has already become a member of the World Trade Organization (WTO), a fact that provoked "an unfavorable reaction from his neighbors."[3] Protectionist policy became the defining factor in the economic relations of the Cen-tral Asian countries and has reduced trade among them to a minimum.

The Transportation Conflict

Simultaneous with the trade problem, a "transportation war" erupted between Kazakhstan (on one side) and Uzbekistan and Kyrgyzstan (on the other). At the bottom of this conflict is the fact that the rail connec-tions from Uzbekistan and Kyrgyzstan to Russia (indeed, this is their primary route for passenger and cargo carriage) must pass through the territory of Kazakhstan. The problem is that Uzbekistan and Kyrgyzstan have accumulated large arrears in the payment due for transit through Kazakhstan and have proposed to pay off the debt in kind, not hard currency. There was indeed a precedent for settling accounts in this way: in 1997, Uzbekistan used natural gas to pay its rail transit debt. This time, however, Kazakhstan insists on being paid in dollars. When Kazakhstan failed to receive payment in May 1999, it interdicted the movement of passenger trains from Uzbekistan and Kyrgyzstan across its territory until such time as these countries paid off their debts with hard currency. Kyrgyzstan also had a transportation dispute with Uzbekistan, after the latter established extremely high tariffs for the movement of trains across its territory.[4]

The Natural Gas Conflict

All of southern Kazakhstan obtains its natural gas from Uzbekistan, but in recent years has suffered from periodic interruptions in the delivery of this fuel. The disruptions are due, once again, to the question of payment: Tashkent demands that it be paid in hard currency, but Kazakhstan proposes barter. This conflict came to the point where, in the spring of 1999, southern Kazakhstan (including Almaty) was left without natural gas. Apparently the ruthless behavior of Kazakhstan in the rail transit issue was a response to Uzbekistan's own refusal to compromise on the question of payments for natural gas. Uzbekistan also regularly cuts off the delivery of natural gas to Kyrgyzstan, thereby causing serious difficulties in the latter country.

"Deliver the Coal and You'll Get Water"

Kyrgyzstan, as just indicated, is an upstream country, and in the spring of 1999 it shut off the delivery of irrigation water to the southern oblasts of Kazakhstan. It did so after Kazakhstan failed to deliver coal, as stipulated in an agreement between the two countries. Kazakhstan also owed Kyrgyzstan millions of dollars for electric power. In turn, Kazakhstan has its own grievances: Kyrgyzstan does not pay for the deliveries of natural gas and (as noted above) for the railway movement across Kazakh territory. Although the governments of these two countries reached an agreement, and Kyrgyzstan has resumed its delivery of water,[5] the fundamental problem—mutual dependence and mutual nonpayment—persists.

Members of the Kyrgyz parliament, with increasing testiness, have urged President Akaev to respond to the challenge by shutting off the flow of water that Uzbekistan uses to irrigate its cotton plantations: "We also have a shut-off valve—let's close it!"[6]

As the foregoing suggests, relations among the countries of the region have become increasingly tense. Each state owes the other; antagonism is mounting; an unwillingness to compromise has gained the upper hand; retaliation has replaced tolerance and compromise in mutual relations and reasonable attempts to resolve differences.

Political Confrontation

Differences in their respective foreign policies reflect the growing split among the states of Central Asia. The two main states—Kazakhstan and Uzbekistan—belong to different blocs in the post-Soviet realm. These blocs consist of two groups. The first includes Russia, Belarus, Armenia, Kazakhstan, Kyrgyzstan, and Tajikistan; the second consists of Georgia,

Ukraine, Uzbekistan, Azerbaijan, and Moldova (GUUAM).* The schism emerged when, five years after the formation of a defensive alliance of all Commonwealth of Independent States (CIS) members (save Ukraine), three members—Georgia, Azerbaijan, and Uzbekistan—did not renew their membership and made use of their right to withdraw upon the expiration of the five-year agreement.

Having lost half of the members of this defensive alliance, Moscow proposed that the remaining states establish closer military ties than had hitherto been the case. These remaining members of the earlier defense pact supported this proposal to create a new military union at a summit held in Erevan in May 1999. At this meeting, the members also discussed the principles for creating "coalition contingents of troops in regions of collective security for joint defense."[7] Moreover, the purpose here was not simply to coordinate a unified system of air defense; it is not known whether that arrangement will continue to exist. Rather, the explicit objective here was to create a force of ground troops. The Erevan agreements (which were signed by Russia, Belarus, Armenia, Kazakhstan, Kyrgyzstan, and Tajikistan) indicate some far-reaching intentions on the part of the signatories. For example, they adopted proposals "on the composition of the contingent of troops included in the coalition forces to resolve goals of joint defense."[8] In other words, any military threats that emerge within the framework of a single defense space will be suppressed by "coalition forces." The agreements also provide for joint military exercises.

The lure of a military alliance with Russia, despite the obvious signs of degradation in its military power, includes *inter alia* one that is extremely important for all: Russia promises to provide them with weapons on the basis of preferential credits. Specifically, former President

---

*If the term "bloc" denotes a military-political association, the pro-Moscow defensive alliance fits the definition. However, GUUAM does not constitute a military-political alliance; rather, it is a grouping of states in opposition to the pro-Moscow alliance. GUUAM member-states share a common desire to oppose Moscow's ambition to preserve its hegemony in the post-Soviet space. They are seeking Western support and endorsement for their actions in pursuit of this objective. Formed in the spring of 1999, GUUAM does not seem likely to become a strong and enduring association. The anti-Moscow sentiments of its member-states could change quickly as a result of changes in their economic or political circumstances and they could readily adopt more Russia-friendly positions. Therefore, the existence of this quasi-bloc should not be seen as a permanent political factor.

Boris Yeltsin of Russia ordered his Ministry of Defense to make direct deliveries of weapons to participants in the new military coalition.

As a counterweight to the military consolidation of the pro-Moscow bloc, the countries of GUUAM are increasingly disposed to demonstrate their devotion to Washington and NATO. At a meeting during the anniversary celebration for NATO in Washington (in May 1999—i.e., almost simultaneously with the Erevan summit), the GUUAM countries declared their intention to "develop mutual cooperation within the framework of the Council of European-Atlantic Partnership and the NATO program of Partnership for Peace, and to strengthen their relations with respect to "the resolution of conflicts and crises."[9] The Erevan meeting of defense ministers and the creation of a military bloc were organized by Moscow to demonstrate its continuing control over part of the former Soviet empire and to counter the efforts of GUUAM to become a client of Washington and NATO.

Apart from the demonstrative effect, the real opportunities for a pro-Moscow military bloc and its unity must be taken with a large dose of skepticism. For Armenia (which finds itself mired in a phony war with Azerbaijan) and for the government of Emomali Rakhmonov (which controls only part of a war-torn Tajikistan), a military alliance with Moscow is extremely important. In the case of Kazakhstan and Kyrgyzstan, by contrast, this political game holds little attraction. But play they must, for neither country can permit a deterioration in its relations with Moscow. That is because each has close economic ties with Russia, at least formally belongs to a common customs union, and hence is still disposed to talk about the formation of a "single economic space."

It is still premature to talk about a confrontation of the two blocs and, especially, the consequences of this new geopolitical structure for the preservation of stability in Central Asia. Nevertheless, the drift of Central Asian states in different directions carries an inherent threat of destabilization.

One of the key factors that might trigger destabilization is the growing tension between Uzbekistan and Tajikistan. The interminable Uzbek-Tajik conflict has many dimensions and many causes. But one factor (perhaps the most important, one suspects) is the intention of Tashkent to establish control over the contiguous region of northern Tajikistan (Khudzhent, formerly Leninabad oblast), where a significant part of the population consists of ethnic Uzbeks. According to a belief widely shared in the Uzbek political elite (but, of course, not expressed publicly), by all rights—i.e., in economic and geographic terms, in ethnic composition—Soviet map-makers should have assigned this territory to Uzbekistan. To quote President Islam Karimov of Uzbekistan: "Look at the map and our border with Leninabad oblast of Tajikistan, and you will see that a tongue has been thrust out into our territory."[10] The reference, of course, is to the "tongue-shaped" Khudzhent oblast, which cuts a huge notch into eastern Uzbekistan. The strong man of Uzbekistan is not only a wily politician, but also an experienced, professional economist. He knows perfectly well that this "tongue" is extremely rich in natural resources and constitutes the most economically developed territory in all of Tajikistan. At the present time, when Tajikistan exists only nominally as a sovereign state, the tantalizing idea of seizing this "tongue" cannot fail to incite the imagination of the ruling elite in Uzbekistan. To be sure, it would be extremely risky to take concrete actions and to become embroiled in the internecine strife and carnage of Tajikistan, especially since Uzbekistan already has enough problems of its own. However, the opportunity is there, the historic moment appropriate, the temptation enormous, and the will to resist weak.

Although much ink has been spilled over the economic crisis in Central Asia, it is no less important to attend to the political consequences. Quite apart from the obvious threat of domestic turmoil, the economic crisis has exacerbated interstate tensions, shattered the myth of "regional unity," and opened the door to a desperate struggle for resources, rights, and even territories. The politics, no less than the economics, of Central Asia augur ill for stability, especially in the short term, but probably in the longer perspective as well.

II. Individual States and Their Problems

The relative importance of the five states of Central Asia is, of course, quite uneven. By and large, stability in Central Asia depends upon political and economic developments in the three key countries in this region: Kazakhstan, Uzbekistan, and Turkmenistan. The first two states, because of their population and economic potential, play the leading role in the region. Turkmenistan ranks far below the other two countries in terms of these indicators, but it possesses enormous reserves of natural gas and, in the post-Soviet era, has assumed a significant place in the geoeconomic and geopolitical alignment of forces and interests. Far less important are the two remaining states, Tajikistan and Kyrgyzstan. The former, caught in the throes of a sanguinary civil war, for the foresee-able future will continue to be a source of tension and conflict in the region; it is also the principal supplier for the narcotics produced by neighboring Afghanistan and by domestic growers. As for Kyrgyzstan, this tiny mountainous state will follow in the wake of Kazakhstan's poli-tics, which are oriented toward Russia; its president, Askar Akaev (the least authoritarian of all the Central Asian leaders) has made it his top priority to avoid any complications in his country's foreign relations, whether with countries within or outside the region.

In assessing the current state of affairs in these countries, it is abso-lutely essential to acknowledge and critically assess the paucity and unreliability of much of the statistical information emanating from this region. Particularly important is the lack of accurate data about the scale of the shadow economy, which some experts estimate to be as high as 40 percent of the GDP. Much is also written about the enormous magni-tude of the drug business; in the apt phrase of some, the medieval "silk route" has turned into the "narco-route." Despite the importance of such illicit activities, it is impossible to determine the actual scale of produc-tion and trafficking.

Caspian Hydrocarbons

Apart from the numerous concrete problems of producing and shipping hydrocarbon resources from the Caspian Sea Basin, the future of this region really depends upon three fundamental issues: (1) while the re-gion clearly possesses hydrocarbon reserves, their magnitude is still unknown; (2) it is still undetermined how, and over what routes, these are to be delivered to end-users; and (3) it is unclear how these countries will obtain necessary investments to extract the hydrocarbons and to construct the pipelines to deliver them. This complex of contradictions and problems—political, economic, and ecological—is so immense, and the number of countries with an interest in this region is so great, that (at least in the near future) one can hardly count on any significant exploi-tation of the Caspian hydrocarbon reservoir. At the present time, the transnational petroleum corporations have made only modest financial commitments, but these have been used primarily to stuff the pockets of powerful elites in Azerbaijan, Kazakhstan, and Turkmenistan. These questions have also ignited endless discussions in the local and Western press about the best routes for transporting oil and gas and about the confrontation of powers involved in playing this modern version of Rudyard Kipling's "Great Game." One gains the impression that the principal strategy of the leading world petroleum companies is to stake claims to potential resources, but not to make—at least for the present— any serious investments for their development. The practice of attracting outside capital by exaggerating resource potential is hardly something new; the Caspian littoral states are no exception, as they seek to appear before potential investors in the best possible light. One can virtually drown in the sea of contradictory reports about the intentions of the petroleum companies, about the confirmed and unconfirmed reserves, about the routes to be taken for the new pipelines, and about the scale of investment needed for their construction. It is impossible to determine what is hard fact, and what is bluff and disinformation that has been deliberately disseminated to achieve certain objectives.

Apart from questions about the magnitude of the estimated and, more importantly, the confirmed reserves, any attempt by potential investors to estimate the probable return on Caspian hydrocarbon resources must deal with several extremely serious difficulties:

- the inferior quality of Kazakh and Turkmen oil (which contains a high percent of hydrogen sulfide, thereby requiring significant additional expenditures on technology to bring the oil to the normal qualitative level);
- inhospitable climatic conditions (only in Siberia do conditions make it more difficult to produce oil);
- environmental costs (which loom as a dark threat to the unique fauna of the Caspian Sea and, especially, to the caviar-producing sturgeon that produce enormous revenues).

The ecological costs, if only for political reasons, are of direct concern to foreign investors. Geoffrey Kemp points out that "as a result, some exploration has been put on hold while the consortium companies commission environmental impact studies of the possible consequences of further development in certain areas. Environmental reports caution that an enclosed sea such as the Caspian is particularly vulnerable from an ecological standpoint to oil spills and other related sources of pollution."[11] All these factors result in unusually high costs in the production of Caspian oil. Another peculiarity, which substantially undercuts the profitability of Caspian hydrocarbon production, is the fact that this region is geographically isolated: situated in the center of the continent, it is remote from potential world centers of consumption. The transportation factor, of course, affects the end price of Caspian hydrocarbons. This "land-locked" factor has spawned a plethora of proposals for the best pipeline routes, but the expediency of each possibility depends not only (in some cases, not even primarily) on economic, but rather political factors. As Kemp rightly observes:

> Three of the producers—Azerbaijan, Kazakhstan, and Turkmenistan—are surrounded by other countries. They cannot get their energy to market without crossing someone else's territory. Interestingly, in the long and turbulent history of the oil business, this has rarely happened. In the past, all the great gas exporting countries have had direct access to the world's shipping lanes. . . . In the Caspian region, the major foreign countries, as well as the producer countries, must negotiate with adjacent countries, especially Russia, and reach mutually acceptable agreements if the energy is to be exported. If they do not cooperate, the oil and gas will remain in the ground.[12]

The economics of exploiting and exporting Caspian hydrocarbons, complicated in their own right, is further compounded by political barriers.

International corporations, Russia, the United States, Iran, Turkey, China, Pakistan, India, and the Persian Gulf states all have mutually exclusive interests in the Caspian region. This conflict and interplay of so many and such powerful participants in the Caspian "Great Game" block the development of the Caspian hydrocarbon resources and themselves pose a real threat to stability in Central Asia. But even if one assumes that the opportunities for the full-scale development of Caspian hydrocarbon resources will be maximally realized, there is little reason to think that this will lead to economic recovery and improved conditions for the mass of the general population. This gloomy assessment follows from the simple fact that, given the systems that have taken power in the post-Soviet Central Asian states, the lion's share of export revenues flow into a tiny stratum of a new nomenklatura elite, which operates covertly, has no need to fear transparency and public control, and diverts these funds into accounts held in foreign banks.

Turkmenistan

The enormous reserves of natural gas, a large territory (mostly desert) with a small population, an absolutely authoritarian regime, a cult of the personality centered around the "Turkmenbashi" (President Niiazov) and inflated to grotesque proportions—all these features constitute the defining characteristics of post-Soviet Turkmenistan. The dream of the early 1990s that this country would become a second Kuwait never came to pass. The principal problem of the economy is the lack of access to a market with solvent clients; that is, with end-users of natural gas who are capable of paying for deliveries. Only if Turkmenistan resolves this problem does the country have a chance of achieving stable economic development.

Moscow's Natural Gas Policy

In the post-Soviet era, the pipelines linking the natural gas deposits of Turkmenistan with its customers crossed through the territory of Russia. With the breakup of the Soviet Union, Ashgabat has continued to be dependent upon Moscow because this pipeline is still the only shipping route for its exports. However, the principal markets inherited from the Soviet era (above all, Ukraine) are not in a position to pay in full for the natural gas imports and instead seek to use barter deals to settle accounts. But Ashgabat has toughened its stance; it now insists that it be paid in hard currency and at prevailing world prices.

This constantly smouldering conflict explains President Niiazov's attitude toward every aspect of economic relations with the countries of the CIS, above all with Russia. Gazprom (representing Russia) impedes the transportation of Turkmen gas to markets in Western countries by denying Ashgabat access to the former "all-Union" pipeline; Moscow also refuses to purchase and re-export natural gas from Turkmenistan. In fact, with good reason, Moscow now regards Turkmenistan as a primary competitor in its battle for a place in the world's natural gas markets. Hence, it is certainly not in Moscow's interest for Ashgabat to construct an alternative pipeline route and thereby enable its natural gas to gain direct access to markets in Europe, Turkey, China, and Japan. An expansion of exports would enable Ashgabat to invest more in the exploration of new deposits, which in turn would expand its export opportunities—again, something that runs contrary to Russian interests. This is why Moscow has done (and will continue to do) everything in its power to preserve Ashgabat's dependence and thereby restrict the volume of natural gas exports from Turkmenistan. Ashgabat is fully cognizant of Russian intentions, and that in turn explains its coldness toward its "elder brother."

Problems Facing Natural Gas Production

Despite its clear vested interest, Moscow does not have great possibilities to block Turkmenistan's development. Western oil and gas companies have manifested an interest in various schemes to build an alternative pipeline network as well as to explore and develop gas deposits. The thrust of Niiazov's policy is to attract diverse sources of investment and to avoid a situation where a single company holds an excessively large share of his country's "natural gas pie" and hence a dominant role in the main sector of the Turkmen economy. As Niiazov rightly fears, the latter scenario might restrict his government's capacity to conduct an independent foreign and domestic policy.

During the post-Soviet period, many foreign countries (including the United States, Japan, Turkey, Iran, China, and the countries of the Persian Gulf) and the largest petroleum companies (Shell, Unocal, Exxon, and others) have indicated a willingness to invest in the exploration, exploitation, and transportation of Turkmen gas. But first they must resolve a complicated tangle of problems (economic and political) concerning the production and shipment of natural gas from Turkmenistan —problems that, significantly, have impeded the realization of specific projects and that foster significant doubts about the prospects for the development of Turkmenistan's riches in natural gas.

Thus, the tantalizing lure of Turkmen gas has sparked a conflict of interests between several important states—for example, between Russia and the United States, between the United States and Iran, between Iran and Turkey, and between Russia and Azerbaijan. But perhaps the most important and politically sensitive conflict concerns Washington's adamant opposition to any plans to ship Turkmenistan's natural gas through Iran and, indeed, to any cooperation between Ashgabat and the far more powerful government in Tehran. Nevertheless, Turkmen-Iranian cooperation has been developing successfully, and Iranian companies lead all those involved in the oil and natural gas sector of Turkmenistan. Of the multitude of proposals to transport Turkmen gas so as to avoid Russian territory, only an Iranian pipeline has actually been constructed: in December 1997, the two countries opened a new pipeline from Korpedzhe (Turkmenistan) to Kuy (Iran). Tehran has given a guarantee to Ashgabat that it will annually purchase 12 billion cubic meters of natural gas from this pipeline for the next twenty-five years.

The realization of other projects to ship the "blue fuel" in western, eastern, and southern directions continues to be the principal subject of day dreaming in Ashgabat. But such schemes must overcome the significant hurdles that cause uncertainty and indecisiveness among potential investors. The latter is hardly diminished by suspicions that Turkmen authorities have falsely inflated the actual scale of potential reserves—a tendency inevitably driven by the huge gap between Ashgabat's export ambitions and the scale of known reserves. However, in this respect, Turkmenistan is hardly unique. All the post-Soviet states that produce oil and natural gas tend to exaggerate estimates of their reserves. But such machinations only sow the distrust of official assessments that now constitutes a normal phenomenon in professional circles.

Niiazov's Pragmatism and Neutrality

The main thrust of Turkmenistan's foreign policy has been to navigate between the conflicting interest of three main foreign powers: Russia (which is still the main conduit for the transshipment of Turkmen gas), the United States (not only because it controls investments and technologies, but also because its recognition and support are important to Ashgabat), and Iran (which has already established business ties and which is also important for reasons of national security). Thus the cardinal principle of Turkmenistan's foreign policy is neutrality.

But neutrality does not connote inertness. In particular, the strongman of Turkmenistan cannot reconcile himself to the losses incurred through barter deliveries of natural gas to Ukraine and Georgia. That loss was further compounded by the high costs of shipping natural gas through Russian territory, all the more galling because Moscow's natural gas diplomacy is unabashedly directed against Turkmenistan's interests.

These factors explain why Turkmenistan has not joined the CIS or participated in any other blocs. Indeed, Turkmenistan has been remarkably consistent in its hostility toward the CIS. From the very moment that this organization came into being, Niiazov acknowledged it to possess a purely consultative role and openly proclaimed the principle of priority for bilateral relations between the post-Soviet states.

Still, the overriding leitmotif in the foreign policy of the Niiazov government is its determination to avoid becoming embroiled in any kind of intra-regional conflicts, which might spoil good relations with neighbors and somehow lead to an open confrontation with Moscow. In the case of Russian relations, Niiazov seeks to downplay any problems between Moscow and Ashgabat, be it unresolved issues pertaining to the division of the Caspian reserves or the ever-present tensions in relations with the natural gas monopoly Gazprom.

In the final analysis, the foreign policy of Turkmenistan appears highly contradictory. On the one hand, Ashgabat issues declarations about closer partnership with the CIS countries, above all with Russia;[13] on the other hand, it takes openly unfriendly actions against Russia and other countries in the CIS, including its Central Asian neighbors. One telling example was its sudden reversal of policy on visas for citizens from other post-Soviet states; since 1992, all of these newly independent republics had refrained from requiring visas for citizens from the other former Soviet republics. Turkmenistan became the first state, indeed, in a unilateral fashion, to over-turn this policy: in June 1999, Ashgabat announced that it would require visas for all those coming from post-Soviet states, with no exceptions.

For all practical purposes, nothing currently links Turkmenistan to the CIS and Russia: it categorically refuses to participate in any of the economic or military-political organizations headed by Moscow. To be sure, Turkmenistan periodically issues declarations for the purpose of tranquilizing Moscow, even as it—at the very same time—energetically seeks to assure Washington of its fidelity. But the facts speak for them-selves: in May 1999, Ashgabat demanded that Moscow withdraw the troops that guard the Turkmenistan border, thereby liquidating a rem-nant of the Russian military presence in his country. Simultaneously, the Turkmen government announced that it intended to sign an agree-ment with NATO to establish a special program to train military and civil personnel (at NATO expense) and to participate in the NATO pro-gram of "Partnership for Peace."[14] It bears noting that Ashgabat launched this demarche in May 1999, at the very time of a Washington summit of GUUAM leaders who came to celebrate NATO's anniversary. It appears that Niiazov, while not a member of the GUUAM alliance, made haste to affirm his support for the pro-NATO, pro-Washington position of this organization. It would seem that, despite the *pro forma* declaration of neutrality, in fact Ashgabat has become increasingly disposed to em-brace an overtly pro-Western policy.

Kazakhstan

It is difficult, indeed virtually impossible, to fathom the economic strat-egy and foreign policy of Kazakhstan. That incoherence stands in marked contrast to the other two Central Asian leaders, Niiazov in Turkmenistan and Karimov in Uzbekistan, who, from the very outset of the post-Soviet era, formulated an economic and foreign policy and, apart from some unavoidable deviations, have generally adhered to it. The leader of Kazakhstan, Nursultan Nazarbaev, has not demonstrated such consistency. On the contrary, his policies have been characterized by frequent gyrations, with constant changes in basic conceptions, programs, favorites, foreign advisors, premiers, and ministers. All that attests, first and foremost, to the absence of clear, precise points of orientation.

Foreign Policy

To be sure, one must acknowledge that the foreign policy situation of Kazakhstan is far more complicated than that facing Turkmenistan and Uzbekistan. Above all, Kazakhstan finds itself pulled by two opposing poles of gravity (Russia and China), even as it believes that it must demonstrate its fealty to Washington. All this leaves the Kazakh leadership in an extremely awkward position. The key point is that, precisely because the government must constantly try to strike a proper balance in this triangle (itself so loaded with contradictions), it cannot achieve either consistency or coherence in its foreign policy.

With all the means at its disposal, the Kazakh leadership in the new capital of Astana seeks at once to maintain good relations with its powerful neighbors and to exhibit a strong sensitivity to any kind of encroachment on the country's territorial integrity. Although at the official level both Russia and China display friendship and avoid giving grounds for accusing them of aggrandizement, covert distrust and suspicion (and even fear) undergird Astana's relations to Moscow and Beijing. The Kazakh political community is perfectly well aware that the Russian jingoists cannot accept the idea that Kazakhstan is really truly independent; nor can Astana ignore their claims to the northern and eastern territories of Kazakhstan. Similarly, visceral mistrust of China is widespread and deeply rooted, among not only policy-makers, but also broad masses of the population.

Kazakhstan-China Relations: Tensions Behind the Facade of Friendship

In the post-Soviet period, the top Chinese leaders have frequently reprised the view that specifically Kazakhstan is to play a key role in their strategy for Central Asia and therefore ranks as their most important partner in the region.[15] Notwithstanding the superficial cordiality in relations with China, the states of Central Asia nourish an abiding distrust of Beijing and even an abiding sense of profound pessimism in the face of China's growing power. This sense of helplessness is widespread among the political elites; it has also become firmly entrenched in popular consciousness.

One need only recall that, in the last century, a significant part of Central Asian territory belonged to the Chinese Empire. Thus, in 1994 *Guofang* ("National Defense"), a publication of the People's Liberation Army, published an article that listed, as part of the historical boundaries of China, "the region to the west of Xinjiang" (manifestly a reference to the eastern part of Kazakhstan) and "Lake Balkhash" (likewise located on the territory of central Kazakhstan).[16] Indeed, according to some scholars, Beijing still regards the fertile Fergana Valley as Chinese territory: "although Beijing has been careful to avoid public mention of these territorial controversies, it has not forgotten the Chinese past of these Central Asian territories, and it sees the breakup of the Soviet Union as an opportunity to expand China's Central Asian leadership."[17]

The public pronouncements of Chinese irredentists, while unofficial and less explicit than the claims expressed in Russian publications, nevertheless have attracted a predictable response in Central Asian capitals, above all in Kazakhstan. As a result, there is a prevailing sense that good relations with China are temporary, a sentiment grounded in deep distrust of the true intentions of Beijing.

To be sure, both Astana and Beijing attempt to keep their mutual disputes hidden from public view. Notwithstanding the frequent declarations about friendship and good neighborly relations, in fact the relations between them are far from idyllic. Thus, the Kazakh press is highly critical of an agreement on state borders that their country's parliament confirmed in the spring of 1999. The problem of disputed territories is an old one, not a product of the last decade: when the Soviet Union still existed, China laid claims to a significant part of the territory of Kazakhstan. In the post-Soviet era, the dispute has concerned a relatively small area of land. The two sides did reach an agreement, the text of which has not been published, to divide this disputed territory into equal parts.[18] However, a number of Kazakh experts do not think that this agreement has put an end to the territorial disputes. From 1993 to 1996, the two sides regularly signed documents reaffirming the absence of territorial claims against the other. Nevertheless, the ink on these documents had barely dried when Beijing would reiterate its view that the territorial issue had not been completely resolved.

Moreover, Kazakh public opinion is greatly concerned by the fact that China plans to construct a canal to divert part of the water from the Chernyi Irtysh (which crosses through both countries) in order to provide irrigation water for Xinjiang and for the industrial development of the Karamay oil field. As it is, Kazakhstan already suffers from a shortage of water, with half of its water supply coming from the territories of neighboring states (a significant part of which is the Chernyi Irtysh River in China). If China does increase the diversion of water from the Irtysh River, that will have severe economic and ecological repercussions for Kazakhstan. Astana is reluctant to lodge any serious protests with Beijing over the matter. Nevertheless, Altai Tleuberdin (President Nazarbaev's former chief of staff) has offered this diplomatic comment: "The Irytsh crosses national borders, and the state through which it passes has the right to use these water resources so long as it does not inflict harm on the water consumption of another state."[19] After insistent appeals from Astana, Beijing finally agreed to hold negotiations, with the Kazakh position becoming more active after protests in the press and accusations that authorities were passive, only covered up problems, and had no desire to defend national interests.[20]

Astana has still other reasons for concern. First of all, in 1996 Kazakhstan (together with Russia, Kyrgyzstan, Tajikistan, and China) signed the Shanghai agreement, which provides for the demilitarization of a 100 km border zone. The problem is that during the Soviet period the government constructed all its fortifications close to the border. As a result, the new demilitarization agreement creates enormous difficulties for Kazakhstan, which simply does not have the wherewithal to construct a new line of border defense and hence must leave its borders virtually unprotected.[21] Moreover, the government of Kazakhstan is deeply concerned about the immigration of Chinese into the country. It has classified all statistics on this question, but that has not prevented the most fantastic figures from circulating among the general population. The Kazakh leadership is making a maximum effort to elicit a favorable disposition from their powerful eastern neighbor and to avoid giving any grounds for dissatisfaction. But the Kazakh government finds itself in very difficult straits, since it must withstand a public opinion that is strongly anti-Chinese.

This latent conflict between Astana and Beijing sometimes comes to the surface. That is even true in the case of Kasymzhomart Tokaev, who was earlier the Kazakh minister of foreign affairs and became prime minister in October 1999. Yet even Tokaev, an extremely cautious professional diplomat of the old Soviet school, could not conceal the contradictions in Kazakh-Chinese relations. And one issue (perhaps the most important in terms of mass psychology) is the intensive migration of Chinese into Kazakh territory, that is, the "peaceful Sinification" of immense, unpopulated, economically undeveloped territories of the country. It is a moot point whether this Sinification is actually occurring, or whether it is merely the hallucination of a paranoid populace. The abolition of visa requirements between the two countries, a step taken in the early 1990s, effectively eliminated any controls over Chinese migration to Kazakhstan. The Kazakh press has been conducting an anti-Chinese campaign, with a steady stream of reports that the Chinese are resettling in massive numbers and buying up housing and property in Kazakhstan. As a result, the Kazakh authorities were forced to act unilaterally and reestablish their former visa requirements in an effort to establish control over Chinese travel to their country. Tokaev does not conceal the fact that "negotiations on this matter were rather complicated," and affirms that "the position of the Kazakh side was quite firm and explained, to a large degree, by the pressure of public opinion and the means of mass communication." The latter, he declared, was due to "the natural fear of assimilation by a multitudinous neighbor."[22]

Beijing, for its part, does have a vested interest in supporting and preserving the secular regimes of Central Asia: they all seek to prevent the dissemination of Islamic extremism and, more generally, the diffusion of politically active Islam in Central Asia. After all, that same threat hangs over the predominantly Muslim region of Xinjiang, which since the early 1990s has witnessed a plethora of explosions, assassinations, and other terrorist acts by Uighur separatists. The Chinese leaders cannot fail to be concerned about the activities of Islamic militants in those areas of Central Asia that border on Xinjiang. The penetration of Islamic extremists, weapons, explosives, and religious teachings from neighboring Pakistan and Afghanistan into Xinjiang has bolstered the Uighur movement and encouraged its demands for the secession of Xinjiang from China. As has been pointed out, "in the year of conflicts in Kosovo, East Timor, Daghestan, and Chechnya, Kashgar [one of the two largest cities in Xinjiang] serves as a powerful reminder that China is also vulnerable to the forces of ethnic fragmentation that have atomized other, once seemingly impregnable, authoritarian states."[23]

The Xinjiang situation lends credibility to press reports that Beijing is putting pressure on Pakistan to suspend its support for the Taliban in Afghanistan. According to these reports, China gave Pakistan to understand that it opposes that country's pro-Islamic foreign policy, and that is why Beijing withheld its support during the most recent Kashmir crisis. The Chinese regard Pakistan as a key element in its strategy to block the activities of Islamic fundamentalists, and fear that the Taliban are serving as Islamabad's main base for the export of aggressive Islam into Central Asia and Xinjiang.[24]

Slowly but surely, the Central Asian states are being drawn into the Chinese orbit, in the first instance economically, but also politically (if more gradually). This tendency is most apparent in China's two contiguous neighbors, Kazakhstan and Kyrgyzstan. In general, however, one must acknowledge that Beijing has thus far conducted itself—at least to all external appearances—in a very peaceful manner, displaying much caution in relations with its Central Asian neighbors.

Kazakhstan and Russia: Neither Together nor Separate

Notwithstanding the current importance of Kazakhstan's relations with China, in the immediate future Russia will continue to hold top priority. But the relations between the two countries are quite problematic. A storm of indignation among Kazakhs ensued in the wake of declarations by Alexander Solzhenitsyn (proclaiming the northern—and most economically valuable—part of Kazakhstan as Russian territory) and the provocative rhetoric of Vladimir Zhirinovskii that evoked a strong resonance among Moscow irredentists. However, neither former president Boris Yeltsin nor numerous post-Soviet Russian governments have given reason for the Kazakhs to accuse them of expansionist intentions. There is some reason for concern with respect to the activism of the so-called Ural Cossacks, heirs of a Urals Cossack host in Tsarist Russia but assigned to Kazakhstan when Moscow drew up the boundaries of Soviet Kazakhstan. The demands by the Cossacks that they be united with Russia and that Moscow reconsider its boundaries with Kazakhstan (that is, claim the territory that the Cossacks now inhabit) evoke a favorable response from the Slavic population of Kazakhstan (approximately 40 percent of the country). Such movements could provoke conflict between the two countries.[25]

In recent years, however, Moscow's irredentist ambitions with respect to Kazakhstan have gradually receded. The proponents of a Russian "Monroe Doctrine" have fallen silent. One no longer finds statements in the press to the effect that Russia cannot escape "its destiny" and therefore "cannot refrain from sending her soldiers to Central Asia."[26] Likewise, the clamor about "Eurasianism" as the ideology of Russian irredentism has also died down. Moscow politicians, concerned about preventing the breakup of Russia itself, are hardly in a position to fantasize about the annexation of Kazakh territory.

For whatever reason, mass consciousness of the Kazakhs (not to mention the non-Kazakh population) is not seriously concerned about Russian expansion. The cultural ties with Russia are still strong; the Russian language, as before, still prevails in Kazakhstan. The majority of the population watches Moscow television, and the Russian press fills the newspaper stands.

Relations with Russia are considerably more important for Kazakhstan than for Uzbekistan and Turkmenistan. Kazakhstan is regarded as one of the loyal allies of Russia in the post-Soviet realm, and a supporter for the maximum possible integration within the structure of the CIS. President Nazarbaev stubbornly propagates the idea of a "Eurasian Union," but thus far has found no support among leaders in the other post-Soviet states. He can no doubt be called "Integrationist No. 1." Kazakhstan (together with Russia, Belarus, and Kyrgyzstan) was the initiator and creator of the Customs Union in the CIS. Russia, indeed, is the chief foreign trade partner for Kazakhstan. Astana follows the main lines of development in post-Soviet Russia; it borrowed, in fact, its very ideology of economic reform from Russia.

The unbroken, if weakened, connection with Russia has strong historic roots. More than any other republic in the former Soviet Central Asia, Kazakhstan developed demographically, economically, and culturally during the Soviet era and, therefore, more than others reflected the Russian heartland. Therefore, during the first years of independence, the Kazakh leadership copied virtually all the policies of Moscow; elements of such borrowing, indeed, are still apparent.

Moscow created the industry of Kazakhstan, especially its most developed branches in the northern and eastern parts of the country, as an integral component of the technological complex in the Urals and Western Siberia. Approximately fifty of the largest industrial enterprises of Kazakhstan were part of the military-industrial complex of the USSR.

Economic relations with the industrially developed regions of the Urals and the southern part of Western Siberia have since tended to intensify. In recent years, a large part of Kazakhstan's exports of vital food products—meat, milk products, and cereals (including wheat)—go to Omsk, Tiumen, Novosibirsk, Kemerovo, Tomsk, and other oblasts of the Urals and Western Siberia.[27] Moreover, these Russian oblasts have signed bilateral economic agreements with neighboring Kazakh oblasts (for example, the "Omsk Agreement"). Economic (including technological) cooperation of Kazakhstan with the industrial oblasts of the Urals region and Western Siberia is becoming a reality in today's world and a tendency for the future as well. Moscow has virtually no control over this development; the authorities of these Siberian oblasts act independently and at their own discretion. For its part, Astana generally encourages this kind of contact. The fact that Slavs dominate the ethnic composition of the population of northern and eastern Kazakhstan also plays an important role in the mutual penetration in the business activities of Siberia and Kazakhstan.

Notwithstanding all this, relations between Astana and Moscow are subject to constant tension. Economic problems doubtless constitute the principal cause. For example, the two countries in the end failed to reach a mutual agreement on the value added tax (VAT) for the customs clearance of transit goods. As a result, a customs war broke out in January 1999, when Astana, despite its membership in the Customs Union, imposed a strict ban on the import of twenty-one categories of food products from Russia. This protectionist action resulted from the fact that after the devaluation of the ruble in August 1998 Russian food products became considerably cheaper than those produced domestically (with obvious negative consequences for the domestic producers). Another reason, perhaps even more important (though not publicized by Kazakh decision-makers), that Astana launched this attack on Moscow lies in the fact that after the devaluation of the ruble it was no longer profitable for Kazakhstan to export its own goods to Russia. After the Kazakh leadership (emulating the Moscow example) devalued its own national currency in April 1999, Astana promised to remove the protectionist barrier against Russian goods. In fact, however, the trade war has not only persisted but has even intensified. Astana accuses Moscow of subsidizing its own producers by providing cheap domestic prices for energy and low rail tariffs; it has therefore announced that it will investigate the alleged dumping.[28] Another source of constant tension is Moscow's arrears in paying the lease for its space launching site at Baikonur. An accident involving the rocket Proton in July 1999 (the debris from which landed on the territory of Kazakhstan), compounded by Moscow's haughty response to Kazakh demands for compensation to cover the material damage, further strained relations between the two states.

Moscow displayed the cooling in its relations with Kazakhstan by taking measures to strength the common border with this partner in the Customs Union. After the breakup of the Soviet Union, the Russian-Kazakh border was virtually open and little more than symbolic. In June 1999, the Russian government issued a "Decree on the Strengthening of Borders and the Creation of Control Points," the purpose of which was to regulate and restrict all movement across its border (above all, with respect to goods).[29]

However, despite outbursts of mutual irritation and despite the erosion of partnership in economic relations, for the present Kazakhstan preserves its loyalty to Russia in the military-political spheres. Thus, it has remained a member of the "Treaty on Collective Security" (which is now semi-defunct). Moscow encourages Astana to participate in a refurbished military coalition by providing weapons under extremely favorable terms or even gratis. In early 1999, for instance, Moscow reportedly sent the Kazakh Air Force a dozen SU-27s and a surface-to-air missile defense complex S-300.[30]

Relations with the United States: Ups and Downs

For the greater part of the post-Soviet period, relations between Kazakhstan and the United States have been very good, but these began to go sour in 1998. From the very outset, it was important for Washington to cooperate with Kazakhstan in order to address several strategically vital matters—the elimination of all Soviet nuclear weapons located on its territory, ensuring American participation in the development of hydrocarbon resources (which lay in the interest of American corporations), and channeling the shipment of these commodities over routes that Washington deemed in its best interest. The transformation of Kazakhstan into a nonnuclear state and its signing of the nonproliferation treaty led to the establishment of particularly warm relations between the two governments. This process was further abetted by a tight monetary policy (which Washington approved), strict adherence to the IMF's prescription for the transition to a market economy, the rapid pace in the transformation process, and also the relative liberalism of the governing regime (especially when compared with the overtly authoritarian rule in Turkmenistan and Uzbekistan). At least public opinion and the mass media in Kazakhstan are considerably freer than in these two neighboring states. All this created the impression of internal stability, while the tantalizing opportunities to develop a broad range of mineral resources (which are so rich in Kazakhstan) made this country highly attractive to foreign investors, including Americans. The prospects for a productive business and political partnership with a country situated in the center of Eurasia evoked considerable enthusiasm in Washington.

There is scarcely any need to explain why the Kazakh side has been so acutely interested in a partnership with the United States, given the prospects of engagement with its private and public sectors and, especially, the allure of financial assistance and political support from Washington. As the Clinton administration formulated and began to implement an energy strategy with respect to the Caspian region, it gave top priority to Kazakh oil exports and the direction these would flow in any East-West pipelines. For Washington, the principal strategic objective was to ensure that this pipeline bypass both Iran and Russia. The U.S. government designated Kazakhstan to play a key role in the Central Asian region; as its ambassador to that country, it dispatched one of its most capable and best-trained diplomats, William Courtney. This extraordinary interest in Kazakhstan, reinforced by accounts in Western mass media, gave rise to great expectations and encouraged a tendency to exaggerate.

The apogee in U.S.-Kazakhstan relations came in late 1997, when President Nazarbaev came to Washington to participate in a session of a bilateral commission. Thereafter, however, a distinct chill settled on relations between the two countries. Kazakhstan's poor economic performance (aggravated by the economic crisis in East and Southeast Asia and in Russia), the fall in the prices of Kazakhstan's exports, rising doubts about the real magnitude of its unexplored hydrocarbon resources, and more sober assessments of the scale of investment required to develop and transport these commodities to world markets—all served to erode the economic interest of the American government and business circles.

However, the most important reason for Washington's cooling toward Kazakhstan was the domestic policy of the Nazarbaev regime. Hopes for a liberalization of public life and for the development of democracy proved illusory. In particular, Kazakhstan failed to meet OSCE standards when it conducted presidential elections in January 1999 and parliamentary elections in October 1999. The intervention of the executive branch in the voting, the outright falsification of voting returns in many parts of the country, and the suppression of opposition provoked an extremely negative reaction among the governments and public organizations of the United States and Europe, with a correspondingly negative impact on relations with Kazakhstan. Another serious blow to U.S.-Kazakhstan relations occurred in the summer of 1999, when Astana sold MiG-21s to North Korea for 8 million dollars—an act that made Kazakhstan a target of American sanctions. It will require considerable effort and much time to repair the harm that this deal by the Kazakh leadership—which is difficult to fathom in rational terms—has inflicted on relations with the United States.

Still, one should anticipate that even if Kazakhstan does not recover its former top-priority status in American eyes, then it will at least see some improvement in its relations with Washington. The Americans will be driven to favor a rapprochement by their own vested interest in having Astana support its proposals for a pipeline that skirts both Russia and Iran and, specifically, passes through Turkey to the port of Ceyhan. At the European summit meeting in Istanbul in November 1999, President Nazarbaev did in fact join with the presidents of Azerbaijan and Turkmenistan in signing an agreement to build a pipeline that will carry Caspian oil through Turkish territory. In so doing, Nazarbaev chose Washington over Moscow, an act that should earn the gratitude of the U.S. administration.

Intensification of the Domestic Crisis

By the end of the 1990s, the social and economic crisis in Kazakhstan had already reached ominous proportions. During the post-Soviet period, after all, the population here had to endure a profound economic decline and depression. In 1994, for example, industrial production declined by one-third from the previous year; compared with 1990 (the last year before Kazakhstan became independent), industrial output had fallen by half. But by then the regime had already become firmly entrenched. Nor had the euphoria over the newly acquired independence as yet dissipated. And it still seemed credible when the political leadership explained the objective inevitability of economic recession because of the transition period, the breakup of a single economic space with

Russia, and the introduction of a national currency. At this point, expectations still loomed large that the export of enormous mineral resources and especially oil would lead to a veritable boom in the economy.

It must be said that the Kazakh leadership, without giving the matter serious consideration, leaped into a whirlwind of radical reform—emulating Moscow and unconditionally following the recommendations of the IMF and the World Bank. The government placed all its hopes for economic recovery on a program of massive privatization, and the process of economic reforms has entailed fundamental changes in the structure of ownership, with a strengthening of nonstate forms of property. At the same time, the regime understood the idea of "minimizing state intervention in the economy" essentially to mean that it could divest itself of responsibility and transfer this onus to the new, efficient class of private owners. The government conducted this transformation in pell-mell fashion, uncritically replicated the Russian model, neglected to make the necessary legal and practical preparation, and as a result failed to achieve its goals. Above all, its frenetic campaign of privatization failed to create a class of efficient private owners; instead, it merely spawned a tiny stratum of *nouveaux riches*, the "new Kazakhs" (the local equivalent to the "new Russians"), while subjecting the great majority of the population to systematic immiseration. Hence its reforms served not to ameliorate, but to aggravate, social tensions.

Although the period of 1995–97 did witness some improvement in economic indicators, one finds little reason to think that the population experienced any real changes in their standard of living. To be sure, if one looks at the conditions in Almaty (at that time, still the capital), one cannot fail to see the external signs of growing prosperity. For example, if measured in terms of the most expensive foreign automobiles per thousand inhabitants, Almaty ranked among the top capitals in the entire world. However, if one looked beyond the capital, a very different picture obtains: the general population has experienced destitution, not prosperity; the decline in living standards has been particularly pronounced in small towns and rural areas. Characteristically, the lack of electricity has now become routine in many of these areas.

Thus privatization, in the perverted version that it took in Kazakhstan, failed to create the much-vaunted class of "efficient private owners." And this failed effort came at a high price: the government sold off the country's vast natural and industrial wealth for a small fraction of its real worth. One of the most reliable economic journals in Russia offers this gloomy assessment of the privatization process in Kazakhstan:

> In less than two years' time the government of Kazakhstan managed to sell off almost 90 percent of the country's industry. The total value of the property thus sold amounted to no more than three billion dollars. The identity of many of the new owners of Kazakh property remains unknown. All the participants and observers of this "mad privatization" either refuse to comment on these events or remain incognito.[31]

In the post-privatization period of 1996–97, the economy of Kazakhstan showed a striking polarity. In the words of Petr Svoik:

> At one pole are just fifteen to twenty large enterprises (for the most part, belonging to "foreign investors"),[32] which operate in a relatively stable fashion and provide the main volume of exports. The general number of people employed in these enterprises does not exceed 250,000 to 300,000, who in effect "feed" the entire country. At the other pole are several large firms that specialize in the import of food products, which of necessity have a "cover" in the upper echelons of the regime, but also until recently included 150,000–200,000 "shuttle traders," who handle the delivery of virtually the entire assortment of non-comestible consumer goods. Moreover, up to one million people are active in the infrastructure for the sale of imported goods. The domestic production of goods consists chiefly of spirits and vodka. In addition, the flour mills and bread-baking industry of Kazakhstan satisfy domestic demand, but the meat-processing industry covers significantly less.[33]

In the judgment of other Kazakh experts, "Kazakhstan's own industry, which already supplies less than 15 percent of domestic demand, is either expiring or already dead."[34]

The conditions that underlay the crisis at the end of the 1990s differ from those of 1994 in this respect: world prices have plummeted on virtually all of the raw-material products exported from Kazakhstan, and that in turn has severely restricted or completely eliminated opportunities to sell off state property. The regime has no new ideas that are capable of rekindling hope (as privatization did earlier); its old ideas are completely discredited in the eyes of the population and now have zero propaganda effect. The hope of reaping enormous revenues from petroleum has also faded. Even if there is a boom in the oil industry, people no longer believe that their lives will improve: such a windfall would only enrich the ruling clan-bureaucratic elite and its entourage. The published declarations by Nazarbaev (such as the program for "Ten Simple Steps to Help People" or the Program for the Development of the Country by the Year 2030) are so pathetic and so devoid of specifics that they can only evoke irony and irritation among the people. The populace now exhibits an enormous fatigue and indignation with the ruling regime. The reserve of patience has decreased significantly from its former level in 1994. According to a public opinion poll published in February 1999, nearly two-thirds of the respondents characterized the current condition of society as "catastrophic" or "critical." In the opinion of the Kazakh sociologists who conducted the poll, such results "give reason to think that the potential of patience is quite small." More than half of the respondents (55.6 percent) declared that "one cannot be patient for long" or "it is impossible to be patient."[35] All these are warning signs of impending social disorder.

The authoritarian regime of Nazarbaev is more liberal in terms of freedom of speech and the openness of the mass media than is the case with Karimov's regime in Uzbekistan (not to mention Niiazov's in Turkmenistan). Of course, one cannot speak of Kazakhstan having "democracy" in the Western sense; even a Russian level of democratization is unacceptable for Nazarbaev. At the same time, criticism (sometimes quite sharp criticism) of the economic, social, and foreign policies of the leadership is a routine phenomenon in the papers of the Kazakh press. The only subject taboo for the press is the first family. Opposition parties and their leaders that operate legally in Kazakhstan, despite their disunity, are nevertheless acquiring an ever greater authority in public life. In principle, one cannot preclude the possibility that in the foreseeable future the political regime in Kazakhstan may make some minor concessions toward liberalization.

Uzbekistan

Of the many problems that face post-Soviet Uzbekistan, the two most important concern the need to repulse the onslaught of Islamic radicalism and to eliminate the conditions that promote its growth and dissemination. The chief task is to avert any further immiseration and increase in unemployment, especially among rural inhabitants (who comprise approximately 60 percent of the population in the country). In every respect, Uzbekistan is the key state of Central Asia. It has borders with all four of the other Central Asian states as well as Afghanistan.

Moreover, ethnic Uzbeks, who comprise three-quarters of the country's population, exhibit a devotion to Islam that is greater than that found among the Kazakhs and Kyrgyz, and is no less fervent than that of the Tajiks. It is perfectly understandable why Muslim radicals want to over-throw the regime of President Karimov and to take full control of Uzbekistan. If they succeed, they will be positioned to exert pressure on the entire region of Central Asia.

The Specter of Tajikistan

Until now, the harsh authoritarian regime of President Karimov has been able to handle this pressure and to keep Uzbekistan from repeating the tragic experience of Tajikistan. Indeed, it is precisely the example of Tajikistan that serves as a warning to the population and poses a clear alternative: either life under the conditions of the existing regime, or descent into the carnage of civil war, with the threat of intercession from neighboring Afghanistan. Fantasies about Uzbekistan establishing a truly democratic system (in the Western sense) are only possible for people who lack a rudimentary familiarity with the history, culture, traditions, and mentality of the Uzbeks.

In the opinion of local experts, contemporary Uzbekistan lacks the necessary ingredients to create an Islamic state in the classic, orthodox mold. The population here, even in rural areas (not to mention in the cities), is not disposed favorably toward the prospect of such a regime. The revival of traditional social and cultural relations in the post-Soviet era does not at all mean a willingness to accept Islamic fundamentalism and to construct a state based on its precepts. If one ponders the alterna-tives to the existing regime, one cannot help but agree with Aleksei Malashenko (an expert at the Carnegie Center in Moscow): "This is more likely to be a moderate Islam, if of course one does not provoke it and drive it into a corner."[36] Even in this form, however, the Islamic movement is capable of creating a situation similar to that in war-torn Tajikistan.

The terrifying thought that the Tajik tragedy might be repeated in Uzbekistan works in favor of the existing Uzbek regime and forces many, if not the majority of the population, to tolerate the decline in living standards and the arbitrariness of a corrupt bureaucracy. And their fears are well-grounded. According to Stuart Horsman, "the situation in both Tajikistan and Afghanistan is without doubt a serious security concern for Uzbekistan, but there is a credibility gap between rhetoric and practice" (discussed below). Although, as he points out, "numerous domestic and international commentators have criticized Tashkent for exaggerating the regional threat of Islamic fundamentalism,"[37] the violent events of 1999 demonstrated that the Karimov regime in fact did not overestimate the gravity of the menace posed by Islamic militants. In August and September 1999, Islamic radicals (who, according to information from Bishkek, included not only Uzbeks but also Afghans, Arabs, and other foreigners) launched an assault from the territory of Tajikistan into the Fergana Valley, with the final goal of overthrowing the Karimov regime ("behind which stands Israel") and to establishing "the law of sharia in Uzbekistan."[38] That was the explanation offered by the Islamic leader of Uzbekistan, Zubair ibn Abdurrakhman, in a telephone press-conference for Kyrgyz and foreign journalists in late October 1999. He bluntly declared that "the main goal is to create an Islamic state on Uzbek territory."[39] The reality is that the deteriorating economic condition (which indeed, for many, is tantamount to the direst impoverishment) helps to make the ideas of Islamic radicalism more acceptable, especially among the mass of unemployed youth in Uzbekistan. It also enables Muslim militants, whether home-grown or foreign volunteers, to recruit supporters and mobilize them for the struggle against Karimov's secular state system and for the "establishment of the law of sharia."

The Leader and the System

Of all the Central Asian autocrats, arguably the most extraordinary is Islam Karimov. Even his adversaries have to concede that he is distinguished by a strong will and intellect. He also exhibits a sense of proportion in the external trappings of power. His official residence, for example, is located in the old and rather modest building of the former republic-level Central Committee of the Communist Party; standing in marked contrast to Nazarbaev, who has two luxurious residences in Almaty and yet another in Astana. Nor does Tashkent flaunt the signs of a grotesque "cult of the personality" like that in Ashgabat, where enormous portraits of the Turkmenbashi hang on every corner and where his sculpture—cast in gold—rises up to dominate the main square. Nor can Karimov's closest associates be described as part of his "family," as it is understood in Kazakhstan, where the president's sons-in-law all hold key positions in business and in state security, and where the elder daughter heads the state television.

It would also be erroneous to think that the Uzbek strongman possesses unlimited power. Like perhaps no one else, he knows the vices of the social order that has developed in Uzbekistan—a fusion of centuries-old ethnic and cultural traits with the special characteristics of the Soviet era that penetrated the social fabric. In essence, Karimov inherited a hybrid "clan-nomenklatura" structure of rule that had developed over many decades. Although reportedly himself not a clan figure, he recognized the inherent qualities of this structure, with its system-building function, and therefore found himself obliged not only to adapt, but to head it and to occupy the top position in this pyramid. In his public statements, he denounces corruption and criminality, as well as regionalism and clan influence.[40] Yet he is in no position to purge society of these evils; it is simply beyond the limits of his real power. He can only rule by operating within the parameters of the existing system, by exhibiting flexibility and circumspection, and by observing its unwritten rules. In essence, Karimov himself is a hostage to this system. He is the supreme arbiter, someone who regulates the mutual relations of clans and endeavors to strike an acceptable balance between the interests of society and the clan-nomenklatura (which seeks to hold onto the property and capital that it has already amassed). Thus Karimov is forced to give the corrupt bureaucracy a piece of the pie, but he must also limit its gluttonous appetite. While it is by no means easy to enforce such restraints, the ruling elite does have a vested interest in seeing that the state retains a leading role in the economy as it carries out modest reforms. Hence, both Karimov's policy and the president himself are fully acceptable to this new "clan-nomenklatura" elite.

While Karimov cannot fail to recognize the urgent need to modernize the economic and social order, he apparently believes that, given the concrete conditions of contemporary Uzbekistan, only the existing system—even with its low (and diminishing) efficiency—is able to sustain the regime and political stability. This assessment presumably explains the half-heartedness of the reforms thus far undertaken. Karimov thus finds himself in a painful quandary: on the one hand he risks losing control in the event of a real liberalization of public life and the economy, while on the other hand he recognizes the need to open safety valves to let off steam before social unrest is ignited and sets off a cataclysmic explosion.

How strong are the stabilizing forces that the regime can summon on its behalf? In essence, two factors are of critical importance here. One is the national character of Uzbeks—namely, their extraordinary patience, the tradition of obedience, the remarkable work-ethic of the *dekhkane* (peasants), and their capacity to survive conditions of minimal material support. The other factor is cotton output and its market price, along with the world prices on other exports, such as gold, uranium, rare metals, and the like. The Uzbeks do display unusual patience, but it is not infinite. The volatility of the second factor is self-evident.

It should be noted that Karimov himself is a professional economist: prior to the time that he became head of the Uzbek Communist Party, he was the minister of finance and head of the republic economic planning commission. Hence it is entirely conceivable that Karimov foresaw not only the positive but also the negative consequences of massive and instant price deregulation as well as a precipitous privatization. He therefore opted for the path of a gradual economic transition—an economic and political ideology that was the direct antithesis to the Russian model that both Kazakhstan and Kyrgyzstan chose to emulate.

As a result, Uzbekistan avoided the catastrophic economic decline that overwhelmed the other post-Soviet republics in Central Asia. In 1990–95, when the GDP of Kazakhstan fell by more than half and that of Kyrgyzstan by 50 percent, the GDP of Uzbekistan declined by just 18 percent. In 1995, the aggregate index for industrial production, which had fallen by 40 to 50 percent in the other Central Asian states, stood at the same level in Uzbekistan as it had in 1990.[41] However, this "slow transition" dragged on for too long and, in effect, turned into a stalemate for reform, even as the economy gradually drifted downward. The regime has exhausted the opportunities to promote economic growth by maintaining the basic elements of a command economy. The result has been economic stagnation. To reverse this negative dynamic, it is essential to accept the risk of real economic transformation, with a decrease in the control over public opinion. Is Karimov prepared to overcome this ruinous, destructive inertia?

Declarations and Reality

To cast this issue into full relief, it is useful to examine Karimov's speech, entitled "Uzbekistan as It Heads for the Twenty-First Century," that he delivered at the fourteenth session of the Uzbek parliament. This programmatic document sets forth the priorities, goals, and methods of development in the country up to the year 2005 and beyond.[42] As its principal idea, the statement proclaims that "the first priority is the liberalization of political and economic life." There is no need here to examine in detail his theses on political liberalization, but it must be said that, however alluring and just such statements might be, it is anything but clear how they are compatible with reality. Take, for example, the following statement: "The fullest possible development should be accorded to a free and independent means of mass information." For the moment, Uzbekistan has a system of strict censorship over the press, radio, and television; everything is just as it was during the Soviet era and, if anything, the control is even more rigorous.

As for the economic section of this declaration, Karimov's announcement of "liberalization" was long awaited. His statement thus promises to reverse the regime's decision to retreat from economic reforms in late 1996, when it established strict controls over hard currency, introduced a system of licensing on imports, and slowed the rate of privatization. Most important, Karimov's declaration sets, for the first time, a clearly defined goal for reform in the sphere of property: "The formation of a diversified economic structure, in which private property plays the leading role." Until now, the Uzbek leader had never assigned a "leading role" to private property. However, with respect to the concrete economic issues raised in this programmatic statement, much remains unclear and confusing. The president identifies various problems, but neither explains what caused them nor offers concrete measures to resolve them. Hence his critique of these shortcomings remains nebulous and fails to detail specific reforms.

Example 1: Karimov declared that "we have adopted a 'Law on the Limitation of Monopolistic Activities,' but it does not really work in practice. Even in trade and the service sector, where the statistical data show that there are virtually no state structures, we encounter monopolistic organizations." All this is quite true. But the fact is that these "monopolistic organizations" exist because of the state's hard-currency controls, its licensing system for imports, and its other forms of state regulation (which all serve to pad the incomes of responsible officials).

Example 2: Karimov also announced that the government has set for itself another goal: "to increase the number of small and private enterprises in the next two to three years and raise their share of the GNP to at least 25 percent." In 1999, this share amounted to far less—between 6.5 and 11 percent (according to various estimates). Even if one accepts the larger figure, Karimov thus proposes in the span of just two or three years to double their share of the GNP—a manifestly unrealistic goal. It is, after all, extremely difficult to establish an independent business, since one must both overcome countless bureaucratic hurdles and arrange financing. The latter is particularly difficult, since small enterprises have virtually no access to credit resources and no right whatsoever to purchase foreign currency from the state. The difficulties facing small business are compounded by the high degree of monopolization; racketeering; and the captious nitpicking (often unfounded) by local authorities, various inspectorates (tax, fire, and health), and numerous other regulatory organs, all of which see the small enterprises as easy prey for extracting bribes. The extremely high taxes (often amounting to about 70 percent of earnings) also have the effect of suppressing the development of small business.

Example 3: Karimov's declaration set the goal of "raising, within the next five years, the minimum wage by 3.5 times, which, together with other factors of economic growth, will make it possible to raise the level of per capita incomes in the country by 1.8 to 2.0 times during this period." Is one really supposed to take this target seriously? One need only reflect on the fact that the per capita income of the population is to surpass the rates of economic growth. In fact, however, for the national income to double during a five-year period, economic growth must be more than 14 percent per annum.[43] It is hardly possible to take such an astronomical rate seriously.

Example 4: In his report Karimov declared that "it is necessary to achieve a reduction in the level of inflation in the next five years— down to a level of 6 to 8 percent per annum." However, it is anything but clear how this goal is compatible with the declared need "to liberalize the system and market for hard currency" and with "the resolution of the question of the complete convertibility of the national currency into a hard currency (beginning in the year 2000)." After all, to achieve these latter goals, it will be unavoidable and necessary to carry out a devaluation and to unify the official and "black-market" exchange rates (which, in 1999, showed a gap of 500 percent). But those steps will inevitably lead to a rise in inflation.

No less astounding is the fact that among the priorities of liberalization Karimov said nothing at all about agrarian reform—that is, about agriculture—the main sector of the Uzbek economy. Unless real reform is undertaken in this sector, it will simply not be possible to achieve stable economic growth. It may be that Karimov regards agrarian reform as something already completed. Yet that would be a strange view, given the fact that the state (as before) still plans the structure of crops sown, sets low procurement prices, controls the production and sale of cotton and grain (which occupy no less than 70 percent of all irrigated land), and licenses the export of all other agricultural products. Nor, as yet, do private farms dominate in the agrarian sector. How then can the regime hope to realize its pronouncements about "the leading role of private property in the economy" if this principle is not applied to the main sector of the economy?

Thus, however attractive the goals in "Uzbekistan as It Heads for the Twenty-First Century" might be, the lack of specifics on their realization suggests that the president has not resolved to embark on fundamental structural reform.

It should be obvious that, to counter the growing predisposition of various social strata toward an Islamic political alternative, it is essential for the regime to make corrections in its economic policy and loosen its tight control over domestic political life. To judge from Islam Karimov's public statements, he is fully aware of this. However, if he does indeed decide to move from words to deeds, he can hardly count on the support of the new, but well-entrenched, nomenklatura. In the mid-1990s, Karimov replaced the old cadres with new people, but we all know what happens when one puts "new wine into old wineskins." Personnel from the new generation, or at least many of them, are also subject to the control of clan groups and faithfully defend their narrow interests.

At the present time, the Uzbek leadership must address two critical issues on its economic agenda: (1) state regulation over the convertibility of hard currency, which clearly needs to be abolished, but which will unleash a surge in inflation and have other untoward consequences; and (2) the unfavorable balance of payments, which cannot fail to be a growing cause of concern for Karimov. After the IMF denied Uzbekistan a stand-by credit at the end of 1996, imports had to be financed to a large degree through export credits granted by the export-import banks of the industrialized countries. This has led to a rather rapid increase in the foreign debt, and the payments to service this debt will increase sharply by the years 2004–2005.

Foreign Policy

It would appear that Islam Karimov's main goals in foreign policy are, first, to defeat attempts by Islamic radicals to topple his regime and, second, to establish his dominance as the principal leader of Central Asia. His campaign against Islamic fundamentalists not only enjoys the support of his neighbors in Central Asia, but also corresponds to the interests of Washington, Moscow, and Beijing. Although his aspirations to leadership are not openly articulated, no one can doubt the existence of this grand design and his personal ambitions (which, it must be admitted, are not unfounded). All the fluctuations, flip-flops, and gyrations in Karimov's foreign policy over the last decade are subordinated to achieving both these goals. The anti-Iranian policy in the first half of the 1990s gave way to a cautious, wait-and-see posture in the second half of the decade. The stormy love affair with Turkey from the beginning of independence suddenly ended in 1999, with a marked chill in their relations. Similar shifts have also been characteristic of Uzbekistan's relations with Russia and its neighbors in the region.

Karimov assigns top priority to becoming a member of Washington's circle of client states and to establishing close ties with NATO. As already pointed out, in 1999 Tashkent joined the pro-Washington GUUAM bloc, decided to open a mission at NATO headquarters, and supports Washington in virtually all of its actions (including the operation in Kosovo). Karimov not only supports American policy in the Middle East but has also established close economic and political ties to Israel—a step that has earned him particular enmity in extremist Muslim circles. Tashkent's loyalty to Washington and NATO has not gone unrewarded. Whereas the West favored Kazakhstan in the first half of the 1990s, it shifted its priority to Uzbekistan in 1997. Washington and its Atlantic partners close their eyes to the lack of democracy in Uzbekistan, pretend to take seriously the cosmetic measures to liberalize the regime,[44] and rely on Uzbekistan as the key strategic partner to press their interests in Central Asia.

At the end of 1999, Tashkent and Beijing established much closer relations. That improvement in ties was at least partly due to their mutual interest in suppressing the militant Islamic movements, which had become far more active and threatened not only to destabilize Uzbekistan, but also to fuel disorder among the Muslim population of western China (the Uighurs of Xinjiang). In November 1999, Karimov made a state visit to Beijing and held two meetings with President and Party Chairman Jiang Zemin. While in Beijing, Karimov declared that both countries "are united by the effort to combat international terrorism and to maintain regional security." As a result, Uzbekistan—which itself has tens of thousands of Uighurs—became China's ally in the struggle against Uighur separatist movements. Significantly, the Uighur diaspora in Uzbekistan has remained neutral in the struggle by the Uighurs of Xinjiang to gain their independence from China; Karimov assured President Jiang that the Uighurs in Uzbekistan will not become a problem for China in the future. In return, the Chinese leader offered his country's assistance to Tashkent in the struggle against Islamic extremists, including the Taliban in Afghanistan. Both sides also agreed to work together in the struggle to suppress the drug trade. During this visit, Karimov signed a number of agreements for trade and economic cooperation.[45]

Moscow represents the most complicated sphere of foreign policy for Uzbekistan, with periods of frosty relations alternating with short thaws. The key point is that Moscow simply cannot reconcile itself to the fact that Central Asia is slipping out from under its domination. While Nazarbaev periodically tries to tranquilize Moscow politicians by playing integrationist games and by espousing the idea of a single economic space, Karimov—from the very outset—has openly voiced his irreconcilable opposition to integration with Russia, even in the most innocent symbolic form. In essence, the hegemony of Uzbekistan in the region is incompatible with the active presence of Moscow.

Tashkent has therefore sought to exclude Moscow from any significant role in regional affairs. As one observer points out, "the Russian vector in Uzbek policy, while remaining substantial and sometimes a painful zone of Uzbek foreign policy striving, is increasingly dropping to secondary (after the West) and even tertiary importance."[46] Russia participates very little in the investment programs of Uzbekistan, and the commercial and economic relations between these countries have been reduced to a bare minimum. Tashkent has also minimized the presence of Russian mass media in the country.

Nevertheless, the states of this region recognize, however reluctantly, that Russia is the only state upon whom they can count in the struggle against the Islamic threat. Even Tashkent, which has created the most combat-ready army in the region, turns to Moscow for support whenever a crisis situation arises. It is quite another question whether Moscow can render this support on all occasions and to all these states.

Karimov cited such doubts in February 1999 when he justified his decision to withdraw from the Moscow-led "Treaty on Collective Security." Specifically, he accused the Russian government of failing to provide the requisite support against the Islamic militants from Afghanistan: "When the Taliban seized the northern part of Afghanistan and were practically at the bridge linking the territory of Uzbekistan with Afghanistan," Tashkent appealed to Moscow for assistance and asked the latter to send some rocket launchers. Although then-prime minister Viktor Chernomyrdin promised to send these weapons immediately, in fact the Uzbeks never received them. Karimov emphasized that there had been a number of such incidents.[47]

It is not easy to follow and explain the real motivation between this hot-and-cold fluctuation in the relations between Moscow and Tashkent. Thus, during a visit by President Boris Yeltsin to Tashkent in October 1998, the two sides signed a "Declaration on Comprehensive Cooperation," but particularly in the military sphere. Yet only a few months later, in February 1999, Tashkent unilaterally withdrew from Moscow's military union.

The relations between Moscow and Tashkent are tightly intertwined in a complex web of relations with other countries in the region. On the one hand, the other countries fear Moscow's control and encroachment on their independence; on the other hand, they also seek Moscow's protection not only to combat Islamic extremism but also to restrain the ambitions of Tashkent. Moscow of course exploits these fears as an opportunity to maintain its presence in the region. The most contentious sphere of conflict between Moscow and Tashkent concerns Tajikistan. For its part, Tashkent simply cannot abide Moscow's dominance in Dushanbe, which leaves Tajikistan in virtually total political, economic, and military dependency on Russia. Nor is Tashkent willing to accept the inclusion of the Islamic opposition into the Tajik government (an event fraught with far-reaching implications), or the ever-increasing flow of narcotics from Tajikistan.

But that raises the question of what would happen in the event Tashkent had its way—namely, that Russia withdraws from Tajikistan, thereby throwing open the Tajik-Afghan border. Who would assume the role of a stabilizing force, which the Russian 201st division—for better or worse—currently plays? Would the Uzbek army take over this responsibility? It is highly doubtful whether it could even cope with this task. The Uzbek government can hardly hope that it will withstand the pressure of the unified forces of Tajik and Uzbek militants, reinforced by extremists from other Muslim countries, who come well-trained, well-armed, and well-paid. Nor can one exclude the possibility that the Taliban will exploit this situation to the hilt. It is also difficult to imagine what would happen in Tajikistan if Uzbek troops were to intervene there.

And if not the Uzbeks, then who would replace the Russian forces? NATO? One can well imagine the enthusiasm of Atlantic policy-makers for sending troops to Central Asia, especially in the wake of their recent experience in the Balkans. If in East Timor it was principally Australian forces who were active, who would assume the task of extinguishing a fire in Central Asia should it break out? Possible candidates include China, Iran, Pakistan, and Turkey. It is a bit horrifying, but useful, to play out the hypothetical scenarios should events unfold along these lines.

During the summit in Istanbul in November 1999, Islam Karimov appealed to the world community and to the Organization for Security and Cooperation in Europe (OSCE) to wage a joint struggle against terrorism—by which he meant, above all, Islamic extremism. But such appeals are hardly likely to have any practical results. It may be that the pragmatic Uzbek leader will find a compromise between loyalty to Washington and closer relations with Moscow. The latter, of course, presupposes that Moscow will use sound judgment and not attempt to reclaim its dominant role in the region.

It also requires that Washington give more serious reflection about America's real strategic interests in Central Asia. The statements by American politicians and analysts are nebulous and unconvincing. Will the United States really assume the responsibility of ensuring stability in this volatile region? A former ranking member in the National Security Council of the Clinton administration has recently emphasized that the United States "has a big stake in the future development and political makeup of the South Caucasus and Central Asia," and proposed that Washington (independently and through programs like NATO's "Partnership for Peace") "help the Caspian states build up the military forces needed to control their borders and to protect their pipelines and transportation."[48] One can well imagine the consequences of such an ill-advised attempt to launch a regional arms race in an area already seething with mutual distrust, competing economic claims, and the ambitions of authoritarian leaders.

III. The Soviet Legacy and the Need for Objectivity

It is perfectly obvious that the economic decline in the first post-Soviet years was unavoidable. There was simply no way to avoid a period of dismay and perplexity, as regimes sought to identify an appropriate model of economic development, oriented themselves toward the external world, attempted to find a niche in the world economy, and struggled to foster a market mentality in the general population. But nearly a decade has passed, and it is high time to overcome the decline that was supposed to be transitional, not perpetual.

The leaders and officials of these Central Asian countries, as a rule, attribute the persisting economic crisis to the onerous consequences of Soviet rule and the breakup of a single economic space. While in no wise should one deny the significance of these factors, it is only fair to underline the important advantages that Central Asia inherited from the Soviet Union and that created favorable conditions to keep the economy afloat or, at least, to prevent a deep slump during the critical initial period of national independence. After all, in the course of the many years that Central Asia formed part of the USSR, Moscow systematically created a powerful economic and intellectual potential in the region. At the point when the Central Asian states proclaimed their independence, they possessed quite significant capacities for the production of cotton, agricultural commodities, oil and natural gas, coal, enriched uranium, ferrous and nonferrous metals, gold, and many other goods. At the same time, they had a shortage of industrial capacities to process agricultural products and raw materials. Despite this asymmetry, the economies of Central Asia nonetheless had a powerful export potential, which was the product of enormous investment from Moscow and not simply the creation of the labor and intellect of indigenous peoples. The Soviet regime constructed a gigantic irrigation system, hydroelectric plants, a transportation infrastructure, and the space launching site at Baikonur. At the time the Central Asian states became independent, they possessed a well-developed R&D base in the fundamental and applied sciences, an array of laboratories, research and design institutes, a class of professionals and researchers in industry, medicine, and other branches, and a well-developed system of general and specialized education. What other postcolonial countries possessed the kind of favorable starting position that Central Asia enjoyed? Where else was there such a high educational level in the population?

Rather than berate the legacy of Soviet rule, it is only fair to note that during the post-Soviet era the governments of Central Asia have been guilty of systematically squandering what they inherited from the USSR. And nothing has been more degraded than the human capital and the system for its reproduction—both of which took decades to build. Irreparable harm has been dealt by the emigration of the nonindigenous peoples, who, as is well known, supplied the majority of professionals and specialists in industry.

Nor should one disregard another factor of great importance during the initial phase of independence: when the Soviet Union was dissolved in 1991, industrial enterprises in Central Asia (like those elsewhere in the former Soviet Union) had accumulated billions of dollars worth of reserves ("normative and supra-normative reserves of surplus commodity-material goods"). These included a broad variety of material resources (for example, metals, construction materials, and spare parts for machinery and equipment) that could sustain current levels of production for at least two or three years. At a minimum, these resources should have enabled the post-Soviet regimes to avoid the collapse that occurred in 1992–93. In the end, however, these reserves were plundered and sold at dumping prices abroad, thereby serving not to soften the effect of transition but to enrich the tiny stratum of people in power (especially in Kazakhstan).

The overdramatization of the effects of the breakup of the Soviet Union also has the goal of understating the real economic resources available at the start of independence. In turn, this misrepresentation of the real possibilities for overcoming the shock of transition serves to mask the abysmal performance of authorities and to deflect blame to various "objective factors." In general, one tendency has become increasingly apparent: the leaders of the Central Asian countries, along with the ethnic elite, propagandize among the population a tendentious, self-serving picture of the Soviet past.

While obviously no apologist for the Soviet system, the present writer—when the USSR still existed—wrote critically about the economic and ecological problems of Central Asia and about the human dramas that Soviet rule entailed (beginning with the self-termed "genocide" of the Muslim population in the 1920s).[49] For the sake of objectivity, however, one must also recognize the enormous cultural and economic achievements in the Central Asian republics during the seven decades of Soviet rule. The Soviet period in the history of Central Asia cannot be reduced to simple black-and-white terms, as the current ruling elites in this region are wont to do.

Conclusion

As one examines the post-Soviet economies of Central Asia, the following characteristics are observed:

- ossification of the ruling regimes;
- "primitivization" of the economy;
- a desperate reliance upon natural resources as the main source of economic growth;
- a lack of rational improvements in the industrial structure;
- the incapacity of domestic investments to stimulate growth;
- the increasing limitations on the ability to attract foreign investment;
- the worsening of the balance of payments;
- the growth of foreign indebtedness;
- the incompleteness of reform in the agrarian sector;
- the use of agriculture as a "donor" to support other sectors of the economy;
- an excessive reliance upon import-substitution (which is by no means always justified).

All these negative dynamics threaten to doom the economies of Central Asia to protracted stagnation, at least in the foreseeable future.

The sharp upturn in world prices on oil, metals, and cotton brought about an improvement in the economic situation in Central Asia in 2000 from the previous two years. If one disregards the low starting point, the growth can appear quite impressive. In 1999, Kazakhstan achieved a record level in the production of oil. Despite some delays, the Caspian pipeline consortium is making systematic progress in its project to enable the shipping of oil through the Russian port of Novorossisk. Once complete, this new pipeline will permit Kazakhstan to increase its export of crude oil to profitable markets. However, one should not rush to any conclusions about the stability of this raw-material model; at any moment, a sudden decline in world prices could burst this illusory bubble of prosperity.

During the first two to three years of the coming century, Kyrgyzstan and Tajikistan are most likely to experience a further intensification of the crisis. In the case of Turkmenistan, it is practically impossible to evaluate the economic prospects, partly because of the extremely inadequate quality of information, and partly because everything depends on the opportunities to export natural gas to consumers who can pay in hard currency. As for Uzbekistan, if the government stays its present course and merely spins its wheels on the matter of real market reforms, it will not be able to overcome the stagnation and embark on a trajectory of stable economic growth.

This economic and social-political stagnation also entails social disintegration, with a growing gap between the rich and poor and the elimination of the middle strata (professionals, mid-level managers, and skilled workers) that developed during the Soviet era but have since become destitute and dropped to the bottom of the social pyramid. Such a polarization of society, which juxtaposes the interests of the rich and poor, is inherently riddled with antagonism, instability, and conflict.

Behind the pseudodemocratic decorations, the ruling regimes of Central Asia have adopted the practice of simulating parliamentary government and of holding what are essentially sham elections. The suppression of real political activity reinforces apathy and a cynical attitude toward the government. People have ceased to rely upon the regime or to expect it to render assistance; instead, they have increasingly come to realize that they can only count on themselves. This struggle for survival has unleashed individual initiative, entrepreneurship, and self-reliance: society has become more hardy and adaptable. In addition, there has been a primitivization of needs and reduction of consumption to a minimum. While these changes serve the interests of the authorities (by favoring stability and preservation of existing regimes), they also are fraught with serious dangers: insofar as people demand less from the government, they also are less inclined to give it their support. Society, in a word, is gradually becoming alienated from the ruling elites and their regime.

The growing material polarization and spiritual fragmentation also contribute to the development of social conflicts. While seeking to consolidate society, but without risking to use Islam for these purposes, the regimes of Central Asia are attempting to construct a new ideological base, one based on the glorification of a national past and its heroes. In Uzbekistan, for example, the regime is filling the post-Soviet political vacuum with a new ideology based on the cult of an idealized image of Amir Timur (best known in the West as Tamerlane), who has been transformed into the historical and cultural icon of the nation. Significantly, the Uzbeks, as the heirs and descendants of Tamerlane, are given the leading role in the history of Central Asia. In Kazakhstan, Ablai-Khan (who headed the three Kazakh khanates in the mid-eighteenth century) plays the same role. As in the case of the Tamerlane dynasty, only the positive features are emphasized; his brutality and aggressive behavior toward neighboring peoples is conveniently forgotten. There are even serious attempts to prove that Genghis Khan was a Kazakh, not a Turk. The extreme Russocentric Weltanschauung, implanted by Moscow during the Soviet era, has been replaced by an equally extreme ethnocentrism. Thus, official propagandists exaggerate the size of the population in the past; they also expand the territorial boundaries of areas that their predecessors allegedly occupied. Such myth-making (which, significantly, is devoid of an Islamic component) seeks to implant a stronger sense of national identity, to unite the people, and to serve as a kind of political lightning rod. However, because this idea of national greatness comes from above, it has failed to achieve the desired effect; it is as alien to mass consciousness as communist dogma was in the Soviet era. Propaganda about the special qualities of one's own people, which invidiously implies their superiority over others, can only catalyze a chauvinist mentality and aggravate the problem of multinational tensions in the region. Even without this propaganda, the region is already beset by centuries-old mutual animosities that divide the different ethnic groups of Central Asia.

The militant Islamic forces have directed the main thrust of their assault at Uzbekistan—the bulwark of the entire structure of regional stability. If Uzbekistan fails to withstand this attack, the other secular regimes of Central Asia could also collapse. The coexistence of Islamic radicalism with the ruling regime is hardly a possibility. After the bloody internecine strife and decomposition of the state and social order in Tajikistan, an attempt has been made there to create a symbiosis between Islamic militants and the ruling elites. However, this fragile construction is about to collapse under the weight of centrifugal domestic and foreign forces. In Uzbekistan, for the moment, the regime has succeeded in keeping the influence of Islam within limits set by the authorities. However, as experts have pointed out, Islam—in contrast to Christianity—can neither confine itself to the spiritual sphere alone nor fail to make a claim to political control over society. Hence, one must expect that the soundness of the system constructed by Islam Karimov will be repeatedly subjected to tests in this politically (not merely geologically) dangerous seismic zone.

Russian and Central Asian mass media have spread the claim that there is some kind of pan-Islamic "grand design," which purportedly lies behind the simultaneous assault of Muslim radicals along a broad front stretching from Afghanistan to Chechnya. It is hardly surprising that Moscow politicians and generals are seeking to convince public opinion, both in Russia and in the West, that there is a unified strategy and coordination of activities by Islamic militants in both Central Asia and Chechnya, all of which is directed and financed by a single center. It is understandable too that the Central Asian press, which operates under official control, attributes the upsurge in fundamentalist sentiments to external forces. If one were to believe General Ivashov (a ranking figure in the Russian general staff), he has "proof that the bandit attacks in both Central Asia and in the northern Caucasus are organized and conducted according to a single plan and financed, to all appearances, by the same sources." Vladimir Putin, during an appearance at the upper house of the Russian parliament when he served as prime minister, claimed that the Muslim radicals are planning "the construction of an enormous pseudo-Muslim state from the Caspian to the Black Sea."[50] This conspiracy theory strikes a strong chord in mass consciousness. Such ideas are still more cogent to popular thinking when these can be personified in concrete individuals, such as Osama bin Laden. It is highly convenient to explain the increase of Islamic activism in Central Asia by referring solely to exogenous, not internal, factors. However, as the authoritative specialist on Islam, Aleksei Malashenko, convincingly argues, "there is no organizing center: the political activity of Islam is occurring, above all, at the national level." To neutralize the radical Islamic movement in Central Asia by relying solely upon coercion will hardly succeed. It may be possible to avoid a social explosion by exploiting the depression and political passivity of the population, but not over the long term, especially in the face of a virulent Islamic movement. Protest will inexorably take on a religious form.

The development of the intraregional situation in 1998–99 shows that the growth of an Islamic threat, which is common to all the Central Asian regimes, does not contribute to their solidarity and unity. On the contrary, one finds the reverse tendency: relations between states in this region have become increasingly strained and conflictive. No matter how much they strive to be included in a Western defense system, it is an illusion to fantasize about the physical participation of the United States and NATO to support political stability in the region. The whole experience of the post-Soviet era shows that each new outburst of Islamic activism in the region, and each attack by the Taliban radicals, forces the leaders of Central Asia to overcome their anti-Russian feelings and to seek support in Moscow. Even the figure most overtly inclined to distance himself from Moscow, Islam Karimov, in the wake of the most recent extremist onslaught in late 1999, spoke about the need for a "strategic partnership [with Russia] to repulse Islamic expansion from the south."[51] Despite the constant friction in the relations with Moscow, the latter's role—as a force upon which the Central Asian regimes can rely in their struggle to prevent the Islamization of the region —will persist in the foreseeable future.

Notes

1. Calculated from statistical data supplied by the national statistical services in the Central Asian states and from the database of the International Monetary Fund.

2. See Interstate Statistical Committee, *The Commonwealth of Independent States in 1998: A Digest of Provisional Statistical Results* (Moscow, 1999), p. 115.

3. *Vremia*, 1999, no. 12:1; *Nezavisimaia gazeta*, 6 February 1999, p. 5; Iu. Razgulaev, "Torgovaia voina," *Vremia*, 12 February 1999.

4. S. Kozlov, "Tsentral'noaziatskii soiuz dal treshchinu," *Nezavisimaia gazeta*, 7 May 1999.

5. "Novosti," *Izvestiia*, 2 June 1999.

6. Igor' Rotar', "Iskhodia iz sushchestvuiushchikh realii," *Nezavisimaia gazeta*, 7 July 1999.

7. A. Korbut, "Reanimatsiia obshchikh interesov," *Nezavisimaia gazeta*, 21 May 1999.

8. *Izvestiia*, 22 May 1999, p. 3.

9. Korbut, "Reanimatsiia obshchikh interesov."

10. *Vremia*, 13 April 1999, p. 1.

11. Geoffrey Kemp, *Energy Superbowl* (Washington, DC: Nixon Center, 1997), p. 33.

12. Ibid., p. 25.

13. V. Mikhailov, "Niiazov podderzhivaet SNG," *Nezavisimaia gazeta*, 7 May 1999.

14. "Ashgabat polnost'iu vzial na sebia okhranu granitsy," *Segodnia*, 26 May 1999; "Turkmeniia rasshiriaet kontakty s NATO," *Segodnia*, 12 May 1999.

15. See, for example, Kasymzhomart Tokaev, *Pod stiagom nezavisimosti* (Almaty, 1997), pp. 207, 217.

16. Maria Hsia Chang, "Chinese Irredentist Nationalism: The Magicians' Last Trick," *Comparative Strategy* 17 (1998): 87–88.

17. Craig Harris, "China's Policy in the Islamic World," *The China Quarterly* 110 (March 1993): 114.

18. A. Guliaev, "Kitai-Kazakhstan: pogranichnyi spor prodolzhaetsia," *Izvestiia*, 30 April 1999.

19. V. Turov, "Kak Rossiiu ostavliaiut za 'vodo-zaborom,'" *Nezavisimaia gazeta*, 12 May 1999.

20. Ibid.

21. Guliaev, "Kitai-Kazakhstan."

22. K. Tokaev, *Pod stiagom nezavisimosti* (Almaty, 1997), p. 204.

23. Liz Sly, "China's Chechnya: A Powder Keg of Mistrust, Hatred," *Boston Globe*, 19 October 1999, p. A21.

24. *Boston Globe*, 21 September 1999, p. 7.

25. See, for example, A. Serb, "Ural'skoe kazachestvo khochet byt' v sostave Rossii," *Sodruzhestvo Nezavisimykh Gosudarstv*, 1999, no. 4.

26. *Nezavisimaia gazeta*, 17 November 1992, p. 50.

27. *EKO*, 1999, no. 5: 89–105.

28. *Izvestiia*, 16 July 1999, p. 2.

29. Postanovlenie Pravitel'stva Rossiiskoi Federatsii ot 29 iiunia 1999, No. 709 (as reported by ISI Emerging Markets, Internet Securities, Inc.).

30. *Nezavisimaia gazeta*, 26 January 1999, p. 5.

31. *Ekspert*, 1996, no. 48 (16 December): 40.

32. According to *Ekspert* (1996, no. 48 [16 December]: 41), "many of the firms with foreign names that have bought enterprises in Kazakhstan or that run them under a concession agreement are in fact off-shore companies, which are the joint creation of Kazakh and Russian financial circles." It is for reasons of "taxation" that they are registered somewhere like the Virgin Islands or Ireland.

33. *Energiia* (Almaty), 1999, no. 3: 22.

34. *Energiia*, 1999, no. 2: 25.

35. *Energiia*, 1999, no. 2: 33.

36. A. Malashenko, "Pogoda na poslezavtra," *Sodruzhestvo Nezavisimykh Gosudarstv*, 1999, no. 5 (May): p. 3.

37. S. Horsman, "Uzbekistan's Involvement in the Tajik Civil War 1992–1997," *Central Asian Survey* 18 (1999): 40.

38. A. Smirnov, "U Bishkeka poiavilsia svoi Dagestan," *Segodnia*, 26 August 1999.

39. *Nezavisimaia gazeta*, 2 November 1999, p. 5; ibid., 3 November 1999, p. 5.

40. See, for example, I. Karimov, *Uzbekistan on the Threshold of the Twenty-First Century* (Cambridge, MA, 1998), pp. 53–68.

41. B. Rumer and S. Zhukov, eds., *Central Asia: The Challenges of Independence* (Armonk, NY: M.E. Sharpe, 1998), pp. 65, 76–77.

42. *Pravda Vostoka*, 15 April 1999.

43. See J.S. Hogendorn, *Economic Development* 3d ed. (New York, 1996), pp. 12–13.

44. For example, to create the appearances of political pluralism in implementing the parliamentary law "on political parties," which formally established a multiparty system, five political parties were established. But all these quasi-parties serve as transmission belts to implement presidential policies and are completely subject to control by the Karimov administration.

45. Iu. Chernogaev, "Tashkent i Pekin zakliuchili pakt," *Kommersant-Daily*, 12 November 1999.

46. *Sodruzhestvo Nezavisimykh Gosudarstv*, 1998, no. 5 (27 May): 12.

47. *Panorama*, 26 February 1999, p. 5.

48. Sheila Heslin, "Danger at the Crossroads," *New York Times*, 3 November 1999, p. A-29.

49. Boris Rumer, *Soviet Central Asia: A Tragic Experiment* (Boston, 1989).

50. *Kommersant*, 18 September 1999, p. 2; *Nezavisimaia gazeta*, 15 September 1999, p. 3.

51. Iu. Sidorov, "Uzbekistan opredeliaetsia v orientirakh," *Kommersant-Daily*, 3 December 1999.

2

The Economic Development of Central Asia in the 1990s

Stanislav Zhukov

The literature on the problem of economic growth has firmly established the notion of a "lost decade." This term was originally used to characterize the development of Latin American countries in the 1980s. It refers to the accumulation of domestic and foreign disproportions in the economy that first retarded, then completely blocked, the development of Latin American countries for an entire decade.

For Central Asia (as indeed for the entire post-Soviet realm), the 1990s did not constitute simply a "lost decade," but rather represented an era of incredible and incomprehensible economic catastrophe. What has been the scale of the economic and social losses? Has the economic downturn finally reached bottom? What is the main thrust of the structural changes overtaking the countries of Central Asia? And, most important, have these countries laid the necessary foundations so that they can "take off"—that is, launch themselves onto a trajectory of stable economic growth? These questions are the focus of the present chapter.

The Zigzags of Economic Decline

In the first half of the 1990s, all the newly independent states of the former USSR, including those in Central Asia, experienced a profound economic decline. Between 1990 and 1995, the GDP fell by 62 percent in Tajikistan, 49 percent in Kyrgyzstan, 39 percent in Kazakhstan, 30 percent in Turkmenistan, and 18 percent in Uzbekistan (see Table 2.1).

58

Table 2.1

Growth Rates of Central Asian States, 1991–1998 (as percent of previous year)

Indicator/Country	Percent decline from previous year					As percent of 1990	Percent decline from previous year			As percent of 1995	As percent of 1990
	1991	1992	1993	1994	1995	1995	1996	1997	1998	1998	1998
GDP											
Kazakhstan	−11.0	−5.3	−9.2	−12.6	−8.2	61.4	+0.5	+2.0	−2.5	100	61.4
Kyrgyzstan	−7.9	−13.9	−15.5	−20.1	−5.4	50.6	+7.1	+9.9	+1.8	120	60.7
Tajikistan	−7.1	−29.0	−16.3	−21.3	−12.4	38.1	−16.7	+1.7	+5.3	90	34.3
Turkmenistan	−4.7	−5.3	+1.5	−16.7	−7.7	70.4	+0.1	−25.9	+4.5	78	54.6
Uzbekistan	−0.5	−11.1	−2.3	−5.2	−0.9	81.2	+1.7	+5.2	+4.4	112	90.9
Industry											
Kazakhstan	−0.9	−13.8	−14.8	−28.1	−8.2	44.1	+0.3	+4.0	−2.1	102	45.0
Kyrgyzstan	−0.3	−26.4	−25.3	−28.0	−17.8	32.4	+18.8	+50.4	+8.3	177	57.3
Tajikistan	−3.6	−24.3	−7.8	−25.4	−13.6	43.4	−23.9	−2.0	+8.1	81	35.2
Turkmenistan	+4.8	−15.0	−11.0	−33.0	−38.0	32.9	−27.0				
Uzbekistan	+1.5	−6.7	+3.6	+1.6	+0.1	99.8	+2.6	+4.1	+5.8	113	112.8
Agriculture											
Kazakhstan	−10.0	+29.0	−7.0	−21.0	−24.0	64.8	−5.0	−0.8	−19.0	76	49.2
Kyrgyzstan	−10.0	−5.0	−10.0	−18.0	−2.0	57.4	+15.0	+12.5	+4.0	134	76.2
Tajikistan	−4.0	−27.0	−9.0	−10.0	−21.0	45.3	−18.0	+4.0	+6.5	91	41.2
Turkmenistan	−4.0	−9.0	−16.0	−13.0	−28.0	55.0	−29.0				
Uzbekistan	−1.0	−6.0	+1.0	−8.0	+3.0	89.1	−6.0	+4.0	+4.0	102	90.9

Investment

Kazakhstan	+0.5	−47.0	−39.0	−15.0	−37.0	17.4	−39.0	+12.0	+13.0	77	13.4
Kyrgyzstan	−14.0	−25.0	−23.0	−45.0	+82.0	49.7	+19.0	−4.0	−53.0	54	26.8
Tajikistan	−15.0	−42.0	+0.1	−43.0							
Turkmenistan	+11.0	+20.0	+74.0								
Uzbekistan	+5.0	−32.0	−5.0	−22.0	+4.0	55.0	+7.0	+17.0	+15.0	144	79.2

Sources: Interstate Statistical Committee, *Commonwealth of Independent States in 1998* (Moscow, 1999), pp. 214, 229, 274, 286, 304; Interstate Statistical Committee, *Commonwealth of Independent States in 1997* (Moscow, 1998), p. 287; International Monetary Fund, *World Economic Outlook, Spring, 1999* (Washington, DC, 1999), p. 15.

Note: The figures in Table 2.1 are compiled mainly from national statistical sources; they therefore differ from the data on GDP growth cited in Table 3.1, which is based on various IMF publications. Moreover, the data in Table 2.1 and 2.6 are not in disagreement, but refer to entirely different matters. Namely, Table 2.1 presents data by comparing the GDP with the national income in constant prices; Table 2.6 presents aggregate and per capita GDP in nominal U.S. dollars at the official exchange rate (and, for Uzbekistan and Turkmenistan, at the prevailing black-market rates).

The contraction of production was evident in every branch of the economy; there were no exceptions. Thus, during this same period (1990–95), the output of agricultural goods fell by 55 percent in Tajikistan, 43 percent in Kyrgyzstan, 45 percent in Turkmenistan, 35 percent in Kazakhstan, and 11 percent in Uzbekistan. The decrease in the industrial production of the Central Asian states was even more intensive: 68 percent in Kyrgyzstan, 67 percent in Turkmenistan, 57 percent in Tajikistan, and 56 percent in Kazakhstan. Only Uzbekistan, in the middle of the 1990s, was able to maintain industrial production at essentially the same level as in the previous five years. Nonetheless, even here the decline reached 7 percent in 1992.

Concurrent with this decline in the general economy and production branches, profound crisis also overtook the investment sphere. The volume of capital investment for 1995 in Kazakhstan and Tajikistan amounted to less than one-fifth of the level in 1990. During the same period, investment shrank by 60 percent in Kyrgyzstan and 45 percent in Uzbekistan. To judge from official statistics for 1991–93, only Turkmenistan claimed to have had a substantial growth of investment. However, the reliability of these statistics is questionable, and since 1994 Turkmenistan has ceased to publish data on the dynamics of capital investment.

To all appearances, 1996 signaled a turn toward the better in the economies of Central Asia. After five years of negative growth rates, all the countries of the region (except Tajikistan) reported a positive growth in the GDP. In addition, three states—Kazakhstan, Kyrgyzstan, and Uzbekistan—witnessed an increase in industrial production. The growth of GDP and industrial output in these three countries continued into the next year as well. In addition, Uzbekistan and Kyrgyzstan reported that agriculture had also demonstrated positive rates of growth, while in Kazakhstan agricultural output fell by less than 1 percent.

Considered from its extremely low starting point, Kyrgyzstan's performance in 1997 could justify ranking that country in the "league of champions" for economic growth. The GDP here increased by 9.9 percent, but industrial output by an astonishing 50.4 percent. The growth of the GDP, industry, and agriculture in that country continued in 1998. Uzbekistan similarly demonstrated steady, positive rates of growth in both 1997 and 1998.

The situation in Turkmenistan and Tajikistan is rather more murky. In 1997, for the first time in a decade, the GDP in Tajikistan rose by 1.7 percent, and the following year it climbed another 5.3 percent. Tajikistan succeeded in restoring a positive rate of growth, first in agriculture (1997) and then in industry (1998). In the case of Turkmenistan, which had experienced a 0.1 percent growth of its GDP in 1996, the sharp contraction of exports (and, accordingly, the production of natural gas) led to an overall decline in its GDP. According to estimates by the International Monetary Fund (IMF), the GDP in this country plunged by more than one-quarter in 1997, but then showed a small gain of 4.5 percent the following year.

With the exception of Kazakhstan, all the countries of this region continued to exhibit economic growth in 1998. In the case of Kazakhstan, 1998 was one of the worst agricultural years in the last several decades. As a result, agricultural production decreased here by 19 percent, and that in turn caused the GDP to decrease by 2.5 percent.

Notwithstanding the somewhat encouraging dynamics of 1996–98, the macroeconomic results of development in the states of Central Asia in the 1990s give little cause for consolation. In 1991–98, the GDP of Kazakhstan decreased by more than one-third: by 1998, the GDP here was only 61.4 percent of the level reached at the beginning of the decade. Moreover, the modest growth achieved in 1995–97 was wiped out by the next downturn in 1998. As a result, the GDP in 1998 had changed little from the middle of the decade.

In Tajikistan, the growth of 1997–98 was not sufficiently large to offset, even partially, the deep contraction of the preceding years. In 1998, the GDP of Tajikistan was only slightly more than one-third of its level in 1990. Moreover, during the years 1996–98, the GDP dropped another 10 percent from the mid-1990s.

The results of independent development in Turkmenistan were hardly any less dismal. Measured in terms of the intensity of decline in economic activity, this country ranks right behind Tajikistan. Moreover, a substantial decrease in the GDP here not only occurred in the first half of the 1990s, but persisted in the following years from 1996 to 1998.

In Kyrgyzstan, the GDP admittedly did increase by 20 percent in 1996–98 (over the base year 1995). However, if that GDP is compared with the level at the beginning of the 1990s, the economic situation here is hardly any better than in Kazakhstan.

Only Uzbekistan, if one is willing to rely upon the official statistics, was more successful in dealing with the disintegration of the Soviet economy and in finding an adequate response to the challenges of independent development. Here the GDP increased by 12 percent in 1995–

98 and, by the end of this period, the government still claimed it to be 90.9 percent of the level in 1990. Industrial production in Uzbekistan also developed steadily throughout the entire decade; only in 1992 did output decline (7 percent). As a result, by 1998 the volume of industrial production in Uzbekistan was 12.8 percent higher than at the beginning of the decade.

Thus, after the first eight years of independent development, not a single state in Central Asia had managed to regain the level of production it had already enjoyed in 1990. These new states were, in short, well below the level when, in the view of some researchers, they were "colonies" of Russia. Moreover, with the exception of Uzbekistan (which might recover its "late-colonial" volume of production by 2001–2), the other four states of Central Asia will require much more time to achieve that goal. For the sake of comparison, one might bear in mind that even Algeria, despite the destruction of an eight-year war for independence and the enormous economic shock caused by the flight of several hundred thousand Frenchmen (who controlled the most efficient spheres of economic activity), required only eight years to reach and surpass the highest level of production achieved during the period of colonial rule.[1]

Worse still, not in a single state of Central Asia has economic growth acquired a stable character. By the end of 1998, it became perfectly obvious that after the relatively successful years of 1996 and 1997 the region apparently was on the verge of a renewed economic downturn. At some point after late 1997, all the post-Soviet states found themselves in the wake of the great turbulence caused by global price shocks on the markets for raw materials and energy resources. In addition, some of the most important export markets of Central Asia have experienced stagnation or recession. During such periods, the long-term tendency for prices to drop on raw materials and natural resources (vis-à-vis industrial goods) has begun to assume a particularly acute form.

Relatively less important, yet destructive for the financial and economic plans of Kazakhstan and Kyrgyzstan, is another factor: a breakdown of confidence among global speculative investors in these emerging markets. That lack of trust has been paralleled by the increasing difficulty that has faced the Central Asian states as they seek to place government bonds on the world financial markets. It is clear that these and related tendencies will have their greatest impact on the economies of Kazakhstan and Kyrgyzstan. That is because both countries have gone further than the others in the task of creating a modern financial system and opening to international competition.

In September 1997, Kazakhstan placed a Eurobond for 350 million dollars on world financial markets.[2] In 1998, however, the global financial instability prevented the Kazakh government from financing its budget expenditures by placing new Eurobonds. In addition, the instability in world finances prevented Kazakhstan from tapping the full power of the stock markets for domestic enterprises, although these had been regarded as a new mechanism to mobilize financial resources and thereby attract fresh investment.

There are strong reasons to presume that in the coming years the instability in the world economy will intensify, and that the probability of new global turmoil will significantly increase. Such a development, in turn, is fraught with profoundly negative consequences for all the post-Soviet states.

The magnitude of the economic crisis in Russia has dealt a further blow to all the countries of Central Asia. The intensity of the shock varies from one economy to the next, but has left none untouched. Kazakhstan, Kyrgyzstan, and Uzbekistan (where the export-import flows are, to a substantial degree, oriented toward Russia) have all found themselves in particularly difficult straits.

In 1998, only Kazakhstan showed a return to the pattern of a negative rate of economic growth. According to official estimates, in 1999 the GDP here fell by another 1.5 to 3.0 percent.[3] In 1999, however, this regression could come to encompass not only Kazakhstan but also Kyrgyzstan. At the same time, all countries in this region, without any exception, face serious economic difficulties.

Is the Economic Decline Over?

A number of factors make it possible to conclude that all the countries of Central Asia are still far removed from the point where they can embark on a trajectory with a stable rate of positive economic growth. Let us examine these factors in greater detail.

Of critical significance is the problem of investments. In the middle-range perspective, the prospects for investment in the Central Asian region do not provide much cause for optimism. Capital investment—the main dynamo of economic growth—is still in a most lamentable state in the post-Soviet republics.

Capital investment in Kyrgyzstan in the 1990s has been highly volatile. That country experienced a sharp decline in the first years of independence, but then enjoyed a veritable boom in 1995–96, when investment skyrocketed by nearly 100 percent. In 1997 and especially in 1998, however, investments fell by 50 percent and amounted to only one-quarter of the level in 1990 (see Table 2.1).

The situation has been comparatively better in Kazakhstan and especially Uzbekistan. In 1997–98, Kazakhstan showed a 12 percent increase in the annual rate of capital investment; Uzbekistan recovered its pre-independence investment level in 1994 and has shown a steady increase ever since.

Nevertheless, capital investment in Kazakhstan fell in 1995 to 17 percent of the 1990 level and declined to just 13.4 percent in 1998. The level of capital accumulation remains extremely low and indeed continues to fall. The norm for the gross accumulation of fixed capital has decreased here from 24.4 percent of the GDP in 1994 to 17.0 percent in 1997, and then sank to just 10.1 percent in 1998.[4] It should be obvious that, notwithstanding the weak positive steps in recent years, new investments in fixed capital can only provide partial compensation for the gradual depletion of the fixed capital. Nor, of course, can it provide a reliable basis to support stable, positive rates of growth in the middle- and long-term perspective.

In 1994–98, Uzbekistan reported not only an increase in the volume of investments, but also a rather high level of capital accumulation. Therefore, compared with Kazakhstan and Kyrgyzstan, Uzbekistan appears to have much brighter prospects for growth. A word of caution is in order, however: the available statistics do not make it possible to judge the quality of the capital process in Uzbekistan. Indeed, there are many indirect indications that investment resources (the volume and structure of which the state totally controls through administrative measures) are not in fact used in the optimal way. It is highly probable that, as in the former USSR, the emerging economic structure in contemporary Uzbekistan will not be in a position to generate self-sustained growth. Moreover, the total volume of investment in Uzbekistan has contracted substantially since the Soviet era. Thus, in 1995, capital investment here amounted to just 55 percent of the level in 1990; indeed, by 1998, this indicator had risen to just 79.2 percent. Nor is the norm for capital accumulation high when compared with international standards. In 1993–97, it averaged 19.8 percent, rising in some years to 23–24 percent.[5]

Amidst all this economic decline, the countries of Central Asia have also experienced such phenomena as arrears and, on a massive scale, the financial insolvency of enterprises in the productive and service sectors of the economy.

The phenomenon of arrears has been studied in great detail in the Russian case, but it is also endemic to the economies of Central Asia. In effect, arrears represent a special form of interenterprise credit; they resort to this informal credit in order to overcome a shortage of working capital and a limited demand for their products. Described in the simplest terms, arrears allow enterprises to deliver each other their goods without payment and thereby accumulate mutual debts. These firms are calculating (not without grounds, it must be said) that, sooner or later, the government will write off these debts. The latter consideration is indeed a powerful incentive for nonpayment, since the government is regularly unable to pay for state orders from its own budgetary funds. In addition, the government encourages arrears outside the budgetary sphere; for example, it forces petroleum refinery enterprises to make deliveries of fuel and lubricants to the insolvent agrarian sector. It also forbids suppliers to cut off the supply of fuel and energy to bankrupt customers.

Arrears thus represent an auxiliary form of money, one that is emitted by the nonfinancial sectors in order to overcome the limitations of an austere monetary-credit policy followed by financial authorities. Despite all the monetarist rhetoric of the post-Soviet governments, practically all of them close their eyes to this type of monetary emission. Indeed, it is not only the producers but the governments themselves that actively engage in this practice. Any other policy would be tantamount to political suicide, since the great majority of economic organizations inherited from the Soviet past are no longer viable in the new configuration of production costs and demand constraints.

Apparently, for this same reason, the phenomenon of uncontrolled monetary emission has been ignored by international financial organizations. The latter, of course, have provided credits and intellectual guidance for the process of transition to a market system in the post-Soviet realm. The position taken by the Bretton Woods institutions is entirely understandable, however. Had they taken a different tack, it would have been perfectly clear from the very outset of the reforms that the "stabilization programs" sponsored by the International Monetary Fund and the World Bank would have been tantamount to the demolition of the economic structure that the newly independent states had inherited from the former USSR.

Whatever the case, arrears mediate a substantial part of economic activity in the countries of Central Asia. In Uzbekistan, for instance, bills payable represented 40.8 percent of the GDP in 1995 and 40.1 percent in 1996. The indicators for "overdue bills payable" (viz., past due for a term exceeding three months) reached 10.9 percent of the GDP in 1995 and 13.2 percent in 1996.[6] In Kyrgyzstan, where the dismantling of the inherited economic structure has been most systematically implemented, the bills payable rose from 17.5 percent of the GDP in 1997 to 20.3 percent in 1998. Overdue bills payable, however, did modestly decline as a proportion of GDP (falling from 6.6 percent to 5.5 percent over the same years).[7]

The problem of arrears is most acute in Kazakhstan: during the entire period of 1995–98, the overdue bills payable (more than three months past due) never dropped below 34–35 percent of the GDP.[8] In 1998, the overdue bills payable amounted to 35 percent of the GDP, and the sum of all bills payable amounted to 87.5 percent of the GDP. The volume of overdue bills payable was more than four times the M2 money supply.[9]

Moreover, the bills payable are not the only transition ailment to infect the Kazakh economy. By the beginning of 1999, the arrears on wages and salaries here reached 69.1 percent of the total volume of cash in circulation in the national economy.[10] If the government were to pay off these debts alone (and they do not include still others, such as the arrears on pensions and social assistance), that would instantaneously wipe out many years of work aimed at stabilizing consumer inflation.

The phenomenon of arrears clearly reveals that the monetary assessments of the GDP in all the Central Asian states must be seen as highly provisional. From the perspective of the market, a significant part of the economic activity in these countries is a paper fiction and, under normal circumstances, would not be sustained. Even in Kyrgyzstan (which is in a relatively favorable situation with respect to arrears), approximately 5–7 percent of the GDP exists only on paper. In Kazakhstan, at least a third of the GDP would be superfluous under market conditions.

In reality, liquidation of the nonpayment mechanism would trigger a still sharper decline in economic activity than would follow from the ratio of overdue bills payable to the GDP. The point here is that the bulk of the indebtedness falls on the electric power and fuel sector—that is, the branches at the very fountainhead of the production cycle. In an economy that has a dense network of forward and backward linkages, a 1 percent contraction of production in the fuel and energy complex would trigger a far greater decline in the output of branches that consume these intermediate inputs.

Along with arrears and a contraction of investment, the financial condition of enterprises is yet another indicator that the decline in production is still not over. In 1998 in Kazakhstan, for example, 51.5 percent of all enterprises and organizations engaged in economic activities were operating at a net loss.[11] During the preceding year (1997), for which more complete data are available, 30 percent of the enterprises in the industrial branch of Kazakhstan produced a negative added value. More specifically, the proportion of such unprofitable enterprises amounted to 40 percent in electric power, 37 percent in food-processing, 35 percent in machine-building, and 22 percent in fuels.[12] Still more revealing is the fact that Kazakhstan produced 26 percent of its electric power at a loss.[13]

It hardly need be said that operating at a loss (i.e., producing negative added value) is characteristic not only for Kazakhstan, but for all the other countries of Central Asia. In addition, it bears noting that unprofitable production is especially widespread in the agricultural sector.

Finally, it is important to note that the official indicators of economic activity are, increasingly, of dubious reliability and accuracy. As regimes of personal rule become consolidated in the states of Central Asia, local statistical services have begun to resort to highly refined manipulation; the goal, clearly, has been to depict the economic situation in a more favorable light than the facts warrant. For Uzbekistan and Turkmenistan, which are especially characterized by a lack of informational transparency, this "improvement" of the statistical indicators is routine. However, such tricks have also become common in Kyrgyzstan and Kazakhstan, which in general are "open" countries in terms of information. And there are also some instances where international experts take part in this "improvement" in the national statistics.

Concealed behind all these efforts are real economic processes. A significant segment of production in post-Soviet states comes from the unofficial "shadow economy," where economic actors, on a massive scale, seek to avoid taxation. Even in Uzbekistan, where an authoritarian regime would appear to be in total control, according to some estimates "the shadow sector" nonetheless amounts to 28 percent of the GDP. In the agricultural sector of that country, the production outside centralized control accounts for 62 percent of total output. In Kazakhstan, the shadow economy is estimated equal to 40 percent of the official GDP.[14]

Although the statistics are constantly being updated, they suffer increasingly from distortions. In this respect, the case of Kazakhstan is quite revealing. In 1996, the volume of GDP was corrected by adding estimated data on the sector of "households." According to official calculations, in 1996 these household producers accounted for 26.1 percent of the total GDP; moreover, they were responsible for 61 percent of the added value in agriculture, 45.1 percent in transportation, and 34.4 percent in trade. Even in industry, households generated 9.7 percent of the gross added value; they purportedly accounted as well for 12 percent of the added value in construction.[15]

It is natural that such substantial "corrections" (the methodological basis of which is not fully clear) significantly affect any characterization of the rate of growth. Table 2.2 presents the rates of growth for various branches of industry in Kazakhstan; the data present calculations that both include and exclude households. In the span of just two years, the share of output attributed to households jumped from 1.3 to 14.3 percent for construction materials, from 14.4 to 36.5 percent for light industry, and from 30.8 to 37.2 percent for the food-processing industry.

As this table demonstrates, statistical "corrections" completely altered the flow of economic dynamics in 1996. If the calculations omit the sector of "households," industrial production *contracted* by 9.1 percent; if the calculations include this sector, aggregate output *increased* by 0.3 percent.

The same results from statistical "correction" also obtain at the macro level. In 1997, for example, the GDP of Kazakhstan decreased by 3 percent if the households are disregarded, but rose by 2 percent if they are included. The growth in the latter case was solely attributable to the claim that the output of households rose by the fantastic amount of 76 percent.[16] In 1998, calculations that include the household producers also make it possible for official statistics to show a smaller industrial (and therefore general economic) decline.

In short, it is premature to talk about an end to the economic downturn in Central Asia. In principle, it is possible to have economic growth by putting into service those productive capacities that are now idle (on a large scale), and also by attracting an influx of foreign investment in lines of production aimed at export. However, economic growth in this

Table 2.2

Relative Importance of "Household Producers" in Kazakhstan, 1996–1998

			Percent Change in Output			
	Share of household producers in output (in percent)		With household producers		Without household producers	
	1996	1998	1996	1998	1996	1998
Total industrial production	9.7	9.9	+0.3	−2.1	−9.1	−3.5
Wood and timber industry	11.4	29.1	+7.0		−22.5	
Construction materials	1.3	14.3	−31.8	−11.9	−34.7	−13.9
Light industry	14.4	36.5	+14.5	−12.9	−15.7	−15.3
Food-processing industry	30.8	37.2	+32.7	+1.3	−27.1	+0.3

Sources: Natsional'noe statisticheskoe agentstvo, *Sotsial'no-ekonomicheskoe polozhenie Respubliki Kazakhstan za ianvar'-dekabr' 1996 goda* (Almaty, 1997), p. 6; M. Khasanova and Z. Zaitova, "Valovoi vnutrennii produkt: analiz i problemy izmereniia," *Aziia. Ekonomika i zhizn'*, no. 46 (November 1999): 6; "Valovoi vnutrennii produkt za 1996 god," ibid., no. 49 (December 1997): 6; Natsional'noe statisticheskoe agentstvo, *Sotsial'no-ekonomicheskoe polozhenie Respubliki Kazakhstan za ianvar'-dekabr' 1998 goda* (Almaty, 1998), pp. 96–100.

region will continue to be spasmodic and uneven for a number of years. Such will be the case until the mechanism of nonpayment is eliminated, unprofitable enterprises are declared bankrupt, and the norm and volume of capital investment are substantially increased.

Structural Changes

The large-scale contraction of economic activity has been accompanied by a fundamental restructuring of the branch structure of industry and employment. To delineate the structural changes in the economies of Central Asia, one can examine this process through the prism of three major sectors of the economy: agriculture, industry and construction, and services.

Table 2.3 shows the dynamics of the aggregate structure of the GDP for Kazakhstan, Kyrgyzstan, and Uzbekistan in current prices and in constant prices for 1995. The peak in the breakup of the inherited economic structure in all three countries came in the first half of the 1990s. It was precisely in the first years of independent development that Kazakhstan, Kyrgyzstan, and Uzbekistan experienced de-industrializa-

Table 2.3

Shifts in the Structure of Production and Employment
(in percent)

Country	Sector	GDP						Employment		
		Current Prices			Constant Prices (1995)					
		1991	1995	1998	1991	1995	1998	1990	1995	1998
Kazakhstan	Agriculture	28.8	13.0	8.8	12.4	13.0	10.8	23	22	24
	Industry and construction	36.7	31.5	27.8	45.4	31.5	33.3	32	22	18
	Services	34.5	55.5	63.4	42.2	55.5	55.9	45	56	58
Kyrgyzstan	Agriculture	37.2	43.9	43.8	38.7	43.9	49.2	33	46	48
	Industry and construction	35.4	19.5	21.0	26.6	19.5	22.1	28	16	13
	Services	27.4	36.6	35.2	34.7	36.6	28.7	39	38	39
Uzbekistan	Agriculture	37.5	32.5	30.7[a]	30.3	31.3	29.4	39	41	41
	Industry and construction	36.0	27.7	27.4[a]	28.8	26.8	30.3	24	19	18
	Services	26.5	39.8	41.9[a]	40.9	41.9	40.3	37	40	41

Sources: UNDP, Tsentr ekonomicheskikh issledovanii, *Uzbekistan 1998. Otchet o chelovecheskom razvitii* (Tashkent, 1998), p. 107; *Commonwealth of Independent States in 1998*, pp. 202, 214, 293, 304; *Natsional' nye scheta Kyrgzskoi Respubliki, 1993–1997* (Bishkek, 1998), p. 36; *Natsional' nye scheta Respubliki Kazakhstan 1994–1997* (Almaty, 1998), p. 26; *Statistical Handbook 1996*, pp. 197, 231, 503; S. Zhukov, "The Economic Development of Kazakhstan, Kyrgyzstan, and Uzbekistan in 1990–1995" (paper presented at the Issyk-Kul' Forum, Tokyo, October 1996); also, the sources cited in Table 2.1.

[a] Data for 1997.

tion on a massive scale. That process in turn entailed a contraction in the relative share of the GDP produced by industry and construction. These three countries also experienced growth in the service sector, with a noticeable growth in the contribution of services to total GDP.

Furthermore, the decline of industry was particularly noticeable in Kyrgyzstan, while in Kazakhstan the service sector strengthened its position. The relative significance of the agrarian sector in each country changed in different ways. In Uzbekistan and especially Kazakhstan (if the structure of the GDP is calculated in current prices), the role of agriculture in aggregate output decreased noticeably. In Kyrgyzstan, by contrast, this contribution increased noticeably.

Especially intensive changes in the structure of employment and production were apparent in Kazakhstan and Kyrgyzstan. In Uzbekistan, which retained the administrative-command system of control over the economy, structural changes have been minimal.

In 1995–98, Kazakhstan and still more Uzbekistan palpably reduced the intensity of branch restructuring. It is remarkable that during these same years both countries experienced a partial re-industrialization, which was reflected in an increase in the share of industry and construction in the structure of production. Moreover, in both countries, construction and industry have increased their share at the expense of agriculture.

In Kyrgyzstan, the intensity of structural changes is just as active in the second half of the 1990s as it had been in the first half of the decade. Given the small scale of its economy (small even when compared with the somewhat larger economies of neighboring states), two or three relatively large-scale projects can have a considerable impact on the macroeconomic structure. Moreover, even though industry and construction prevailed in the growth, agriculture also increased its share of the GDP.

The pattern of changes in the employment structure essentially coincided with the change in branch proportions of the GDP in constant prices (see Table 2.3). In all three countries under review here, industry and construction lost their former role as the principal sphere for employing labor. Thus, in 1998, this sector provided employment for only 18 percent of the labor force of Kazakhstan, and the figure for Kyrgyzstan was still lower (13 percent).

The proportion of the labor force employed in agriculture showed virtually no change in Kazakhstan and Uzbekistan. In Kyrgyzstan, however, it increased sharply, rising from 33 percent of the labor force in 1990 to 48 percent in 1998.

In Kazakhstan, the service sector employed 58 percent of the labor in 1998. In Uzbekistan, four-fifths of the labor force were equally divided between the service and agricultural sectors. In Kyrgyzstan, the agricultural sector provided jobs for nearly half of the workforce.

As in the case of production, the intensity of structural changes on the labor market slowed in 1995–98 in comparison with the first half of the decade.

Although the structural changes in production and employment in all three countries are moving in the same direction, the intensity of the contraction in production and the increase in unemployment differed substantially among the three countries (see Table 2.4).

Thus, in Kazakhstan the GDP fell by 38.6 percent, but jobs decreased by just 16.7 percent. In Kyrgyzstan the corresponding decreases were 39.4 for GDP and 3.0 percent for employment. In Uzbekistan, production declined by 9.1 percent, but the number of jobs actually increased by more than 10 percentage points.

The increase in employment despite a fall in production and the slow rate of dismissals compared to the contraction in GDP both indicate a decline in the quality of growth. If one assumes that labor productivity (defined as the volume of output per worker) remained on the same level in 1998 as it was in 1990, this means that the surfeit of labor in Kazakhstan reached 1.26 million people. That is approximately one-fifth of the entire labor force. Similarly, Uzbekistan had 1.58 million excess workers (18 percent of the workforce) and Kyrgyzstan had 635,000 (37 percent of the workforce). Nor should one forget that in the early 1990s a significant part of the labor force in the former Soviet republics already exceeded real needs.

In the event that labor productivity is restored to its 1990 levels, the agrarian sector will have large proportions of surplus labor—44 percent in Kazakhstan, 19.6 percent in Uzbekistan, and 46 percent in Kyrgyzstan.

Therefore, the most important characteristics of economic development in the Central Asian countries in the 1990s have included a profound fall in labor productivity and a diversion of the labor force to those sectors where productivity is lowest.

In Kazakhstan, the productivity of labor for the economy as a whole by 1995 was 71 percent of the level in 1990 (see Table 2.5). The productivity of labor in industry and construction had fallen by 44 percent.

Table 2.4

Contraction of Production and Employment, 1990–1998
(1990 = 100 percent)

Sector	Kazakhstan		Kyrgyzstan		Uzbekistan	
	Production	Employment	Production	Employment	Production	Employment
All sectors	−38.6	−16.7	−39.3	−3.0	−9.1	+10.8
Agriculture	−50.8	−11.7	−23.1	+41.6	−9.1	+13.1
Industry and construction	−67.9	−54.1	−49.9	−43.3	−6.2	−12.5
Service	+7.3	+7.8	−49.8	−4.4	−14.9	+23.7

Sources: See citations in Tables 2.1 and 2.3.

Table 2.5

Labor Productivity in the States of Central Asia, 1990–1998
(1990 = 100)

Country	Sector	1990	1995	1996	1997	1998
Kazakhstan	All	100	71	66	66	68
	Agriculture	100	79	78	69	56
	Industry and construction	100	56	56	66	70
	Services	100	107	65	97	100
Kyrgyzstan	All	100	54	57	62	62
	Agriculture	100	43	50	53	55
	Industry and construction	100	66	84	116	107
	Services	100	60	54	49	52
Uzbekistan	All	100	76	77	79	82
	Agriculture	100	82	77	79	80
	Industry and construction	100	95	98	105	113
	Services	100	65	67	69	69

Sources: See citations in Tables 2.1 and 2.3.

Only in the sphere of services did productivity increase by seven percentage points, but that was mainly due to the deficiencies in Kazakhstan's statistics on that sector. In Kyrgyzstan, labor productivity dropped still more precipitously than in Kazakhstan. The decline was especially pronounced in agriculture and services. Compared to Kazakhstan and Kyrgyzstan, the situation in Uzbekistan appears to be far more favorable.

Compared with 1990–95, labor productivity on the whole increased in all three countries in 1996–98. However, the positive gains were neither so significant nor so sustained as to support the view that the negative tendencies of the previous years have been overcome.

Level of Development

The large-scale economic catastrophe unfolding in Central Asia inevitably had a direct impact on the level of economic development in these countries. The indicator used to measure this level is per capita GDP.

In the first half of the 1990s, the massive liberalization of national economies (with deregulation of the exchange rate as its central element) spawned a phenomenon well known in the history of developing countries—namely, what some specialists have called "overshooting."

That occurs when a supremely powerful deregulation shock drives the value of hard currency far higher than its hypothetical equilibrium level. In turn, the "underevaluation" of the local currency reduces the volume of GDP in nominal dollars. In post-Soviet states, this overshooting has been further augmented by the disintegration of a unitary economic system and the introduction of national currencies. In Central Asia, this effect was most starkly evident in Kazakhstan. In 1994, the GDP in that country was less than 12 billion dollars—which was almost half the average value in the years 1996–98 (see Table 2.6).

As the independent economies and finances became stronger, there was a parallel rise in the value of the national currency vis-à-vis the dollar. That, in turn, led to a rise in the dollar value of the GDP. Thus, Kazakhstan stabilized its GDP (as expressed in nominal dollars) in 1996—that is, three years after the tenge had first been introduced. Kyrgyzstan, which had established its own national currency several months earlier than Kazakhstan, also basically stabilized its GDP in 1996.

The future dynamics of the exchange rate depend not so much on liberalization shocks as on domestic inflation and, above all, the flow of exports and the balance of payments. Another important factor is how realistically monetary authorities have initially pegged the exchange rate (as a stabilization anchor). In Kyrgyzstan, for example, the increasing value of the national currency in 1995–96 occurred against a peculiar background: an unrealistic nominal exchange rate, a quite limited expansion of exports, and a strongly negative balance of payments. Under these conditions, stabilization of the exchange rate could only have been ensured by an expansion of foreign loans. Hence it is not surprising that in 1997–98 monetary authorities in Kyrgyzstan were forced to carry out a controlled devaluation of the national currency. As a result, in 1997 the nominal dollar GDP contracted by 3.3 percent from the previous year, and in 1998 the decrease was another 8.4 percent.

The currency of Kyrgyzstan fell still further against the dollar, given the movement of world prices on gold, the main export commodity from Kyrgyzstan. It will also ensue from the series of devaluations of national currencies in Russia and Kazakhstan—the leading partners in the foreign trade of Kyrgyzstan.

At the present time, it appears to this writer that a realistic level of the GDP of Kyrgyzstan (in nominal dollars) falls within a range of 1.1 to 1.2 billion dollars. That is equivalent to a per capita GDP of approximately 300 to 350 dollars. However, the depressing state of the balance

Table 2.6

Aggregate and Per Capita GDP for Central Asian States, 1990–1998
(in nominal U.S. dollars)

Indicator	Country	Exchange rate	1990[a]	1994	1995	1996	1997	1998
GDP (in billion U.S. dollars)	Kazakhstan	Official	43.2	11.79	16.65	21.0	22.33	22.33
	Kyrgyzstan	Official	6.8	1.11	1.485	1.827	1.767	1.619
	Tajikistan	Official	5.9	0.81	0.649	1.053	0.925	1.317
	Turkmenistan	Official	6.0	3.15	3.90	1.9	2.41	2.689 (1.882)[b]
	Uzbekistan	Official	27.1	6.52	10.187	13.907	14.893	14.303
		Black Market		3.40	7.955	8.804	6.604	5.958
Per capita GDP (in U.S. dollars)	Kazakhstan	Official (per census) population	2,600	715	1,020	1,320	1,415	1,430
	Kyrgyzstan	Official	1,570	250	330	400	385	345
	Tajikistan	Official	1,130	140	110	180	155	215
	Turkmenistan	Official (per census) population	1,650	720	870	415	525	545 (385)[b]
		Official (estimated population)		780	945	450	560	615 (430)[b]
	Uzbekistan	Official	1,340	295	450	600	630	600
		Black Market		155	350	380	280	250

Sources: Commonwealth of Independent States in 1998, pp. 112, 201–2, 216–17, 261–62, 291–92; *Statisticheskii biulleten' SNG*, 1991 no. 1: 68; M. Gafarly, "Krizis nanes regionu sil'nyi udar," *Nezavisimaia gazeta*, 28 April 1999, p. 9; *Ekonomicheskie novosti Rossii i Sodruzhestva* (Moscow), no. 2 (January 1998), p. 2.

[a] Data from World Bank.

[b] Data in parentheses is estimated GDP on the assumption that the Turkmenistan manat was overvalued by 30 percent in 1998.

of payments and the continuing deterioration in foreign indebtedness give grounds for drawing more pessimistic conclusions. It is entirely possible that, in the next few years, Kyrgyzstan will slide further downward on the world scale of development.

Apparently, the GDP of Kazakhstan—as measured in dollar equivalents—has still not achieved stable parameters. In 1996–98, the GDP here fluctuated between 22 and 23 billion dollars. However, several factors forced Kazakh authorities in April 1999 to withdraw their support for an unrealistically high exchange rate of the tenge: the unfavorable export dynamics of the past two years, the low level of gold and hard currency reserves, and the devaluation of the Russian ruble. In the span of a single month, the tenge plummeted in nominal terms 35 percent against the dollar.[17] In its present condition, it seems that the economy of Kazakhstan (as measured in a dollar equivalent) does not exceed 18 to 19 billion dollars, which is approximately 1,000 to 1,100 dollars per capita. Moreover, according to an official forecast (which nonetheless appears to this author to be somewhat exaggerated), in 1999 the GDP of Kazakhstan may amount to 19.5 to 20 billion dollars.[18]

It should be noted that the growth in the per capita GDP of Kazakhstan (in nominal dollars) was largely due to the fact that the population of the country was no longer growing, but actually decreasing. Specifically, in 1991–97, Kazakhstan had a negative migration flow that amounted to 1.7 million people. The peak of the migration came in 1994; however, even in 1997, the negative migration balance was 291,000 people.[19]

The situation in the three other states of Central Asia is less clear. In 1998, the dollar equivalent of the GDP of Tajikistan increased over the previous year by 400 million dollars and reached a value of 1.3 billion dollars. It is possible, moreover, that 90 percent of the population operates outside the framework of the monetary economy, which is largely limited to the production of aluminum, gold, and cotton exports. That monetary economy amounts to a per capita GDP somewhere in the range of 200 to 250 dollars.

It is still more difficult to evaluate the parameters of the Uzbek economy, since this country has a system of multiple hard-currency exchanges. There are essentially two main exchange rates: (1) the official exchange rate offered by the Central Bank, which is the basis for import-export contracts conducted within the framework of a centralized state program; and (2) a free exchange rate of the "black market," which is used by economic agents and constitutes the real basis for setting consumer prices.

Moreover, the gap between the official rate and the exchange rate on the black market has been constantly growing. These differentials in rates, of course, directly impact the dollar equivalent of the GDP. If the official exchange rate is used, the GDP of Uzbekistan in 1996–98 ranged between 14 and 15 billion dollars (generating a per capita GDP of 600 to 630 dollars). If, however, the unofficial exchange rate of the black market is used, the GDP amounted to just six billion dollars in 1998 (that is, a per capita GDP of 250 dollars).

In this writer's opinion, the exchange rate of the dollar on the black market of Uzbekistan is excessively high. In the event of a liberalization of the exchange rate policy, the latter will apparently stabilize somewhere between the official and black market rates. If this premise is correct, then the size of the Uzbek GDP (in dollar equivalent) will be in the range of 10 to 11 billion dollars (that is, a per capita GDP of approximately 450 dollars). The per capita GDP of Kyrgyzstan provides indirect support for these calculations. Indeed, even a purely visual comparison of the Kyrgyz and Uzbek economy suggests that Uzbekistan unquestionably surpasses Kyrgyzstan in terms of their respective levels of development.

The situation in Turkmenistan is no less confused, for that country makes available statistics that are by far the least reliable for all of Central Asia. Even the demographic data for this country raise a host of questions. Thus, according to official data (which, incidentally, are repeatedly and uncritically reproduced in international statistical handbooks), the population of Turkmenistan in 1992 grew by 11.7 percent.[20] It is difficult to believe this rate of demographic growth—which, by any measure, is positively fantastic—accurately reflects reality. If these data are to be given credence, there are two possible explanations: either Soviet statistics substantially underestimated the size of the population in the Turkmen SSR; or, in 1992, this country had an immigration of at least 350,000 refugees.

The present author, however, prefers a simpler interpretation: for reasons that remain inexplicable, the official statistics of Turkmenistan greatly exaggerate the population of the country. It must be said that, for all the peculiarities of statistics in the former Soviet Union, it could hardly have "missed" several hundred thousand inhabitants. Moreover, no less revealing is the fact that not a single post-Soviet state has experienced an analogous "demographic explosion" like that which purportedly occurred in Turkmenistan. It is hardly likely that Soviet statistics were so selective and discriminatory, and that the phenomenon focused on a single republic, Turkmen SSR. It is still less likely that local and international observers could have overlooked a massive immigration to Turkmenistan. Interestingly, in 1998 the official Turkmenistan statisticians provided additional evidence for the skeptical view offered here, when they claimed to have established a "demographic explosion" and calculated its growth rate at 6.5 percent.[21]

Given the assumption that the real rate of demographic growth for Turkmenistan in 1991–98 was on the level of that in Uzbekistan,[22] one can construct more reasonable estimates of the population and, from these, estimate realistically the per capita GDP. These rough calculations indicate that the statistics of Turkmenistan have greatly inflated the actual growth of the population in 1991–98—on the order of some 15 percent. At the beginning of 1999, the real population here numbers approximately 4.35 million people, not the 4.99 million listed in official statistics.

Further difficulties in determining the actual scale of the Turkmen economy and the level of its development derive from the statistics on national accounts and the administrative control of the exchange rate for the currency, the manat. It bears noting that Turkmenistan is the only post-Soviet state to have virtually no ties with the IMF and World Bank. Without the expert assistance of highly qualified international specialists, the statistical service of Turkmenistan has serious difficulties in preparing national accounts, including calculations of the GDP. The quality of the published materials is particularly low. Therefore, it is no accident that even the Statistical Committee of the CIS (which is hardly exacting with respect to the submitted materials) in 1998 ceased to publish basic economic information on Turkmenistan.

Furthermore, the government of Turkmenistan has retained its administrative control over the rate of exchange. Beginning on 1 December 1998, it suspended the free convertibility of hard currency.[23] According to incomplete information, at the end of 1998 the rate of exchange for the manat on the black market was 1.5 times higher than the official exchange rate.[24]

Taking all these circumstances into account, the author has made some calculations for Turkmenistan in 1998, with a maximum of possible variants. These computations, briefly put, show that the GDP in 1998 amounted to approximately two billion dollars (450 dollars in per capita GDP). In other words, the level of development in Turkmenistan (along with Uzbekistan) lagged—by a large gap—behind that of the regional leader, Kazakhstan. To be sure, in the event that Turkmenistan succeeds in finding more profitable export markets for natural gas, this country could instantaneously jump to the level of a regional leader and achieve a per capita GDP of 1,000 dollars.

Therefore, in terms of the per capita GDP, the five states of Central Asia assume the following rank-order: Kazakhstan (approximately 1,000 dollars per capita), Turkmenistan and Uzbekistan (approximately 450 dollars), Kyrgyzstan (300 to 350 dollars), and Tajikistan (200 to 250 dollars).

This author's estimates of the level of development in the states of Central Asia are somewhat more modest than those offered by international financial agencies. Thus, the report of the World Bank on global economic development in 1998–99 gave higher figures for the per capita GDP in Central Asia for 1997: 1,340 dollars for Kazakhstan, 1,010 dollars for Uzbekistan, 630 dollars for Turkmenistan, 440 dollars for Kyrgyzstan, and 330 dollars for Tajikistan.[25] For a variety of reasons, the next few years will witness a continuing uncertainty with respect to the economic parameters of these transition countries. Thus, the annual report of the World Bank estimates the *gross domestic product (GDP)* of Turkmenistan to be 4.4 billion dollars, but its *gross national product (GNP)* at 2.9 billion dollars.[26]

There can be no doubt that all the post-Soviet states, including those in Central Asia, are drifting toward the ranks of the undeveloped. Indeed, Kyrgyzstan and Tajikistan have already become firmly entrenched in the group of least developed countries. It is fair to surmise that, of the five Central Asian states, only Kazakhstan and (in the most favorable scenario) Turkmenistan will be able to find a niche at a somewhat higher category of states with a low per capita income. Experts from the World Bank believe that Uzbekistan has a similar opportunity; indeed, they rank that country on almost the same level as Kazakhstan and well ahead of Turkmenistan.

However that may be, not only the indicators for the rate of growth and structural change, but also indices on the level of development attest to the extreme fragility of the current economic situation in this region.

Social and Economic Development

In the first half of the 1990s, the social problems in Central Asia were secondary to the task of achieving economic stabilization. However, during these same years, a significant (if not dominant) part of the population in this region plunged into what can only be described as absolute destitution. Along with an economic catastrophe, the region has therefore also experienced a large-scale social disaster.

Official statistics for 1997 report that 71 percent of the population of Kyrgyzstan is in the category of poor (i.e., with a per capita monthly income of less than 45 dollars). Approximately one-quarter of the population has an income actually *below* the minimum subsistence level.[27]

In Kazakhstan, according to the most optimistic official estimates, 41 percent of the population in 1997 had an income below the subsistence level (45 dollars per month).[28] According to more radical assessments based on a monthly subsistence minimum of 81 dollars, the poor of Kazakhstan represented four-fifths of the population.[29] The situation did not improve later. In November 1998, the government reported that 44.6 percent of the population had a per capita income of less than 24 dollars per month, and that 62.5 percent received less than 37 dollars per month.[30] Crudely put, in the fourth quarter of 1998, approximately 80 percent of Kazakhstan lived in absolute poverty.[31]

In Uzbekistan and Turkmenistan (where official statistics on poverty are either unavailable or unreliable), the situation is hardly any better than in Kyrgyzstan and Kazakhstan. In Tajikistan, no less than 95 percent of the population lives in absolute poverty.

Data on wages provide indirect confirmation of these approximate estimates on the expansion of poverty in contemporary Central Asia. Thus, in 1998 the average monthly wage (according to the official exchange rate) was 128 dollars in Kazakhstan, 56 dollars in Uzbekistan (or, 23 dollars at the black-market exchange rate), 39 dollars in Kyrgyzstan, and a mere 11 dollars in Tajikistan.[32]

Evidence on the deterioration of the social situation also comes from such indicators as illness, child mortality, and life expectancy. Thus, an epidemic of tuberculosis is gaining momentum in Kazakhstan. In 1998, this country had 102 tubercular cases per 100,000 inhabitants; officially, the threshold for an epidemic is considered 70 cases per 100,000 inhabitants.[33]

The low absolute level of incomes leads to a consumption structure that is transparently primitive. In Kazakhstan, households spend 51 percent of their aggregate income on food; the corresponding indicator is 55 percent in Kyrgyzstan, 62–63 percent in Turkmenistan, 69 percent in Uzbekistan, and 87 percent in Tajikistan.[34] The very low wages, and often the impossibility of finding any kind of paid job, force the population into the sphere of a primitive natural economy based on self-sufficiency in production. Thus, in Uzbekistan the "in-kind" component of personal consumption (which involves no mediation through an exchange of commodities) amounts to 60 percent of the total volume of personal consumption. In some areas of the Fergana Valley, where poverty and destitution have long since become a way of life, this indicator is more than 80 percent.[35]

From the very outset, the scale of domestic markets in Central Asia has been limited by the relatively small size of the population. Poverty, which is absolute and virtually ubiquitous, reduces the effective domestic demand to an extremely small magnitude. Accordingly, the opportunities for Central Asian states to organize any kind of efficient production are, in most cases, preordained to fail.

An expansion of the zones of absolute poverty imposes social limits on the chances for rebuilding and sustaining a stable pattern of economic growth. The rapid impoverishment of the population and its massive pauperization make a fertile environment for the dissemination of radical ideas. In Central Asia, the indicator of growing social distress is the growth of the so-called Wahhabite movement. Authorities in all the Central Asian states seek to ascribe this extremely diffuse term to virtually every form of social discontent, which, as a rule, takes a quasi-religious form.

In 1996–98, authorities conducted trials of "Wahhabites" not only in Uzbekistan, but also in Kyrgyzstan and even Kazakhstan.[36] Given that this Central Asian "Wahhabism" is primarily a lower-class protest that reflects the growing dissatisfaction with the impoverished conditions of existence, it is simply impossible to eradicate this movement by police repression and demonstrative court trials. What is needed instead is a consistent, expensive social program to deal with the root problems.

If there is not at least a partial reorientation of economic policy toward the needs of the rural population (which is growing in both relative and absolute terms), it is entirely possible that the region will experience a large-scale insurrection under the Islamic banner. In Tajikistan, the Islamic opposition used force to assert its right to participate in the government. At the present time, a repetition of the Tajik variant in Uzbekistan or Kyrgyzstan seems impossible. However, the rapid re-agrarianization of both states (amidst an equally rapid decline in the standard of living for the great majority of the population) could lead to distressing social and economic surprises in the foreseeable future.

The probability of destabilization in the region results from the fact that, geographically, Central Asia is situated next to Afghanistan and Pakistan. Although Iran has not supported radical movements here (most likely because of its desire for good relations with Russia), that has not been true of Afghanistan and Pakistan. Involved in the global trafficking in narcotics and weapons, both states have long since become a "twilight zone" for the contemporary world. President I. Karimov of Uzbekistan has directly accused Pakistan, Afghanistan, and certain political forces in Tajikistan of providing military assistance to Uzbek radicals acting under the banner of Islam.[37] In the fall of 1998, it was revealed that Kyrgyzstan is being used as a staging base for the transfer of weapons to Afghanistan.[38] Still more striking is the fact that 65 percent of the opium from Afghanistan reaches Europe after crossing the territories of states in Central Asia.[39]

These and many other circumstances require one to be extremely circumspect in assessing the economic gains achieved by the Central Asian states in 1995–98. The analysis offered here allows one to conclude that the economic downturn in this region has still not bottomed out, and that the structure of local economies has not acquired the basic characteristics of fully independent states.

Caution with respect to middle- and long-term prospects for the states of Central Asia increases as one becomes familiar with the internal logic of the operating models of economic development that have emerged in Kyrgyzstan, Kazakhstan, and Uzbekistan. In the cases of Tajikistan and Turkmenistan, it is still too early to speak of any developmental model. In Tajikistan, central authorities do not have sufficient control over the entire territory of the country; at this point, they are concerned almost exclusively with securing their own political survival. In Turkmenistan, economic development still bears the strong imprint of voluntarism in its Eastern variant.

Notes

1. A. Mel'iantsev, *Ekonomicheskii rost stran Magriba* (Moscow, 1984), p. 14.

2. *Panorama* (Almaty), no. 37 (26 September 1997), p. 9.

3. *Panorama*, no. 12 (26 March 1999), p. 3; no. 6 (12 February 1999), p. 4.

4. Calculated from the following sources: Natsional'noe statisticheskoe agentstvo Respubliki Kazakhstan, *Statisticheskii ezhegodnik Kazakhstana 1994–1997 gg.*

(Almaty, 1998), pp. 264–66; *Sotsial'no-ekonomicheskoe polozhenie Respubliki Kazakhstan,* 1998, no. 12 (December): 36; and 1999, no. 1 (January): 71.

5. Calculated from Tsentr ekonomicheskikh issledovanii, *Uzbekistan 1998. Doklad o chelovecheskom razvitii* (United Nations Development Project: Tashkent, 1998), p. 100.

6. M. Iusupov, "Krizis neplatezhei i puti ego preodoleniia," *Rynok, den'gi i kredit* (Tashkent), 1998, no. 1 (January): 37.

7. Calculated from data in: Natsional'nyi statisticheskii komitet, *Sotsial'no-ekonomicheskoe polozhenie Kyrgyzskoi respubliki* (Bishkek), January–December 1998, p. 184; Natsional'nyi statisticheskii komitet, *Sotsial'no-ekonomicheskoe polozhenie Kyrgyzskoi respubliki* (Bishkek), January 1999, p. 142.

8. Calculated from data in Natsional'noe statisticheskoe agentstvo Respubliki Kazakhstan, *Sotsial'no-ekonomicheskoe polozhenie Respubliki Kazakhstan,* 1999, no. 1 (January): 7, 131.

9. Calculated from data in ibid., pp. 50, 131.

10. Calculated from data in ibid., pp. 49–50.

11. Ibid., p. 130.

12. A. Tokbergen, G. Suleimenova, and R. Turegel'dieva, "O prichinakh sokhraneniia ubytochnosti predpriiatii v Kazakhstane," *Al' Pari* (Almaty), no. 1 (January-March 1998): 46–47.

13. Ibid., p. 47.

14. *Panorama,* no. 49 (18 December 1998), p. 3.

15. "Valovoi vnutrennii produkt za 1996 god," *Aziia. Ekonomika i zhizn'* (Almaty), no. 49 (December 1997): 6.

16. "Valovoi vnutrennii produkt," *Al' Pari,* no. 1 (January–March 1998): 3.

17. *Izvestiia* (Moscow), 5 May 1998, p. 2.

18. Calculated from data in *Panorama,* no. 6 (12 February 1999), p. 4; no. 8 (26 February 1999), p. 4; no. 12 (26 March 1999), p. 3.

19. Tsentr ekonomicheskikh issledovanii [Center for Economic Research], *Kazakhstan: National Human Development Report, 1998* (United Nations Development Project: Almaty, 1998), p. 34.

20. Natsional'nyi institut statistiki i prognozirovaniia, *Statisticheskii ezhegodnik Turkmenistana. 1996,* vol. 1 (Ashgabat, 1998), p. 12.

21. Interstate Statistical Committee, *Commonwealth of Independent States in 1998 (A Digest of Provisional Statistical Results)* (Moscow, 1999), p. 289.

22. The transfer of the Uzbek demographic realities to Turkmenistan is fully justified. To judge from materials in the last Soviet censuses of 1979 and 1989—the age structure of the population, the special features of reproductive behavior, and the widespread phenomenon of large numbers of children—these two countries are quite similar. See *Narodnoe khoziaistvo SSSR v 1989 g.* (Moscow, 1990), p. 37; *Demograficheskii ezhegodnik SSSR 1990g.* (Moscow, 1991), pp. 39, 60, 63, 69.

23. *Panorama,* no. 47 (4 December 1998), p. 1.

24. M. Gafarly, "Krizis nanes regionu sil'nyi udar," *Nezavisimaia gazeta* (Moscow), 28 April 1999, p. 9.

25. World Bank, *World Development Report, 1998–1999* (Washington, DC, 1998), pp. 190–91.

26. Ibid., pp. 191, 213.

27. *Kyrgyzstan. Natsional'nyi otchet po chelovecheskomu razvitiiu* (United Na-

tions Development Project: Bishkek, 1998), p. 27; V.V. Mikhalev, V.I. Kumskov, V.M. Khamisov, D.A. Adambekov, "Analiz sistemy sotsial'noi zashchity naseleniia v Kyrgyzskoi respublike v usloviiakh perekhoda k rynku," in *Strategiia sotsial'noi politiki: rynok truda, zaniatost' i sotsial'naia zashchita naseleniia* (Bishkek, 1998), pp. 13–14.

28. *Kazakhstan: National Human Development Report, 1998*, p. 27.

29. V. Mozharova and M. Seitkozhaeva, "Sotsial'noe razvitie i uroven' zhizni naseleniia Kazakhstana," *Aziia. Ekonomika i zhizn',* no. 47 (November 1997), pp. 6–7.

30. Calculated from *Sotsial'no-ekonomicheskoe polozhenie Respubliki Kazakhstan*, 1999, no. 1 (January): 64–65.

31. Calculated from data in ibid, pp. 64–65, 67.

32. Calculated from data in *Commonwealth of Independent States in 1998*, pp. 112, 203, 218, 263, and 293.

33. *Panorama*, no. 47 (4 December 1998), p. 2.

34. See *Commonwealth of Independent States in 1998*, pp. 125–26.

35. See A. Ul'masov, "Funktsii sem'i v rynochnoi ekonomike," *Rynok, den'gi i kredit* (Tashkent), 1998, no. 2 (February): 24.

36. D. Solovyov, "Repressive Islamic Sect Detected in Kazakhstan," *The Moscow Times*, 28 October 1998, p. 6; D. Dubnov, "V Uzbekistane rubiat 'khvosty' islamskoi ugroze," *Vremia MN* (Moscow), 8 July 1998, p. 6; I. Rotar,' "Aresty 'vakhkhabitov' v Kirgizii," *Nezavisimaia gazeta* (Moscow), 4 July 1998, p. 5.

37. Islam Karimov, "Mozhet byt' moi nedostatok v tom, chto ia do kontsa formuliruiu svoi tseli," *Vremia MN*, 19 October 1998, p. 6; S. Kiiampur, "Uzbekskie kommandos iz Lakhora," *Russkii telegraf* (Moscow), 22 April 1998, p. 12.

38. Iu. Razguliaev, "Oruzhie v gumanitarnykh tseliakh," *Vremia MN*, 13 October 1998, p. 8.

39. This estimate comes from experts of the UN program on international control of narcotics. See *Panorama*, no. 11 (19 March 1999), p. 5.

3

Basic Problems of Market Transition in Central Asia

Eskender Trushin and Eshref Trushin

The Starting Point for Independent Development

For the countries of Central Asia to create the fundamental conditions for a market system, they must satisfy two fundamental requirements. First, these states must overcome the many disproportions that they have inherited from the totalitarian administrative-command system of the former Soviet Union. Second, these transition states must also resolve the various new problems that inevitably arise to confront newly independent states.

The complexity of the starting point for the Central Asian countries thus derives in large part from the contradictory legacy of the USSR. That inheritance, to be sure, includes several positive elements:

- the presence of many pivotal and viable branches of industry and agriculture;
- a rather well-developed economic and social infrastructure;
- positive social indicators at the start of reform: (a) a high level of elementary, secondary, and higher education among the population; (b) a limited range of inequality in the distribution of income among various groups of the population; (c) a low rate of infant mortality compared with countries in the Third World; and (d) a high life expectancy.

At the same time, the countries of Central Asia also inherited certain problems: above all, fundamental structural disproportions in the development and distribution of various branches of production. The economies of the Central Asian states also suffered from an inefficient system of economic management.

It must be acknowledged that these countries, upon gaining their political independence in 1991, inherited from the former Soviet Union an economic structure that was very badly distorted and disjointed. In general, the financial and price system was simply not viable; it also incorporated a badly dysfunctional form of incentives for work and investment.

Therefore, once the countries of Central Asia had acquired their independence, they all had to begin the process of restructuring their national economies. And as they undertook this task, they all faced roughly the same conditions:

1. *A high degree of orientation toward raw-material production.* On the one hand, Central Asian states were the suppliers of cheap and high-quality mineral and agricultural materials; on the other hand, they were also significant markets for the sale of low-quality finished goods from Russia, Belarus, and Ukraine. In other words, Central Asia played the role of a raw-material appendage. In many branches of the Central Asian economy, enterprises performed only part of the production cycle. Specifically, in many cases production was deliberately confined to the stage of extraction and primary processing of raw materials, or to the production of semi-finished goods. Hence the basic sectors of the economy in Central Asia did not develop as an integrated, self-contained complex, but as an adjunct to the production activities in the Russian and other republics of the former USSR. As a result, output from Central Asian industries that produced finished goods represented only a small proportion of total production. Finally, hi-tech production of competitive goods was virtually nonexistent in this region.

2. *A high level of dependence on food imports (with the exception of Kazakhstan) and consumer durables.* The republics of Central Asia were forced to import all their essential food products—cereal, meat, sugar, and the like. They also had to import a broad assortment of consumer durables.

3. *A high level of degradation of land resources and an especially irrational utilization of water resources.* This particular characteristic of Central Asia led to an ecological catastrophe: the desiccation of the Aral Sea and a sharp deterioration in the quality of life for the people residing in the area.

The most industrially developed republic in Central Asia was Kazakhstan. Three republics in the region—Uzbekistan, Tajikistan, and Turkmenistan—had their own special characteristics and hence differed from Kazakhstan in two important respects.

First, these three countries had the lowest standard of living in the former USSR. Specifically, their per capita republic income amounted to just half of the average in the former Soviet republics. According to official data, in 1989 approximately 40 to 45 percent of the families in these three republics were living beneath the official poverty line; that is, they had a per capita monetary income below the minimum wage. According to expert assessments, in 1990 at least 60 percent of the population in these republics had incomes below the subsistence minimum; by comparison, the same indicator was only 30 percent in Russia and Ukraine. The small monetary income in turn meant an extremely low level of consumption. For example, the inhabitants of Uzbekistan consumed only 46 percent of the all-union average for meat and meat products; similarly low rates were also true for milk and dairy products (57 percent), fish and related goods (28 percent), and even fruits (51 percent). It also bears noting that the consumption of food products was particularly low in rural areas.

Second, these three countries suffered from an acute unemployment problem, especially in rural areas, which still account for approximately 60 percent of the population. In sheer demographic terms, more than two-thirds of the population consists of children, students, and pensioners—i.e., the most socially vulnerable strata in the population. Moreover, the majority of the population in Uzbekistan, Tajikistan, and Turkmenistan is Muslim; they have their own way of life, communal forms of social self-organization, and a low propensity for relocation and migration.

In judging the priorities and pace of economic reform, it is essential to take into account these special characteristics and the problems each country faced at the outset. At the same time, it should be noted that under the new post-Soviet conditions certain peculiar features and disproportions also provided advantages, at least in the initial phase.

For instance, the raw-material focus of the countries of Central Asia proved advantageous in the period when the economies were "opening up" and faced a decline in production and macroeconomic destabilization. Namely, it was easier for countries producing primarily raw materials to reorient their export from the Commonwealth of Independent States (CIS) to the markets of developed countries. Moreover, the rise in world prices for metals and cotton in 1993–95 also contributed to the stabilization in Uzbekistan, Kazakhstan, and Kyrgyzstan. In the specific case of Uzbekistan, several factors were particularly important in contributing to the financial stabilization: the country's general agrarian orientation, the relatively small proportion of manufacturing industries, and the comparatively limited degree of integration into the industrial structure of the Soviet Union. The latter factor, in particular, made Uzbekistan less dependent upon the delivery of industrial goods from the other countries in the CIS. During the first years of independence, under conditions of a rupture in economic relations among the countries of the former USSR, this factor played a positive role.

One well-known problem of Uzbekistan—namely, the hypertrophic development of irrigated agriculture—had long been a target of criticism, even during the time of the Soviet regime. Under conditions of independence, however, this very "problem" proved a godsend. Specifically, it provided a powerful base for steady agriculture production, a source of funding for the state budget and industry, a force for economic stabilization, and a guarantee of a sound economy in general.

The East has a saying: "When a caravan changes direction to go in the opposite direction, the last camel in the caravan suddenly becomes the first." Uzbekistan, which in terms of per capita social-economic indicators ranked among the lowest republics in the USSR, in the post-Soviet era has suffered the smallest contraction in its gross domestic product (GDP); the standard of living has also declined least among any of the former Soviet republics. It would appear that in the first years of independence Uzbekistan was the "last camel" in the caravan of Soviet republics; as all these countries suddenly changed course to move from a planned economy to one based on the market, it was now at the head of the line.

Alternative Approaches to Economic Reform

By the end of the 1980s, specialists in many parts of the Soviet Union were actively debating different models of reform. But such debate was missing in Central Asia. Thus, at a time when economists in the Russian Federation elaborated a host of alternative approaches, specialists in Central Asia found themselves in a kind of intellectual vacuum. In short, for a variety of reasons, the countries in this region did not manifest the kind of active discussion that was unfolding in other parts of the former USSR. As a result, the Central Asian states—in stark contrast to the Baltic republics—were not fully prepared for economic independence and hence oriented themselves toward greater economic integration with Russia. In other words, the Central Asian states were simply not prepared, either psychologically or intellectually, to face the challenges of economic independence.

That all changed in 1993, when these countries were suddenly excluded from the ruble zone of the Russian Federation. That exclusion, together with the fact that they had suddenly been catapulted into economic independence, forced the governments in this region to develop radical programs to stabilize their economies and to elaborate their own conception of reform and development.

It should be noted that even earlier, in 1991–92, the governments of the Central Asian states did not fully embrace the Russian conception of "shock therapy." In particular, they were loath to embrace such policies as the deregulation of prices and the reduction of state involvement in the economy. Indeed, Uzbekistan and Turkmenistan became distinctive by adopting their own approaches to reform and by proclaiming their "own path of development," which was essentially based on strong state regulation of the economy.

Thus, from the very outset, President Islam Karimov of Uzbekistan openly declared that Uzbekistan would not follow the Russian path of "shock therapy." Rather, he vowed that Uzbekistan would follow its "own path" and, specifically, observe five main principles:

- ideology should be totally excluded from economics;
- the state should play the role of chief reformer during the transition period;
- the entire process of renewal and progress must be based on the rule of law;
- only a strong, effective mechanism of social protection and guarantees for the population can ensure both dynamic progress toward a market economy and the preservation of social and political stability;

- the formation of new market relations should be implemented gradually and in stages.[1]

Although Kazakhstan at first embarked on the Russian path of "shock therapy," it too subsequently attempted to define its own special path. In particular, the government of Kazakhstan took an active interest in the path of development taken by South Korea and Japan. As a result, in 1995–96, when the government made some corrections in its economic policy, it resumed an approach that provided for active intervention by the state to assert control over certain spheres of the economy.

Kyrgyzstan initially delayed its economic reforms, but it then also expressed a desire to emulate the South Korean and Japanese economic models. That was apparent in 1993, when Kyrgyzstan adopted the complete convertibility of its national currency and sought to create an image of itself as the "Asian Switzerland." In the latter guise, the country was to change gradually into a world tourist and business center, which would host the offices of leading transnational corporations and banks. President Askar Akaev also established a more liberal political environment (compared with other countries in the region) and demonstrated great enthusiasm in conducting reforms. In the end, however, he adopted a policy of implementing the recommendations of the World Bank and International Monetary Fund (IMF)—in other words, a policy close to "shock therapy."

In Turkmenistan, President Saparmurad Niiazov made it clear that he wanted to transform Turkmenistan into the "Kuwait in Kara Kum."[2] Moreover, the economic interests of Turkmenistan were oriented toward the West and East Asia, not toward Russia or the other countries of Central Asia.

In November 1995, the parliament of Tajikistan adopted a program to guide reform through the year 2000. This program promised to liberalize international trade (with the exception of aluminum, which remains under state control), to extend privatization, and to establish an open and transparent economy with conditions favorable for foreign investment and the development of export-oriented lines of production.

Why did some countries take the path of "shock therapy," while others opted for gradual reforms? What caused the differences in approach to economic reform in the various states of Central Asia? Could these countries have chosen some other path?

In the final analysis, the speed in conducting structural reform depends basically on concrete conditions in a country and on their initial "starting" position.

Under stable political and macroeconomic conditions, where the decline in production and incomes is not substantial and where there is little risk of political and economic chaos, a country has no need for haste in conducting reforms. In these cases, a country can opt for an evolutionary path. Moreover, gradualism is also preferable in the case of a "vulnerable" social structure—that is, one characterized by low mobility, a widespread pattern of large families, and relatively low per capita incomes of the populace. All these factors indicate a situation where the majority of the population is unprepared to adopt and tolerate "shock therapy." The latter strategy thus bears the risk of igniting political chaos. Uzbekistan and Turkmenistan belong to this category of countries.

When a country has enormous macroeconomic disproportions, when the decline of production and incomes is enormous, when the risk of political and economic chaos is significant—in these cases a country cannot take the path of slow and gradual reform. The room for political maneuvering is greatly reduced; radical surgery offers the only treatment. In cases such as these, "shock therapy" is the more acceptable approach. Moreover, to conduct reform successfully by using the "shock therapy" approach, it is essential that society be well prepared: it must have a high level of mobility, an "ameliorated" population structure (with a moderate rate of demographic growth), and relatively high per capita incomes. Kazakhstan and Kyrgyzstan came closest to meeting these requirements.

The branch structure of the economy is another factor in determining how the individual countries of Central Asia chose their approach to economic reform.

Certain categories of states do not need to rush forward with the privatization of large industrial enterprises. Such countries have the following characteristics: (1) they have a large agrarian sector that is capable of satisfying domestic demand for many food products; (2) in rural areas, they have surplus labor that has limited mobility, does not possess specialized training, and can be easily diverted to other branches of agricultural production; and (3) they have a relatively low level of development in the industrial sector and a small working class. Uzbekistan, Tajikistan, and Turkmenistan belong to this category of countries.

Such countries should assign top priority in structural reforms to the agricultural sector, which should have the following elements:

- land reform;
- restructuring of large agricultural enterprises;
- deregulation of prices and trade policy in agriculture;
- creation of a competitive environment;
- an increase in productivity (primarily in the agricultural sector, not in industry).

The foregoing will create conditions favorable for rapid growth in the agro-industrial complex, for an increase in savings and investments, and for the release of surplus labor resources from agriculture to develop industrial production in rural areas. These changes will lay the foundation for other structural reforms (above all, development of the financial sector) and further industrialization.

Compared with the other countries of this region, Kazakhstan is highly urbanized, with 57 percent of its population residing in cities. It does not have a surfeit of labor resources; the bulk of the workforce is employed in industry and has a high level of specialization. In addition, Kazakhs comprise only about half of the population; the rest (and the majority in the working class) consists of European ethnic groups (Russians, Ukrainians, Germans, and others). Political movements, furthermore, are relatively well developed here. Therefore, in Kazakhstan's case the main problem is to reform enterprises in a highly specialized industry; given the more advanced level of specialization among the workers, this inevitably entails a higher rate of unemployment and, correspondingly, a sharper decline in the GDP. These conditions mandate a faster pace in the implementation of the basic structural reforms. In addition, Kazakhstan has an enormous, uncontrolled common border and close economic relations with Russia, which had already embarked on the "shock therapy" route of reform. As a result, Kazakhstan has been forced to synchronize its reforms with those in Russia in order to prevent the diversion of its resources to Russia (where prices are higher) as well as other negative consequences. In short, Kazakhstan has chosen a path similar to the shock therapy strategy.

The situation in Kyrgyzstan is somewhere between that of Kazakhstan and Uzbekistan. On the one hand, the dominant sector is agriculture (which makes it more like Uzbekistan); indeed, urban inhabitants comprise only 39 percent of the total population. On the other hand, it is similar to Kazakhstan in terms of its ethnic composition (with approximately 60 percent of the population being indigenous Kyrgyz) and economic structure. As a result, Kyrgyzstan found it particularly difficult to settle upon its own approach to reform. In the end, however, the country finally chose a path close to that of the shock therapy approach.

However, as the experience of shock therapy in Russia has demonstrated, a fast pace of reform implementation does not guarantee the results that were desired and needed. Nor does it ensure that a country will attain acceptable rates of economic growth. To achieve economic expansion, it is critically important to provide political and macroeconomic stability, establish openness in trade, and create a favorable environment for investment activity.

When a country conducts reform according to the prescriptions of shock therapy, it runs the risk of being inconsistent—that is, failing to ensure certain economic proportions. That is all the more true during a market transformation, which is fraught with a high level of uncertainty. Therefore, it is essential to have and to ensure access to large financial resources, which provide a kind of insurance that a country can eliminate promptly any of the disproportions that naturally arise in the course of the reform.

From this point of view, a gradualist strategy is preferable for most of the countries in Central Asia. The sole exception here is Kazakhstan, which has certain unique features in its economic structure. Although gradualism is advisable for the other states of this region, this should not be construed to mean approval for a lethargic pace of reform. Rather, it simply means that they should seek to avoid shock therapy. Still, it is usually concrete social and political realities that dictate the actual pace of reform, which can move somewhat more quickly (in the case of shock therapy) or slightly more slowly (in the case of gradualism) than the optimal pace of reform.

The principal dangers inherent in gradualism are procrastination and a low pace of institutional reform in the real productive sectors of the economy. In the authors' judgment, countries that employ the gradualist strategy must apply elements of shock therapy. At the same time, one must bear in mind that massive and rapid privatization and commercialization of state enterprises in the real productive sector can guarantee a higher efficiency only if certain conditions are met:

1. subsidies for producer resources are eliminated;
2. production has an export orientation;
3. producers are given an opportunity to receive the main part of their earnings in hard currency;
4. competition by means of imports is increased somewhat.

If these conditions are not met, as the experience of "shock therapy" in Russia has demonstrated, enterprises do not significantly change their behavior after privatization. In effect, they simply continued to adapt to the conservative environment that still enveloped them.

At the same time, countries that undertake reform by adopting shock therapy should conduct some reforms that bear elements of gradualism. For example, when conducting reform in the financial sector, there are good reasons to observe a certain sequence in a program of deregulation. It is desirable, in brief, to observe this procedure in conducting financial liberalization:

1. support the real banking interest rates for all kinds of transactions;
2. develop and strengthen domestic commercial banks;
3. create conditions favorable to competition among domestic financial institutions;
4. deregulate interest rates;
5. reduce the share of targeted state credits;
6. increase the presence of foreign financial institutions;
7. liberalize capital accounts.

The last step, liberalization of capital accounts, represents the final stage in the deregulation of the financial sector and the entire economy.

Reform in all the countries of Central Asia, whether they opt for shock therapy or gradualism, must have several elements in common:

- openness in the economy;
- an increase in exports
- an accelerated (but systematic) development of the financial sector so as to create conditions for an increase in national savings and investment;
- development of a market and production infrastructure.

Regardless of the reform strategy, during the transition economy all countries must assign the state an active role in carrying out the reforms and regulating the economy. In other words, all require a strong government capable of supporting political and macroeconomic stability. In short, one should not prematurely reduce the state's role in the economy, since in the first stages of the transition period only the government can create the basic market institutions, set up the work of market structures, regulate the basic proportions of the economy, support the economy with state investments, and counteract the numerous shortcomings of the market mechanism (for example, by ensuring the rational utilization and preservation of natural resources).

The failure of reform in Russia, and this statement is no less true of Kazakhstan and Kyrgyzstan, was only partly due to the application of shock therapy. The principal cause of the failure lay in the fact that the role of the central government (and the "state" more broadly) was prematurely pared back. As a result, such countries could not, in a timely fashion, carry out some of the essential institutional reforms. Shortcomings in market and state institutions can undermine the effectiveness of liberalization.

On the Openness of the Economy

Jeffrey Sachs and Andrew Warner have classified an economy as "closed" if it has at least one of the following characteristics:

- an average level of customs fees on equipment and materials that exceeds 40 percent;
- a hard-currency exchange rate on the black market that is more than 20 percent above the official rate;
- strict state control over the main items of export or import.[3]

The economy of Uzbekistan meets at least the final two criteria and therefore qualifies as a closed economy under the Sachs-Warner definition. The hard currency exchange rate on the black market exceeded the official exchange rate for American dollars substantially: 30 percent in 1995, 67 percent in 1996, 156 percent in 1997, 125 percent in 1998, and 270 percent in the first half of 1999. This, in turn, generated income for firms with access to the official currency exchange; such revenues amounted to 18 percent of Uzbekistan's GDP in 1996, 24 percent in 1997, and 19 percent in 1998. In spite of such activities, the bulk of these revenues was used to subsidize manufacturing and the construction of new plants. Moreover, the government of Uzbekistan maintains tight administrative control through licenses on commercial transactions;

it thus oversees more than 90 percent of all imports and 75 percent of exports. It also has set the tariffs on certain categories of imports (for transportation and computer goods) at 30 percent.

Uzbekistan and Turkmenistan are distinguished by strict state control over the basic articles of export (raw materials). These governments justify such measures by the need to prevent competition among domestic producers on world markets and by the desire to augment the state budget in a situation where natural resources comprise the country's main exports. Except for Uzbekistan, in the other countries of Central Asia a black-market exchange rate for currency either does not exist or, if it does, remains within 3 percent of the official exchange rate (as in Turkmenistan). Imports and exports have been substantially deregulated.

In general, the situation in Central Asia is as follows: Uzbekistan is the only country with an economy that is still largely closed, whereas the other countries here have almost completed the liberalization of trade. Uzbekistan has not used its geographic position and created conditions to obtain advantages in order to transform itself into a reliable, liberal center for finance and transportation in the region. Instead, this country has chosen to establish complex, opaque rules to regulate the financial sector and to impose strict regulations on customs, hard currency, and commercial activities. The end effect has been to deflect away from Uzbekistan transit freight and passenger flows as well as foreign investment.

In recent years, the economic policy of Uzbekistan has aimed at import substitution. This strategy has not only encouraged the formation of a closed economy, but has also led to an increase in the share of import-substitution sectors that either are not competitive or do not participate at all in export. The main component of this strategy is the highly overvalued, complex exchange rate of the national currency, the Uzbek *sum*. The dynamic real appreciation of that currency since 1997, in the view of these authors, explains the fall in the absolute and relative indicators of exports from Uzbekistan.

The discrepancy in the rates of trade liberalization naturally provokes tensions between Uzbekistan and the other countries in this region. The price for a number of goods is less than in neighboring countries; the import of these goods to Uzbekistan is subsidized by the official, low exchange rate of the American dollar. This policy then constitutes the precondition for their export to other countries. To counteract this problem, the Uzbek side has introduced strict, prohibitive measures on the reexport of such food products; it has also strengthened its customs and border control. None of this, of course, has helped to stimulate the exchange of goods within the region. The rules for the obligatory "registration" of foreigners who come to Uzbekistan also raise a barrier against tourism and the unrestricted movement of labor within the region. The same effect will obtain from Turkmenistan's introduction of a visa regime for citizens from the CIS. In February 1999, Kazakhstan gave a further impulse to the general process of disintegration in Central Asia when it unilaterally elected to introduce a 200 percent customs duty on various foods, spirits, and tobacco products imported from the other states in the region.

The tendency toward a closed economy in Central Asia correlates with the efficacy of investments in each country. The authors' calculation of ICOR (incremental capital-output ratio), based on IMF data for three countries in Central Asia, yields the following results: 8.3 for Uzbekistan (1996–98), 3.3 for Kazakhstan (1997), and 3.8 for Kyrgyzstan (1996–98). In other words, as economic openness increases, the ICOR here has increased—that is to say, greater openness increased the efficiency of investment. A comparison of ICOR figures with other developing countries substantiates the conclusion that the closed economy of Uzbekistan, which follows an import-substitution strategy for development, has a characteristically low level of effectiveness of investments.

Although one cannot assume that the governments of Central Asia have completely and definitively settled upon a model and concrete long-term program of economic development, certain approaches to reform and development have emerged. First, the countries of Central Asia concur that the state needs to assume an active role in managing the economy. Second, all of them strive to create a stable political and macroeconomic environment as something essential for sustained growth and reform of the economy. Third, they all seek to modernize the economy on the basis of an accelerated development of industry, which they propose to achieve through cooperation with large transnational corporations.

Constructing a Market Economy: Basic Problems, Partial Solutions

From the moment when the countries of Central Asia became independent in 1991, their economies have been exposed to traumatic economic shocks. That turmoil was due both to the disruption of their former commercial ties and to the economic reforms undertaken by their current governments. In the initial phase of development, the countries of this region shared some common economic problems as well as certain baseline characteristics. These included:

- a fall in production;
- hyperinflation;
- the introduction of national currencies;
- the adoption of programs to achieve macroeconomic and financial stabilization;
- the establishment of a legal framework for economic transformation;
- the implementation of reforms that involved prices, institutions, and trade policy;
- the construction of the basis for a market infrastructure.

Although the states of Central Asia quickly obtained political independence, in 1991–92 they still depended heavily on trade with the other republics of the former Soviet Union. Thus, trade with the former Soviet republics represented a high proportion of total trade (exports plus imports): 96 percent in Tajikistan, 91 percent in Kyrgyzstan, 89 percent in Kazakhstan, 85 percent in Uzbekistan, and 84 percent in Turkmenistan.[4] Hence, the disruption of relations among enterprises in the various republics of the former Soviet Union inevitably had a profound impact. That was all the more the case given almost total absence of imports from the "far abroad" (i.e., countries outside the former USSR). Thus, with the introduction of price liberalization in January 1992, these countries soon experienced a precipitous fall in production, which was due to the fall in demand as well as the decrease in the supply of resources and component parts. The aggregate contraction of the GDP for 1991–95 was 18.9 percent in Uzbekistan, 48.3 percent in Kazakhstan, 59.9 percent in Kyrgyzstan, and 78.5 percent in Tajikistan. Since 1991, Turkmenistan has not had a single year of positive growth in GDP; during the entire period of 1991–97, the total decline amounted to 81.1 percent (see Table 3.1). A host of factors brought about this decline in the GDP, including: the suspension of substantial subsidies from the former Soviet Union, an end to the practice of adding nonexistent output to the reports on the physical volume of production, and the outbreak of civil war in Tajikistan.

Table 3.1

Dynamics of the Main Economic Indicators for the Countries of Central Asia, 1990–1998

Year	1990	1991	1992	1993	1994	1995	1996	1997	1998
Growth of real GDP (percent decline from preceding year)									
Kazakhstan	-0.4	-13.0	-5.3	-9.2	-12.6	-8.2	0.5	2.0	-2.5
Kyrgyzstan	3.2	-5.0	-13.9	-15.5	-20.1	-5.4	7.1	6.5	1.8
Tajikistan	-1.6	-7.1	-29.0	-11.0	-18.9	-12.5	-4.4	1.7	4.0
Turkmenistan	2.0	-4.7	-5.3	-10.2	-19.0	-8.2	-7.7	-26.0	4.0
Uzbekistan	1.6	-0.5	-11.0	-2.3	-4.2	-0.9	1.6	2.4	2.8
Balance of state budget (as percent of GDP)									
Kazakhstan	n.d.	-7.9	-7.3	-1.3	-7.2	-2.5	-3.1	-3.8	-5.5
Kyrgyzstan	n.d.	n.d.	-17.6	-14.0	-7.7	-13.5	-6.3	-6.9	-2.2
Tajikistan	n.d.	-16.4	-31.2	-25.0	-10.5	-11.2	-5.8	-3.4	-3.2
Turkmenistan	n.d.	2.5	13.3	-0.5	-1.4	-1.6	-0.8	0	-2.0
Uzbekistan	n.d.	-3.6	-12.2	-10.4	-6.1	-4.1	-7.3	-2.3	-2.6
Inflation of consumer prices (percent rate at the end of the year)									
Kazakhstan	n.d.	137.0	2,984	2,169.1	1,160.3	60.4	28.6	11.3	7.0
Kyrgyzstan	n.d.	170.0	1,259.0	1,363.0	87.2	31.9	30.3	14.8	12.0
Tajikistan	n.d.	204.0	1,364.0	7,344.0	n.d.	2,100.0	40.5	163.6	43.0
Turkmenistan	n.d.	155.0	644.0	1,500.0	1,328.0	1,262.0	446.0	21.0	17.0
Uzbekistan	n.d.	169.0	910.0	885.0	1,281.0	117.0	64.0	50.0	29.0
Current account balance of payments (as percent of GDP)									
Kazakhstan	n.d.	n.d.	-34.0	-2.8	-8.6	-3.1	-3.6	-4.2	-5.6
Kyrgyzstan	n.d.	n.d.	-18.3	-16.0	-11.2	-16.2	-24.0	-11.0	-22.6
Tajikistan	n.d.	n.d.	-18.1	-31.0	-21.0	-9.0	-7.4	-5.5	-7.2
Turkmenistan	n.d.	n.d.	n.d.	20.0	2.0	1.0	2.0	-32.0	-40.0
Uzbekistan	n.d.	n.d.	-11.7	-7.8	2.1	-0.2	-7.2	-4.0	-0.7

Official reserves (in months of imports)								
Kazakhstan	n.d.	0	1.5	3.2	3.2	3.1	3.2	4.1
Kyrgyzstan	n.d.	0	1.1	2.5	2.5	1.8	2.6	2.5
Tajikistan	0	0	0	0	0	0.3	0.6	1.9
Turkmenistan	n.d.	0	6.0	7.0	9.0	9.0	15.0	12.0
Uzbekistan	0.6	0	3.8	5.9	6.9	5.4	3.7	5.2
Total foreign debt (in millions of U.S. dollars)								
Kazakhstan	1,478.0	n.d.	1,848	2,717	3,428	3,890	4,587	7,525.0
Kyrgyzstan	0	n.d.	290.0	413.8	584.7	752.6	1,256.1	1,500.0
Tajikistan	0	n.d.	509.0	760.0	817.0	868.0	n.d.	n.d.
Turkmenistan	0	n.d.	168.0	418.0	550.0	668.0	1,360.0	n.d.
Uzbekistan	62.0	n.d.	1,039.0	1,107.0	1,781.0	2,330.0	2,594.0	3,223.0
Total foreign debt (as percent of GDP)								
Kazakhstan	29.6	n.d.	11.7	24.5	20.0	18.7	20.4	36.2
Kyrgyzstan	0	n.d.	21.7	37.3	36.0	43.0	55.4	90.0
Tajikistan	0	n.d.	75.0	92.0	134.0	84.0	n.d.	n.d.
Turkmenistan	0	n.d.	4.0	9.0	30.0	32.0	74.0	n.d.
Uzbekistan	3.0	n.d.	18.6	19.3	17.8	17.1	18.0	22.7

Sources: O. Havrihin et al., "Recovery and Growth in Transition Economies 1990–97: A Stylized Regression Analysis," IMF Working Paper, no. 141 (September 1998), p. 5; *Progress with Fiscal Reform in Countries in Transition*, World Economic Outlook: IMF Staff Estimates (Washington, DC, 1998), pp. 98–120; "Republic of Kazakhstan: Recent Economic Developments," IMF Staff Country Report, no. 98/84 (August 1998); "The Kyrgyz Republic: Recent Economic Developments," IMF Staff Country Report, no. 98/8 (January 1998); "Republic of Tajikistan: Recent Economic Developments," IMF Staff Country Report, no. 98/16 (February 1998); "Turkmenistan: Recent Economic Developments," IMF Staff Country Report, no. 98/81 (August 1998); "Republic of Uzbekistan: Recent Economic Developments," IMF Staff Country Report, no. 98/116 (October 1998); "The Kyrgyz Republic: Enhanced Structural Adjustment Facility Policy, 1998–2000" (Policy Framework Papers [www.imf.org.]); "IMF Concludes Article IV Consultation with the Republic of Tajikistan" (Public Information Notice); "IMF World Economic Outlook," Spring 1999, part 1, p. 15 (advance copy: www.imf.org.).

The deregulation of prices in Russia provoked a high rate of inflation not only in that country, but also in Central Asia. The inflation, however, ran at a somewhat lower rate than in Russia itself. The sole exception was Kazakhstan, where inflation pulsed at nearly the same high rate as in Russia; this comparatively higher rate was due mainly to the larger volume of trade between southern Russia and northern Kazakhstan (the zone where Slavs comprise the majority of inhabitants).

Elsewhere in Central Asia, inflation was distinctly lower. In the case of Uzbekistan, the government introduced price controls on basic food-stuffs as well as energy and fuel; these measures allowed it to keep in-flation at a lower rate than in the other countries of Central Asia. But such measures only provided temporary shelter from the price shock. Until these countries introduced their own national currencies (in the course of 1993 for four states, with Tajikistan following in 1995), the principal factor driving inflation upward was the devaluation of the ruble.

As a result of the introduction of stabilizing measures in 1993–95 (a policy based on fiscal and monetary austerity), from late 1995 to early 1996 three countries (Kazakhstan, Kyrgyzstan, and Uzbekistan) began to resume economic growth. In their fiscal policy, the countries of Central Asia took measures both to increase revenues for the state budget and to reduce expenditures. Some measures were common to all the countries of Central Asia: the reduction in the money supply, the intro-duction of a value-added tax, an increase in the tax rate on personal incomes, and a cutback in subsidies for enterprises (parallel to the move-ment toward privatization) and for social needs.

When the countries of Central Asia first acquired independence, none sought to introduce its own national currency. Rather, they found it ad-vantageous to remain within the "ruble zone," which allowed them to maintain, or restore, trade and payment relations with enterprises lo-cated elsewhere in the CIS and especially Russia. Moreover, the newly established central banks of the Central Asian countries lacked the req-uisite experience to regulate currency flows; until mid-1993, in fact, they relied upon the Central Bank of Russia to perform this task. That arrangement came to an end in July 1993, when Russia unexpectedly introduced its own national currency. As it did so, the Russian Federa-tion made the following proposal to the states of Central Asia (except Kyrgyzstan, which had adopted its own currency in May of that year): if these countries wished to use the Russian ruble, they must keep their national gold reserves and hard currency in Russia. Of the countries in

Central Asia, only Tajikistan agreed to these terms; the others were forced to introduce their own national currencies.

After Kyrgyzstan introduced a national currency, it chose to undertake a total liberalization of hard-currency transactions. Specifically, it established a free-floating exchange rate for the som; henceforth the Central Bank of the Kyrgyz Republic was to determine the exchange rate through daily hard-currency auctions. The government planned to keep that exchange rate within a certain hard-currency "corridor" mainly through changes in the volume of hard currency offered by the Central Bank. Nevertheless, until mid-1994, the som gradually fell in value, primarily because of the sharply increasing demand on the dollar by the European ethnic groups emigrating from Kyrgyzstan. As a result of a stabilization program (based on a tightening of credit and monetary policy), the government reduced inflation to 87 percent by the end of 1994. The som remained stable in 1995, lost value again in 1996, but then stabilized in early 1997 (through expanded intervention by the National Bank and through an increase in the reserves held by banks).[5] As a result, the som gained slightly in value and remained stable until early 1999.

During the period of stabilization in Kyrgyzstan, the government financed its budget deficit through foreign loans and assistance from the International Monetary Fund, the World Bank, and the Asian Development Bank. In March 1995, Kyrgyzstan adopted Article VIII of the IMF Agreement (requiring the complete convertibility of national currency for current accounts and nondiscrimination against the circulation of foreign currencies). The huge deficit in the current account balance of payments for 1995–96 (16 to 24 percent) was due primarily to the massive imports of equipment in the construction phase of the gold mining project at Kumtor; that deficit, however, dropped to 11 percent in 1997 when the country began to export gold from these same reserves. Kyrgyzstan maintained its competitiveness in foreign trade in 1994–96 because salaries remained low (in dollar equivalents) and because of the gradual devaluation of the real exchange rate of the som.[6]

After Kazakhstan introduced its national currency, it established daily auctions of hard currency as well as an interbank market for foreign currency. However, in addition to the official and "commercial" exchange rates of the tenge, there was a "black market" on foreign currency. The latter arose in response to the continuing requirement that enterprises sell 30 percent of their hard-currency earnings to the state at the official exchange rate. Indeed, in 1994 the government increased this quota to 50 percent. The tenge did not lose value in real terms until the first few months of 1994, but then began rapidly to become stronger vis-à-vis the American dollar (because of the significant influx of direct foreign investments). As a result, the tenge increased its value in real terms by 63 percent.[7] Despite the stronger tenge, Kazakhstan's exports continued to be competitive, largely because its wages were lower than those in Russia. The government had substantially liberalized foreign trade during the initial phase of reform, and the export of goods and services in 1994–96 grew at a faster rate than imports. The deficit in current accounts of the balance of payments was due chiefly to the large-scale import of equipment to develop the exploitation of mineral resources. In 1993–96, the government adopted a policy of stabilization with the goal of reducing inflation; the cornerstone of this policy was a reduction in the money supply and the issuance of high-yield state treasury bills. This policy had several major consequences:

- it shifted domestic capital from the productive to the financial sector;
- it led to a further demonetization of the real productive sector;
- it caused the financial condition of enterprises to deteriorate;
- it brought about a decline in profitability;
- it increased the number of insolvent enterprises.

By the end of 1996, nearly half (48.7 percent) of all enterprises in Kazakhstan were operating at a loss.[8] In essence, the government financed its budget deficit by making foreign loans and issuing state bonds (Eurobonds).

Turkmenistan and Uzbekistan took a somewhat different path. When Turkmenistan replaced the ruble with its own manat in November 1993, the government established a multiple exchange rate against the American dollar: (1) an official rate, which was used for state transactions; (2) a commercial rate for permissible private transactions; and (3) a special rate, which was applied for transactions involving natural gas and in use from April 1994 until February 1995. Beginning in 1993, however, Turkmenistan lost its access to the European market for natural gas—its principal export product. That sudden turn of events was due to the fact that Russia and Iran (the countries with the largest reserves of natural gas in the world) denied Turkmenistan a quota for transshipment through their gas pipelines. As a result, the export of Turkmen gas was limited to

Ukraine and the Trans-Caucasus, which, however, were unable to pay for the gas deliveries. Because of this sharp contraction in gas exports, the GDP of Turkmenistan dropped by 40 percent in 1993–95. At the same time, Turkmenistan began to increase its international reserves; the amount rose from the equivalent of six months of imports to nine months. It achieved this by increasing foreign loans and by cutting back on imports (through limits on access to foreign currency). These policies not only led to a sharp increase in the foreign debt (from 4 percent of the GDP in 1993 to 30 percent in 1995), but also were responsible for persistent financial instability and a high inflation rate (over 1,200 percent per year).[9]

Turkmenistan developed a parallel, official exchange market that functioned legally for two years. Its emergence was due to two factors: (1) restrictions on the purchase of foreign currency (no more than $1,000 per transaction, though the number of transactions was unlimited); and (2) the requirement that firms surrender foreign currency earned through the sale of certain goods. To restore macroeconomic stability, in 1996 the government began to conduct a program of reform. Specifically, it first devalued the manat in real terms by one-third of its original value; in mid-1996, it unified the multiple exchange rates into a single rate.

Despite these measures, the government of Turkmenistan failed to obtain a major effect for stabilization. There were several reasons for this:

- the government decided to double the salaries and wages of those employed in the state sector (even though not paid in full);
- Turkmenistan had continuous difficulties obtaining payment from the consumers of its natural gas;
- the country's cotton yield dropped sharply in 1996;
- the government increased direct state credits to state enterprises.

Nevertheless, the policy of monetary and fiscal austerity in 1995 did achieve a significant reduction in inflation, which, by the end of 1996, had dropped to an annual rate of 446 percent. Although the prohibition of any unofficial circulation of the dollar made the official exchange rate of the manat more stable, the increasing pressure on the hard-currency market was reflected in a growing gap between the official and commercial exchange rates (which rose to 30 percent at the end of 1996).[10] The government maintained a small deficit in the state budget during 1994–97 (less than 1.5 percent of GDP) by reducing expenditures and by accumulating indebtedness to the state sector. This policy enabled the government to compensate for the reduced income from the natural gas exports and for the difficulties in selling the goods it obtained from its natural-gas consumers (as payment in kind for outstanding debts). In 1997, because of the fall in the production of cotton fibers (which was due to the decreased output of raw cotton in 1996) and also because of the impossibility of supporting natural gas exports (given the diminished purchasing power of the trade partners), the GDP of Turkmenistan fell by another 26 percent. At the same time, its current account balance of payments—for the first time since the country became independent—reached an unprecedented negative level (32 percent of the GDP). Concurrent with these difficulties was a sharp increase in arrears—from 24 percent of the GDP in 1996 to 41 percent in 1997.

Nevertheless, by substantially increasing its foreign loans, Turkmenistan was able to enlarge its official reserves to the equivalent of 15 months of imports. However, in the course of 1997, the total foreign debt rose twofold and came to represent 74 percent of the GDP. Still, notwithstanding the sharp contraction in GDP, in 1997 Turkmenistan succeeded in reducing its inflation to an annual rate of 21 percent; it accomplished all this by selling foreign currency on the market and by collecting cash from the population. Such measures enabled the government to stabilize the exchange rate of the manat; by the end of 1997, the national currency of Turkmenistan had regained some of its erstwhile value and indeed stood at 45 percent of its original face value. At the same time, the need to pay salary arrears, in combination with the large-scale allocation of preferential credits to state enterprises, posed a threat to the financial stability hitherto achieved. In April 1998, the official exchange rate of the manat fell by 20 percent and became identical to the commercial rate. Commercial banks obtained the right to conduct transactions with foreign currency, including its purchase and sale to the general population. However, "juridical entities" (i.e., corporate bodies) were forbidden to buy foreign currency from banks; they were only allowed to sell, not buy, hard currency. As a result, the "black market" for foreign currency still exists in Turkmenistan, but it offers a very low return (just 2 to 3 percent above the commercial rate of exchange).[11]

Since November 1993, Uzbekistan has imposed an obligatory requirement that enterprises sell foreign currency to the state at the official exchange rate. However, because of the restrictions on the purchase of hard currency by private individuals, the country saw the formation of a parallel black market. Ever since the introduction of the sum (first as an interim measure, then on a permanent basis from July 1994), this national currency has undergone a gradual devaluation (save for a minor increase in value in 1995–96). In 1995, the government established a "commercial" exchange rate alongside the official rate; authorities also tightened procedures on the weekly hard currency auctions of the Central Bank and the interbank hard-currency exchange.

After the introduction of a permanent national currency, Uzbekistan also embarked on a program of stabilization. That program reduced the budget deficit from 10.4 percent in 1993 to 4 percent in 1995; it also caused inflation to drop from 1,281 percent in 1994 to 64 percent in 1996. In the wake of all this, the GDP ceased its decline in 1995 and even showed some growth the following year. As a result, Uzbekistan had the lowest cumulative decline in GDP among all the countries of the former USSR. It must be said, however, that this relatively better performance was due to a more favorable structural situation at the starting point. Namely, Uzbekistan had the following advantages:

- a lower general level of industrialization based on the Soviet model;
- a smaller degree of integration into the industrial complex of the former Soviet Union;
- a larger proportionate share in the agricultural sector, which was essentially independent of resources from other parts of the Soviet Union;
- the dominance of cotton and other products (gold, copper, and uranium) in production, since, after the collapse of the Soviet Union, these could be easily exported to the markets of developed countries for hard currency, which in turn could be used to cope with the acute crisis in balance of payments.

Moreover, privatization began here relatively late and proceeded at a slow pace. Hence the preservation of old structures for medium-sized and large enterprises, along with state financial support, made it possible to avoid a massive downward spiral in industrial production. The presence of oil and gas resources, together with a policy of import-replacement in energy and fuel, enabled Uzbekistan to avoid almost any import of these goods. Moreover, in 1994–95, Uzbekistan had a rich cotton harvest; because of the rise in world prices on cotton and other export goods, this republic was able to increase significantly its revenues from export. As a result, the deficit in the current account in the balance of payments during the period of stabilization was very small. Put in specific terms, the foreign indebtedness of Uzbekistan—a total of 18 percent of the GDP—ranks among the lowest in this entire region.

However, the moderately austere monetary policy of the government of Uzbekistan (which sought thereby to hold down inflation) had this side effect: a problem of nonpayment. The arrears assumed especially painful forms, such as arrears in wages and salaries as well as delinquency in payments due the state treasury. As is well known, the problem of nonpayment arose throughout the countries in the CIS in connection with the spontaneous deregulation of prices in 1992. More precisely, enterprises failed to pay their bills because they were spending more on material resources and energy than could be recovered by the prices on finished goods. In Uzbekistan, this tendency was intensified in the main sector of its economy—agriculture—by two additional factors: (1) the low state procurement prices set for cotton and grain; and (2) the low prices paid by the monopolistic industrial enterprises that process agricultural raw materials. As a result, the increase in the prices of industrial goods significantly exceeded the prices of agricultural products. Although similar tendencies (to a lesser degree) also appeared in Kazakhstan and Kyrgyzstan, the situation in Uzbekistan was more grave because of the primary role that agriculture played in the national economy of that country. Thus, the low level of solvency or the unprofitability of agricultural enterprises had an especially multiplying effect of arrears throughout the entire economy of Uzbekistan. Nevertheless, in 1993–96 the government was temporarily able to stem an increase in the nonpayment problem by following a policy based on the import-substitution of oil and the establishment of state control on fuel and energy prices.

In the fall of 1996, however, Uzbekistan experienced both a smaller cotton harvest (which provides the country with about half of its foreign currency) and a significant increase in imports. As a result, the Central Bank of Uzbekistan sold part of the official reserves and temporarily prohibited the exchange of the sum for foreign currency. That rule applied even to the main foreign investors in Uzbekistan—Daewoo and British-American Tobacco. At the same time, the government rescinded all the licenses that it had previously issued authorizing the purchase of foreign currency. These measures almost entirely eliminated the partial liberalization of hard-currency transactions in current accounts. In addition, the government of Uzbekistan established a new licensing system to regulate imports. At the end of 1997, the unofficial exchange rate for the sum (in dollars) was nearly twice the official rate; by 1998 the difference was threefold, and by mid-1999 it had risen to nearly fourfold.

In 1993, Tajikistan adopted the national currency of the Russian Federation—the new Russian ruble. At the time, conditions were highly unfavorable for the establishment of a separate national currency. Most important, this country had a weak economy and monetary instability, which were primarily due to the outbreak of civil war within Tajikistan and the continuous military conflict along the border with Afghanistan. The principal financial source for the government was the income from cotton and one aluminum plant; the state also received insignificant taxes from the acutely impoverished territory under nominal government control. After the formation of a new government in late 1994 and early 1995, the country had an opportunity to begin economic reform. Thus, in May 1995, the government adopted a national currency (the Tajik ruble), and by the end of 1996 it conducted a strict monetary policy. Under these new conditions (which included a shortage of cash, state control over most prices, and reduction of the state's budget deficit), inflation decreased sharply: it dropped from 7,344 percent in 1993 to 2,100 percent in 1995, and then to 40.5 percent in 1996 (see Table 3.1). The beginning of structural reforms also proceeded successfully, as the government took the following steps:

- it deregulated the prices on cereals and bread;
- it replaced price subsidies with targeted compensation to specific consumers;
- it levied fees for the use of irrigated water;
- it abolished the requirement that enterprises sell the state their hard-currency earnings from exports;
- it eliminated almost all the licenses on the export and import of goods;
- it announced a deregulation of the prices and trade on cotton (beginning with the 1996 harvest);
- it adopted a program for land reform.

From mid-1996, however, the government of Tajikistan unofficially imposed limits on access to hard-currency auctions and allowed arrears on the payments to the population to accumulate.

Worse still, by the end of 1996, as the civil war once again engulfed the country, the increase in military expenditures undermined the government's monetary policy and led to an increase in the budget deficit. The result was a new surge of inflation, which rose to 163.6 percent in 1997. The national currency weakened against the American dollar, as the exchange rate jumped from 300:1 to 750:1 (by September 1997). The government resorted to direct management and strict control over the economy. Specifically, it replaced the auctions of foreign currency with administrative distribution, increased the excise tax (on exports as well), established high import duties (up to 50 percent), and reasserted control over the cotton trade. Not until the government concluded a peace agreement with the opposition in mid-1997 was there a new opportunity to give more attention to economic stabilization and structural reforms. The government thereupon returned to its policy of monetary and fiscal austerity, liberalized trade policy, resumed the auctions of foreign currency, and sharply reduced the state budget deficit.[12]

Structural Reform

Price Reforms

The transition to a market economy required that the Central Asian states conduct fundamental structural reforms. Indeed, beginning in 1992, all the countries of Central Asia embarked on reform, as they took steps to liberalize prices and to eliminate (or reduce) direct state subsidies to the population and enterprises.

Uzbekistan eliminated direct control over prices for the majority of food products, consumer goods, and services, but did not relinquish state control over many key prices. Thus, the government here still continues to regulate the prices of many goods and services:

- oil, natural gas, gas condensate, and coal;
- pipeline shipping;
- the production and transportation of electricity and thermal energy;
- railway, airports, telecommunications, the water supply, and sewage;
- the output of the main enterprises in machine-building, light industry, and construction materials.

In addition, the state controls the trade and pricing for grain, raw cotton and cotton fibers, and also certain foodstuffs (flour, bread, sugar, and vegetable oil).[13] The government also continues to regulate apartment rents, fees for utilities, public transport, and communications.

In the course of the transition period, the prices of all these goods and services repeatedly rose to keep pace with inflation. As a result, many prices on fuel and energy already approached or exceeded world levels (e.g., for petroleum), although there was a slight differentiation of prices on energy for branches of the economy and the population. Individual groups of the population also receive additional state funds to pay for public utilities; for example, teachers and doctors in cities receive subsidies in the amount of 50 percent for electricity, natural gas, and water; in rural areas, these utilities are free for teachers. The assessment for using irrigated water supplies, which was first introduced in 1997, covers only an insignificant part of the actual cost and, as before, essentially represents a kind of subsidy from the state budget.

In Turkmenistan, the government controls the trade and prices on key goods and services—including energy, oil and petroleum products, natural gas, construction materials, transportation, and communications. In agriculture, it has total control over the trade and pricing of two key products—cereals and cotton. State procurement prices for grain and cereal, and all the resources for agriculture, are still subsidized from the state budget (with irrigated water being free and the prices on fertilizer and seeds reflecting a 50 percent subsidy).[14] The government has deregulated retail prices on meat, milk, vegetable oil, rice, sugar, and tea; it also eliminated state subsidies for all these goods from mid-1997. However, the government still provides subsidies for flour, bread, and children's food; it even dispenses salt free of charge. Moreover, the government also provides electricity, water, and natural gas gratis within a certain limit; beyond that level, it supplies these same goods at low prices. Housing and public utilities (water, heat, and sewage) are also free of charge.[15]

In Kazakhstan, authorities at the regional (oblast) level continue to regulate the fees for public utilities as well as the services of urban and local transport. The central government establishes general wholesale prices on natural gas, fuel, and electricity. However, the state liberalized prices on oil, gasoline, and coal in mid-1994, and later that same year extended the deregulation to bread as well.[16]

Kyrgyzstan deregulated almost all its prices. However, the government has retained the price controls on electricity, heat, grain,[17] and transportation and communications services.[18]

By the end of 1995, Tajikistan had deregulated virtually all prices, with the exception of cotton, grain, and bread. In the case of cotton, beginning with the harvest of 1996 the government abolished state procurement orders on cotton and also deregulated its price. In addition, it de-monopolized cotton procurement and trading organizations; henceforth it permitted private trading in cotton, thereby allowing farmers to sell their cotton freely to any private trader. In 1997, the government set up a cotton commodity exchange and also made plans to privatize all of the cotton-processing industrial enterprises. With respect to grain and bread, in the spring of 1996 the government extended price deregulation to this sphere as well. It also eliminated the subsidies to producers (which had been equal to 14 percent of the GDP); it replaced the subsidies to the population (in the form of the cheap price of bread) with targeted monetary compensation to needy strata. The government also abolished the remaining subsidies in agriculture, which had been in the form of irrigated water and electricity. It did, however, continue to subsidize electricity for industry and for family households. In effect, state control remained only for the prices on water supply in cities, rents, utilities, and public transport.[19]

Privatization and Enterprise Reform

Although there is no ideal share of the private sector in a national economy, for the sake of efficiency it should nonetheless be dominant. The principal structural reform in post-Soviet states has been the privatization of state property, along with the creation and development of new private enterprises. According to the European Bank Reconstruction and Development (EBRD), in 1997 the share of the economy produced by the private sector amounted to 60 percent in Kyrgyzstan, 55 percent in Kazakhstan, 45 percent in Uzbekistan, 25 percent in Turkmenistan, and 20 percent in Tajikistan.[20] The countries of Central Asia envisioned a denationalization by distributing privatization coupons among their citizens (who would use these to purchase shares of enterprises). In other words, they employed the so-called voucher method for the denationalization of state assets. Kazakhstan and Kyrgyzstan followed this method (with certain corrections). However, they also conducted privatization through monetary auctions and, on a case-by-case basis, they also used various individual procedures. In Kyrgyzstan, the government also permitted managers and employees to purchase their own enterprise. Turkmenistan and Uzbekistan gave preference to the privatization of small enterprises (by allowing management and employees to buy them out); these countries also allowed the sale of medium-sized and large enterprises on an individual basis.[21] In all the countries of Central Asia, mass privatization began with small enterprises, which were sold mainly to the employees themselves. Government here also embarked on the privatization of state apartments, which were almost entirely sold to their residents. After this came the privatization of middle-sized and large enterprises.

In Kazakhstan, the government adopted a policy whereby many enterprises in different branches were transformed into trusts under the management of foreign companies. In 1996, the government concluded forty-one contracts involving eighty-nine enterprises. In the case of oil and coal-mining enterprises, the government concentrated on privatizing the profitable ones and shutting down the unprofitable ones. The authorities also transferred the administration of oil resources to the state company "Kazakhneft;" and created relatively favorable conditions for foreign investment in the petroleum sector.

In Kyrgyzstan, the government used monetary auctions to privatize nearly half (4,460) of the relatively small state enterprises in 1991–93. Beginning in 1994, the government privatized and auctioned medium-sized and large enterprises through voucher auctions; by mid-1997, it had privatized more than 1,900 firms (approximately two-thirds of all medium-sized and large enterprises). At this stage of the so-called mass privatization among the population, the government distributed approximately 3.5 billion privatization coupons, which could be used to purchase up to 25 percent of each enterprise available for purchase. Another 5 percent of the value of each enterprise was available for redemption by management and plant employees; the remaining shares were sold in general auctions for cash. In mid-1997, the government suspended the process of privatization and launched investigations into the alleged manipulation of enterprise prices and other forms of corruption. The government later renewed privatization according to a new plan, whereby approximately 300 medium-sized and large enterprises (including state monopolies) were to be privatized by the year 2000. In 1997, the government put up for privatization important state monopolies (for example, Kyrgyz Telekom, Kyrgyzenergokholding, and Kyrgyzgaz). The value of these assets was put at several times the retail value of all privatization coupons previously issued to the population.

In 1993–97, Uzbekistan privatized and auctioned off approximately 82 percent of all enterprises. The privatization rate varied according to the size of the firm: it was highest for small enterprises (96 percent), but much lower for middle-sized firms (21 percent) and large enterprises (17 percent).[22] At the end of 1996, the republic adopted a new system based on "Privatization Investment Funds" (PIF). According to this scheme, the government planned gradually to sell 30 percent of the stock in six hundred large enterprises to these PIFs; in turn, these investment funds would issue and sell stock to the general population. The whole idea was not to have the population control large enterprises directly, but rather to do so through investment funds and management companies. This led to the creation of more than fifty privatization investment funds and sixty management companies; approximately 100,000 citizens of Uzbekistan bought stock from these funds. At the sixteen auctions conducted in the course of 1996–97, the stocks of more than 150 enterprises were sold to these privatization funds. As a rule, the government retains at least 51 percent of the stock in the privatized enterprises. In mid-1997, however, it suspended this policy based on PIFs.

In 1991–92, Tajikistan completed the privatization of state housing and began to denationalize the small enterprises. However, the outbreak of civil war delayed this process and, by 1996, less than 8 percent of state enterprises had been privatized. Once the armed conflict had ended, by the end of 1997 the government had privatized 30 percent of state enterprises, the majority of which were small in size. In 1997, the government resolved to auction off medium-sized and large enterprises and to complete the privatization of small enterprises by the year 2000.[23]

In Turkmenistan, by 1996 the state had privatized and auctioned 81 percent of all legally registered enterprises, with the majority of privatized firms being small and concentrated in the sphere of trade and services. In general, Turkmenistan lags behind in the process of privatizing enterprising; the country plans to complete the privatization of trade enterprises by the year 2000.

Agrarian Reform

The implementation of agrarian reform in Central Asia does not envision the creation of unrestricted private ownership of agricultural land, but rather provides for a long-term lease to collective and private enterprises. The governments also plan to transform the former sovkhozes (state farms) and kolkhozes (collective farms) into new forms—primarily collective enterprises (such as joint-stock companies, associations, co-operatives, and the like)—as well as to create individual family farms based on long-term land leases.

Kazakhstan completed the large-scale redistribution of the land of former state farms and collective farms by the end of 1997. As a result, these reforms transformed 1,267,919 agricultural producers into the following categories:

- private plots of "auxiliary" or part-time growers (96 percent of all producers and occupying 0.06 percent of all agricultural land);
- individual farms of full-time producers, with the right of long-term land leases (representing 3.5 percent of all producers and holding 12.1 percent of the agricultural land);
- collective enterprises in the form of joint-stock companies, associations, cooperatives, and other nongovernmental enterprises (0.4 percent of all producers and occupying 81.8 percent of all agricultural land);
- state enterprises (0.1 percent of all producers and holding 6.04 percent of all agricultural land).[24]

Within the framework of nongovernmental agricultural enterprises, employees have been able to privatize the right to shares of land and the other property that belongs to these collective enterprises. These rights to land and property can legally be sold, bought, used as collateral, and so forth. In practical terms, however, it is difficult to exercise these rights. Therefore, nongovernmental enterprises occupy almost 94 percent of all agricultural land, but the overwhelming majority of the land is being utilized by collective enterprises. In short, the reform has not succeeded in making the transition to family farming. Private family farms in Kazakhstan produce only 4 to 5 percent of all agricultural output in the country.[25] At the same time, Kazakhstan has carried out a deregulation of prices and trade on all agricultural products.

Land reform in Kazakhstan is more advanced here than in any other countries of Central Asia. However, it still has not reached its final goal of enabling a transition to private farming. Within the framework of collective enterprises, land has still not been given to the peasants as such (with the allocation of concrete plots of land on the territory of collective enterprises). As a result, the peasants in effect cannot leave the collective enterprises and create independent, private farms. Hence it is not surprising that after such a land reform has been conducted, and despite the liberalization of prices on agricultural products, productivity in crop cultivation and animal husbandry continues to fall in Kazakhstan.

In Kyrgyzstan, the government transferred to private farmer producers approximately half of all agricultural land (primarily in the southern half of the country) on the basis of a long-term (99-year) lease. The other half of the land, located in the Chui River valley to the north, is populated primarily by European ethnic groups; for political reasons, the land there has not been converted to long-term private leases. In general, land that has not been converted to private leases is used by collective and state enterprises. Moreover, private farmers face a host of serious difficulties—in particular, gaining access to water supplies (because of the poor functioning of the irrigation systems), acquiring inventory and materials (e.g., machinery, seed, and fertilizer), obtaining credits and loans, and establishing channels to market their products. As a result, many private farmers prefer to give back to the collective enterprises their right to land and then to work as employees on the collective farms. Such behavior is also due to the fact that the real rights of private farmers to land remain uncertain; in particular, they are not free to transfer their rights to long-term leases, to bequeath them as inheritance, or to use them as collateral for bank credits. As a result, private farmers actually hold only about one-third of the agricultural land; hence two-thirds of the land and labor employed in agriculture remain under the control of collective enterprises. At the same time, Kyrgyzstan has liberalized the prices and trade policy for all agricultural products; private farmers are free to sell the cotton, wool, vegetables, fruits, and the other products that they grow. In 1996, private farmers accounted for about 40 to 50 percent of the total production for such crops as cotton, wheat, and rice. Because the government has set for itself the political goal of achieving self-sufficiency in grain production, it continues to play a major role in encouraging the production and procurement of grain. In addition, many industrial enterprises that process and store agricultural products (sugar and grain) have not yet been privatized.[26]

Uzbekistan, after gaining its independence in 1991, converted all state agricultural enterprises into collectives. In 1997, such enterprises numbered approximately 1,400. These collective enterprises occupy about 70 percent of all cultivated land and produce virtually all the cotton and the overwhelming mass of the grain. De jure the collective enterprises are autonomous, but de facto they are still controlled by the government, which appoints the administrators and, at least in the case of cotton and grain, regulates the delivery of resources, production, and sale. The employees of collective enterprises usually receive a low salary (paid partly in kind and often with delays), which encourages them to divert part of the resources and grain harvest from collective purposes for their personal use.[27] By the end of 1997, approximately 30 percent of all irrigated land (1.3 million hectares) was leased under the following terms:

1. Approximately 750,000 hectares (18 percent) was transferred to families to use as personal, auxiliary garden plots (with the area not to exceed 0.25 hectares). The lease does not have a specified time limit; the land in effect was to become a "life-long inheritable possession." Although the land can be used as collateral for loans, it cannot be sold or subleased.

2. Approximately 400,000 hectares (10 percent) was used to create about 20,000 private family farms. Such private farms occupy an average of 20 hectares and hold the land on the basis of long-term leases (up to fifty years).

3. Approximately 180,000 hectares (4 percent) are allocated on the basis of one-year leases to 13,000 employees of collective enterprises. Moreover, these contracts of a "family type" can be annually renewed at the discretion of the heads of collective enterprises on the condition that the lessees increase the yield, not lower the quality of the soil, and sell the majority of products to the collective enterprise at set prices.[28]

Private family farms produce no more than 7 to 9 percent of all agricultural output in Uzbekistan. The government has not deregulated the prices and the trade (domestic or foreign) involving cereals and cotton—the two key products of agriculture. Moreover, the state budget continues to subsidize the production resources needed to raise these two crops. Notwithstanding these subsidies, the low procurement prices and the state trade in cotton and cereals—through the hidden mechanism of state orders—ensure that financial resources are diverted from agriculture to the state budget, where they are then used to subsidize industrialization in the cities. The state did formally deregulate the prices and trade on all other products of agriculture. However, the mass production of fruits, vegetables, meat, milk, and other products is limited by the low prices that the monopolistic commercial and industrial processing enterprises pay for these goods. Thus, as a result of this agrarian policy, Uzbekistan has still not created the conditions needed to raise the productivity of irrigated land and to ensure a stable growth in the production of agricultural goods.

In Tajikistan, the de facto division of the country into areas controlled by the government and by the opposition has led to different policies in the use of agricultural land. On territories subject to the control of Dushanbe, local authorities have been given the right to lease land, if it is not used by collective enterprises, for terms up to ten years if the lessee agrees to produce grain (which is in short supply). At the end of 1996, parliament adopted a program of land reform that provides for the redistribution of land in large collective farms to private farmers for unlimited lifetime and inheritable leases. Such rights may also be reassigned on the open market. Consequently, the share of arable land cultivated by private family farms increased from 6 percent in 1995 to 18 percent in 1996 and then to 25 percent by the end of 1997. Contrariwise, the share of land cultivated by state enterprises (sovkhozes) fell from 44 percent (1995) to 30 percent (1996).[29] In eastern Badakhshan, the government created peasant cooperatives with financial support from Ismaili leader Aga Khan (as assistance to the members of the Ismaili sect of Islam who reside in Tajikistan).[30]

Turkmenistan announced a program of land reform at the end of 1996. According to this program, the majority of cultivated land would be leased to private farmers for ten to fifteen years on the condition that they grow cotton and wheat, that they fulfill the state order for a specified volume of production, and that they sell their harvest to the government at state procurement prices. If, at the end of the leasing period, a local association of peasants decides that the performance of a specific farmer has been satisfactory, and if that decision is confirmed by a national commission (headed by the president of the country), this farmer will be given the right of ownership to the land. Although he will not have the right to sell the land, he will have the right to choose freely what he grows and will not have to satisfy any state procurement orders. In accordance with this program, in the course of 1997 the government leased 76.5 percent of the total arable land (1.7 million hectares) and converted another 90,900 hectares into private property. At the end of 1997, the government also privatized the majority of livestock (including 82 percent of the cattle and poultry, 50 percent of the sheep, and 25 percent of the hogs). The government also abolished state orders for meat and milk. However, the government did retain the system of low procurement prices for the entire harvest of cotton and grain. It also kept the subsidies for production resources used in agriculture: the free use of water for irrigation and the 50 percent discount on fertilizers and seed.

Reform of Trade Policy

Kyrgyzstan, Kazakhstan, and Tajikistan have achieved significant progress in liberalizing imports and exports and in providing complete convertibility of the national currencies in current accounts. Turkmenistan and Uzbekistan have had limited progress in the sphere of trade policy, and both allow only partial convertibility of their national currencies for current transactions.

Kyrgyzstan allows full convertibility of its national currency for both current accounts and for capital accounts. It levies a 10 percent tariff on imports from non-CIS countries; goods from CIS countries can be imported duty-free. This country does not use nontariff barriers or impose administrative limitations on imports; import licenses exist for only five categories of goods and are used to protect the health of society, the environment, national security, and the well-being of consumers. There are no export duties; export licenses exist only for weapons and military equipment, nuclear materials, and drugs.[31] In December 1998, Kyrgyzstan became the first country in the CIS to join the World Trade Organization (WTO).

Kazakhstan has, to a significant degree, liberalized its foreign trade and also has established the convertibility of the tenge in trade transactions. In 1997, the government abolished the requirement that private agricultural enterprises register export contracts at the commodity exchange. However, the government did retain the system of state orders for cereals (although reducing the volume to 200,000 tons) and introduced licenses on the import of alcoholic beverages.[32]

In 1996, Tajikistan abolished the state orders for cotton, cereals, and aluminum. It also abrogated the requirement that exporters exchange a specific part of their hard-currency earnings for the national currency; henceforth, it simply mandates exporters to repatriate their hard-currency earnings (i.e., through an obligation to bring these funds into the country). Such products as cotton, cement, wool, fruits and vegetables, leather, silk, tobacco, and metals can be exported only through the commodity markets. Tajikistan requires import licenses for goods that can harm the health, security, and cultural legacy of the country; licenses are also needed for the import of pesticides, natural gas, and electricity. Export licenses are required for metals, tractors, bulldozers, construction equipment, electricity, and petroleum. Tajikistan has also expressed its intention to join the customs union of four countries (Belarus, Kazakhstan, Kyrgyzstan, and Russia), and it is also preparing an application to join the WTO.[33]

Uzbekistan, after a process of gradual deregulation of foreign trade in 1992–95, underwent a policy reversion in the wake of the poor cotton harvest of 1996. Because of the ensuing difficulties in its balance of payments, the government required the registration of import contracts and also increased customs duties in an attempt to reduce imports. In 1997–98, together with insignificant progress in the liberalization of exports (the elimination of export licenses on cotton, oil, and ferrous and nonferrous metals), the government introduced additional duties on exports. It also preserved direct state control of foreign trade involving cotton, cereals, metals, and other goods. Although the maximum duty on imports was 30 percent, the government substantially increased the average tariff duty—from 17 percent in late 1996 to 28 percent in early 1997. In addition to import tariffs, Uzbekistan also levies excise duties on imports. From the end of 1996, the government made it obligatory to register import contracts with the Ministry of Foreign Economic Activity. In early 1998, it abolished this measure for imports where the importer uses his own sources of hard currency, but left it binding for all other transactions involving imports. Importers must register to purchase foreign currency from official sources and go through customs procedures. However, the above restrictions are not applied equally to all enterprises. Namely, the government grants significant privileges to firms with foreign investments as well as firms that export their own products for hard currency.[34]

Turkmenistan requires exporters to repatriate their hard-currency earnings and to exchange these funds at the official rate. Until 1997, it required that 30 percent of the earnings from oil and natural gas be exchanged at the central bank; it took another 40 percent as a tax assessment. The government also demanded the obligatory exchange of 50 percent of the earnings from the export of other commodities produced in the state sector (except cotton). It made no demands for the obligatory exchange of hard currency earned from the export of cotton or other goods produced in the private sector. From the end of 1997, however, the government established a 50 percent tax on the earnings from the export of natural gas; it also required that 25 percent of the earnings be exchange for the national currency. Once these conditions have been fulfilled, enterprises are permitted to hold the remaining funds in hard-currency accounts in Turkmen banks; these enterprises can then use the remaining hard-currency earnings as they see fit, without any restrictions. Imports to Turkmenistan are free from any kind of limitation; there are no import licenses. Nor does the country have any customs duties on imports (except for a 0.5 percent administrative customs fee).[35]

Reform in the Financial Sector

In the Soviet period, Gosbank—the central bank of the former USSR—was responsible for the movement of all financial resources within the country. Once the republics of Central Asia became independent, they transformed the branches of Gosbank into national "central banks." They also converted some or all specialized banks into joint-stock companies (with the government still possessing a controlling or significant share) and allowed the formation of new commercial banks. The introduction of national currencies enabled the Central Asian states to conduct their own monetary policy and to develop and restructure the financial and banking system. Although the majority of countries here have succeeded in avoiding a general collapse of the banking system (by undertaking measures to restructure their finances and operations), these financial networks remain very fragile. The financial sector in Central Asian countries has several principal characteristics in common: a dominant (or substantial) role of state property in the capital of the banking system, the weak development of private commercial banks, and the unstable financial condition of banks.

In Kazakhstan, during the initial period of independence, the main goal for the government in this sphere was to prevent the collapse of the banking system. Hence the government concentrated its efforts on the financial restructuring of large banks and raising the requirements for newly established banks. Only after it had achieved a certain stability in banking did the government take steps to modernize banking operations and improve the legal and regulatory foundations of this system. Nevertheless, the weakness of banking controls and the policy on the granting of licenses for banking activity led to a rapid increase in the number of banks with insufficient capital as well as a growth in problematic credits. Therefore, in 1995 the government of Kazakhstan increased the required minimum amount of banking capital, liquidated about 60 of the 177 commercial banks, and transferred loans (equal to 11 percent of GDP) to three companies that were specially created to administer assets. In 1995–97, the government conducted broad-scale changes in financial regulation and accounting in order to meet international standards. In Kazakhstan, the share of unpaid loans (as a proportion of total credits) dropped from 19.9 percent (1996) to 7.7 percent (1997).[36]

Kyrgyzstan adopted a national currency in May 1993—that is, prior to the collapse of a single ruble zone—and therefore was able to minimize the foreign financial shocks from the rapid devaluation of the ruble. With the technical and financial assistance of the World Bank and IMF, the government designed and then, in 1996–97, implemented reforms in the financial sector that sought to do the following:

- create a competitive and effective private banking system;
- liquidate the two dominant but financially weak state banks (Agroprombank and El'bank) and replace them with a Savings Corporation to service rural areas;
- reestablish two large state banks that existed earlier (Promstroibank and AKB Kyrgyzstan Bank);
- create a temporary agency to restructure debts by assisting in the collection, conversion, sale, and writing off of bad debts and by accelerating the restructuring or liquidation of enterprises;
- create a new system of financial regulation, supervision, accounting, and financial infrastructure that corresponds to international standards;
- develop nonbanking financial institutions.

The government also issued banking licenses to two banks with foreign capital. In 1997, Kyrgyzstan had twenty commercial banks, including three with foreign capital. The share of bad loans dropped from 72 percent in 1995 to 7.5 percent in 1997.[37]

Since 1996, Uzbekistan has moved to modernize its financial and banking system so as to come into line with international standards. This has included the introduction of its own national currency, the creation of a two-tiered banking system, a policy aimed at financial stabilization, the transformation of state banks into joint-stock companies, and the formation of new commercial banks. In early 1996, the government established a new financial instrument—government securities (which are traded on the hard-currency exchange). Beginning in the spring of 1997, the Central Bank and commercial banks of the republic shifted to a new system of accounting and underwent audits by well-known international firms. A distinctive feature of the banking system in Uzbekistan is the relatively small number of banks. By the end of 1998, Uzbekistan had thirty-one commercial banks, four of which included foreign participation. That is partly due to the high requirements for minimum bank capital; in 1997, the government adopted a plan whereby all commercial banks by the year 2000 are to have capital of at least two million ECUs (one million ECUs in the case of rural and regional banks). The government also adopted other measures that prescribe the procedures for registration, licensing, regulation, and liquidation of banks. All this made it possible to reduce the volume of bad loans held by the banks (from 10 percent at the end of 1995 to 4 percent at the end of 1997).[38]

In Tajikistan, after an initial period of difficulties, the government deregulated the interest rates on loans and deposits in May 1995. A year and a half later, it adopted a law on the Central Bank, set uniform demands for reserves in banks of all types, authorized the participation of foreign bank capital, and established a minimum capital for commercial banks (equivalent to two million dollars for banks in which foreign participants hold over 50 percent of the capital; three hundred thousand dollars for national banks). In 1997, Tajikistan had twenty-four commercial banks, none of which included foreign participation.[39]

In Turkmenistan, the Central Bank regulates the rather weak structure of commercial banks. The latter consist of seven banks in which the government has the exclusive or majority holding, one bank in which the government holds equal shares with foreign capital, one bank with an insignificant state share, four local private banks, and two branches of foreign banks. Twelve banks hold licenses to engage in the entire spectrum of financial operations (including nonresidents and hard currency); two banks have licenses to engage only in domestic transactions. Turkmenistan does not use financial instruments that could circulate in the market; nor does it have nonbanking financial institutions, although insurance firms have begun to develop. The majority of banks have become involved in narrow branch transactions or service individual state enterprises; competition in the financial sphere is only beginning to develop. With the support of the World Bank and IMF, in 1996–98 the Central Bank of Turkmenistan introduced an international system of bank regulation, with the establishment of minimum require-ments for the volume of bank capital and other financial norms and rules.[40]

Barriers to Economic Growth

All the countries of Central Asia have encountered similar difficulties that, when taken together, pose substantial impediments to the task of unleashing economic growth.

The Low Level of Savings and Investment Activity

Table 3.2 presents the balance of savings and investments for Kazakhstan, Kyrgyzstan, and Uzbekistan in 1997. The general level of both national savings (from 8.7 to 12.0 percent of the GDP) and investment (from 12.9 to 16.0 percent of the GDP) in the countries of Central Asia is relatively low, especially when compared with the countries of East Asia, where the norms of savings and investment—until the crisis of 1997–98—amounted to 30 to 40 percent of the GDP. Among the countries of Central Asia, Uzbekistan has the highest level of general savings and investment; moreover, the savings and investment activity there are almost equally divided between the private sector and the state. Of these three coun-tries, Uzbekistan also has the largest state savings and investment, which is almost twice that of the state sector in Kazakhstan and Kyrgyzstan. At the same time, Kazakhstan has the largest savings in the private sector; Uzbekistan, by contrast, has the lowest level of private savings and in-vestment. In 1997, only Uzbekistan had a negative savings-investment balance of the private sector.

One can clearly establish the linkage between the level of private savings in the countries of Central Asia and the character of incentive provided by the interest rates on bank deposits. Kazakhstan and Kyrgyzstan have maintained positive interest rates (i.e., above infla-tion) for deposits by the population and enterprises. Kazakhstan has maintained this policy of positive interest rates since 1996; because banks offer such incentives, the level of private savings in Kazakhstan is twice that of Uzbekistan. However, the high level of private savings in Kazakhstan and Kyrgyzstan does not mean that the level of private in-vestment is also high. On the contrary, private investment in all three countries is approximately the same (8.5 to 9.2 percent). In Uzbekistan, the interest rates on banking deposits—when adjusted for inflation—

Table 3.2

Savings-Investment Balance in Kazakhstan, Kyrgyzstan, and Uzbekistan (1997) (as percent of GDP)

Indicator		Kazakhstan	Kyrgyzstan	Uzbekistan
Investment	Total	12.9	13.1	16.0
	Government	3.7	4.2	7.5
	Private	9.2	8.9	8.5
Savings	Total	8.7	4.8	12.0
	Government	−5.0	−5.4	5.2
	Private	13.7	10.2	6.7
Savings-investment gap	Total	−4.2	−8.3	−4.0
	Government	−8.7	−9.6	−2.3
	Private	4.5	1.3	−1.8

Sources: "Republic of Kazakhstan: Recent Economic Developments," IMF Staff Country Report, no. 98/84 (August 1998), p. 45; "Kyrgyz Republic: Enhanced Structural Adjustment Facility" (Policy Framework Paper, 1998–2000 [www.imf.org]); "Republic of Uzbekistan: Recent Economic Developments," IMF Staff Country Report, no. 98/116 (October 1998), p. 12.

are strongly negative, and that in turn has reduced the potential investment activity by the private sector.

In the countries of Central Asia with a more liberalized economy (Kazakhstan and Kyrgyzstan), the share of investment in fixed capital (measured as a percent of the GDP) is still at a low level. On the whole, the financial and banking systems of the countries in Central Asia do not as yet correspond to what is needed to increase economic growth or to satisfy international standards. The majority of credits are short-term and used to augment working capital and to pay wages and salaries.

In Uzbekistan, the share of banking credits in the total volume of capital investment has sharply contracted in recent years, falling from 26 percent in 1993 to 7 percent in 1997. The main cause of the decrease in capital investment through bank credits is the fact that banks are not suitable for providing credits for projects when the inflation rates are high, since the latter essentially mean a negative interest rate on credits (as was the case in 1995–96).

The countries of Central Asia have shown a general tendency to reduce the role of the state budget in financing investment. In Uzbekistan, the share of funds from the state budget in the total volume of capital investment shrank from 47 percent in 1990 to 27 percent in 1997. In

Kazakhstan, the role of the state budget in financing investment declined from 19.7 percent in 1993 to 13.2 percent in 1997. The bulk of these government funds has gone to the state sector. However, there has been a contraction in the investment opportunities of enterprises because of the deterioration in their financial condition.

The high level of inflation has also limited the investment opportunities of the general population. In Uzbekistan, the population's share of total investment was 10.1 percent in 1997 (about half the level of 1992). In general, the funds of the population are used to finance the construction of private housing. Bank deposits in the countries of Central Asia represent an extremely small proportion of the GDP, a pattern that reflects the general distrust of the banking system. In Kazakhstan, bank deposits—measured as a percent of the GDP—did show a modest gain, rising from 1.4 percent in 1996 to 5 percent in 1997,[41] but were still extremely small. In Turkmenistan, bank deposits were equivalent to a mere 2 percent of the GDP.[42] In Uzbekistan, this indicator stood at 9 percent in 1997;[43] in Kyrgyzstan, it was 4.2 percent in 1996.[44]

Given the above, it has been incumbent on the countries of Central Asia to seek foreign sources of financing. Thus, an important source of finance for investment projects in recent years has been direct foreign investment and investment credits. Uzbekistan offers an instructive example: whereas in 1993 the share of foreign investment and credits represented 0.07 percent of the total volume of capital investment, by 1998 this quotient had jumped to 27 percent.

Therefore, the countries of Central Asia strive to attract foreign investment. The latter is given a significant role both for purposes of obtaining additional capital (and thereby compensating for the negative balance of payments), and to increase the effectiveness of domestic investments by tapping foreign technologies and management. Kazakhstan and Kyrgyzstan have created favorable conditions for foreign investors, sold many deposits of useful minerals and components of the infrastructure (including airports as well as heating and electric power systems), and also granted preferential tax treatment.

Uzbekistan has also created favorable legal conditions for foreign investment. Thus, major foreign investors receive a tax holiday (from five to seven years), conditions of free trade, access to very advantageous exchange rates at the official exchange, and all kinds of legal guarantees. Nevertheless, according to data from the EBRD, during the period of 1989–96 Uzbekistan accumulated the smallest amount of per capita investment of any country in Central Asia—a mere 7 American dollars (compared to 33 dollars in Kyrgyzstan, 118 dollars in Turkmenistan, and 187 dollars in Kazakhstan).[45] The principal reason is apparently the fact that foreign companies find it difficult to increase investments in Uzbekistan, since the government sets quotas to limit access to official hard-currency exchange, and exports are not increasing because of the general import-substitution policy.

In the opinion of the present authors, the countries of Central Asia should not lay particularly great hopes on the assistance of foreign investors. That is because the markets of the individual countries are too small; they simply do not have sufficient purchasing power to sustain the large-scale industrial production of consumer goods. In the case of Kazakhstan, its liberal policy on imports and the overvalued exchange rates for the national currency have served to stimulate imports, not domestic production. Furthermore, the geographic isolation of these countries and the high transportation costs (to import parts and components as well as to export finished goods) have also had a negative impact. These two factors make it difficult for transnational companies to operate assembly plants here (as they typically do in the countries of Southeast Asia).

World practice has shown that in situations like those obtaining in Central Asia, foreign investment cannot be the main locomotive of economic growth. The reason is that the domestic economies are weakly developed, and hence each country, by itself, represents an insignificant market. Ordinarily, the domestic private firms must sustain rapid economic growth, which in turn can attract foreign investors, not the other way around.[46]

Although the private sector represents a rather substantial proportion of the GDP in Kazakhstan and Kyrgyzstan, it is nevertheless not prepared to provide active investment in long-term projects. In the countries of Central Asia, the private sector does not have sufficient incentive for investment in production—given the relatively high risk of substantial inflation, the adverse changes in the economic milieu, the lack of adequate institutional support, and so forth. Because the regulatory legal framework is subject to quite frequent alterations (including new decrees by the president and directives from the government), the private sector has no confidence that the general thrust of these changes will serve to protect and guarantee the profits from their investment in the real sectors of the economy. The governments of Central Asia are much better at protecting the foreign investors than domestic private investors.

In those countries of Central Asia with a more pronounced *étatisme* (Turkmenistan, Uzbekistan, and Tajikistan), the government budget and the state sector play the main role. As a result, they have been able to achieve a relatively higher level of national investment.

To be sure, given the conditions of hyperinflation that prevailed in Central Asia in 1992–94, private investment could hardly be significant, since the inflation rendered the returns too uncertain. Under those conditions, only the state could ensure the requisite level of investment.

In Uzbekistan, the increase in the norm of investment in 1993–96 also served to depress effective aggregate demand, which in turn aggravated the problems of selling output, the rising creditor and debtor indebtedness, and arrears. According to the calculations of the authors (based on the method of investment multiplier), the efficiency of gross investments in Uzbekistan gradually decreased during these years. In other words, an increase in the rate of investment gave a smaller increment of growth in the GDP. Thus, whereas each sum invested yielded 2.2 sum in 1994, this indicator had fallen to 1.7 sum by 1997.

Moreover, the mobilization opportunities of the state budgets in Central Asia are close to being exhausted. In 1997, the share of state expenditures in the GDP amounted to 33 percent in Uzbekistan, 29.2 percent in Turkmenistan, 27.1 percent in Kazakhstan, 23.3 percent in Kyrgyzstan, and 15 percent in Tajikistan.[47]

As the foregoing suggests, it is essential for the countries of Central Asia to develop their financial systems. They can then stimulate savings and channel them into the most effective investment projects.

Arrears, Low Level of Monetization, and Weakness of the Financial Sector

The financial systems in the countries in Central Asia have continued to show strong signs of instability, reflected, above all, in the large volume of bills receivable and bills payable. The problem of nonpayment lies in the fact that the indebtedness of some economic actors mounts quickly; as the proportion of overdue bills increases, this process rather quickly engulfs the entire economy. Buyers do not pay for the delivered goods on time; enterprises have no way to pay the wages due their employees, the interest owed to the banks, and the taxes assessed by the government. And the government, in turn, cannot pay on time the salaries of its own employees. The crisis steadily grows like a snowball; it soon comes to paralyze the operation of the financial system, the delivery of tax payments, and especially the real sectors of the economy (simultaneously reducing investments and aggregate demand).

The following data provide some indication of the scale of this phenomenon in the countries of Central Asia. At the beginning of 1997 in Uzbekistan, the volume of overdue debts in the economy amounted to 70 percent of the M2 money supply; by mid-1998, these debts amounted to approximately 150 percent of the M2 money supply.[48] In Kazakhstan, by the beginning of 1998 the volume of overdue debts in the economy was 5 times the M2 money supply.[49] In Turkmenistan, these overdue bills amounted to 6.2 times the M2 money supply in 1997.[50] This whole phenomenon of nonpayment can be attributed to the following factors:

- a decrease in the share of the monetary supply in the GDP (as a result of the struggle against hyperinflation during the stabilization period);
- the backwardness of the financial system;
- the low level of private savings in the economy;
- the low level of competitiveness in most of the industry (which should lead to bankruptcies on a massive scale, but these have been artificially averted for fear of increasing unemployment);
- price inelasticity (because of monopolization and the control of tax organs over producer prices, especially the numerous state enterprises, whereby price reductions to increase operating capital are regarded as tax evasion).

Arrears can be regarded as a kind of interest-free loan that one economic actor (the consumer) obtains from another (the supplier) in the event of late payment for goods received. An austere monetary policy, which was intended to combat inflation, made it more difficult to secure credit; because of the high interest rates, the agricultural and industrial sectors were unable to repay loans and credits. In a sense, arrears represent a kind of "quasi-money," something that appeared in response to the shortage of regular currency and a reaction to the low coefficient of monetization of the economy.

The countries of Central Asia did adopt laws to deal with the problem of bankruptcy. However, the ineffectiveness of sanctions and bankruptcy procedures, the serious deficiencies in the laws that regulate commerce, the weak control over the banking sphere—all these factors created conditions highly favorable to the mounting crisis of nonpayment.

Agriculture and mining constitute the main economic sectors in Central Asia. Because of the higher growth of prices on industrial goods, agriculture generated lower earnings and even became unprofitable; the low incomes of the rural population, in turn, led to a stagnation in the demand on products from many branches of industry. In Uzbekistan and Turkmenistan, the government reinforced this tendency through its low procurement prices on cotton and grain (which had the effect of extracting still more income from agriculture). The government is often late (sometimes by several months) in paying agricultural enterprises for cotton and grain deliveries. The agricultural sector, in turn, cannot pay its suppliers, a process that then has a domino effect on other sectors, with a significant multiplier effect on the entire economy.

Thanks to its efficient tax collection, for the moment the government of Uzbekistan has succeeded in paying wages on time and in limiting the volume of nonpayment to less than 25 percent of the GDP in 1997. In part, Uzbekistan was able to achieve such a low rate of nonpayment because trade with countries in the CIS constituted only about 30 percent of total foreign trade turnover (compared to 51 percent for Kazakhstan and 61 percent for Kyrgyzstan). As a result, it has restricted the "import" of nonpayment from countries in the CIS, where this problem has escalated into a national calamity (for example, in Russia). Moreover, the tax revenues in Uzbekistan constitute about 30 percent of the GDP, whereas the M2 money supply is 16.5 percent of the GDP. In other words, the tax levies are nearly twice the money supply, which allows a state-run economy to finance the majority of state-owned enterprises directly from the state budget. In Uzbekistan, the tolerance of a rather high inflation rate ameliorates the problem of nonpayment; in Kazakhstan and Kyrgyzstan, a more stringent monetary policy aggravates the problem of nonpayments.

In 1997, the volume of M2 to GDP (the coefficient of monetization of the economy) varied in Central Asia as follows: 16.5 percent in Uzbekistan, 12.0 percent in Kyrgyzstan, 10.4 percent in Kazakhstan, 8.8 percent in Turkmenistan. It bears noting that the minimal threshold significance for the coefficient of monetization is 19 percent[51] and the normal level is 30 to 40 percent in countries with an average level of per capita income (a category to which the republics of Central Asia nominally belong). At the same time, the proportion of M2 to the GDP is a key criterion and factor in determining the development of a country's financial system as well as the financial condition of enterprises in the real sector of the economy.

As Berthlemy and Varoudakis have noted,[52] it is possible to obtain the full economic effect from an increase in labor productivity only if there is an unimpeded redistribution of investment resources among different sectors of the economy. For all practical purposes, that kind of redistribution is impossible to achieve under conditions where the financial system is backward and undeveloped. To obtain the full effect from the liberalization of foreign trade, it is essential to have the option of a flexible reallocation of financial resources among branches and sectors in accordance with their comparative advantages. A financial system that is inadequately developed inhibits the mobility of capital; as a result, the needed investments must be financed at the expense of foreign sources. In essence, an undeveloped financial system renders domestic capital immobile and becomes an impediment to economic growth.

The foregoing leads to the conclusion that the inadequate development of the financial system in the countries of Central Asia makes industrialization inefficient and blocks the development of branches that are technology and research intensive. The government cannot assume the function of effectively allocating economic resources; in reality, it can only perform this role during the early stages of development and in a simple economic system.

Among the negative factors for long-term economic growth in the countries of Central Asia, one should note the great gap between the real interest rates for credits and deposits. This gap fluctuates within a range of 10 to 20 percent. The real interest rates for credits in Turkmenistan and Kyrgyzstan are high (on the level of 27 to 35 percent per annum) and have the effect of deterring investment in industry and agriculture. These sectors are simply not in a position to pay such high interest rates.

Nor do the countries of Central Asia have a well-developed stock market, which is reflected in the indicators of its capitalization. Thus, in 1997 the level of capitalization of the stock market (measured as a percent of the GDP) was 5.9 percent in Kazakhstan, 3.9 percent in Uzbekistan, 2.8 percent in Kyrgyzstan, and 0 percent in Tajikistan.

In sum, the basic weaknesses of the financial system in the countries of Central Asia include the following:

- a low level of financial depth (M2/GDP);
- a significant undercapitalization of some banks;
- a supervisory framework that, while in theory adequate, is actually still in the initial stage of implementation;
- a low rate of national (especially private) savings;
- a low efficiency of investment;
- a high spread between the interest rates on deposits and loans;
- a pronounced concentration, segmentation, and statification in the banking sector;
- a high level set for minimum reserves;
- a low volume of transactions on the stock exchange;
- the lack of market-based skills (especially risk-assessment and risk-management) among banking personnel;
- inequities in the treatment of banks (with some having uncontested, special government privileges);
- the lack of confidence in the banking sector.

Thus, one may conclude that, notwithstanding progress in certain areas, the banking and financial systems of countries in Central Asia still do not meet the conditions for economic growth or conform to international standards. The bulk of credits are short-term, especially in Kyrgyzstan and Kazakhstan, and they are used to supplement working capital and to pay wages, not to address long-term goals of economic growth.

Industrial Policy

Among the most important problems facing industrial policy makers of countries in Central Asia, one should draw particular attention to the following:

1. Inadequate Competition and Distortions in the Economic Structure

This factor is expressed in the high level of raw materials used, in the small proportion of machine-building production, in the significant level of physical depletion of fixed production capital, and in the high level of energy consumption of the GDP (which exceeds, by 2.5 to 5.0 times, the rate in developed nations).

2. The Limited Efficiency of Foreign Trade Policies

The unfavorable foreign economic situation and the growth in the real exchange rate of the national currencies of Uzbekistan and Kazakhstan led to a fall in the volume (Uzbekistan) and a slower rate of growth (Kazakhstan) for exports in 1997–98. The loss of some traditional markets (machine-building, fruits and vegetables, textiles, and other products) and the lack of a clearly focused marketing policy to create new competitive positions on international markets for manufactured goods have sharply undermined the efficiency of investment and worsened the balance of payments for countries in Central Asia.

3. Low Level of Activity by Small Business

In Central Asia, small business accounts for only 3–8 percent of the GDP.[53] This underdevelopment of small and medium-sized business can lead to a greater monopolization, a deterioration in the competitive environment, and retardation of progress toward the formation of a national class of property-owners. In Uzbekistan and Turkmenistan, monopolies control not only the production of the most important categories of goods, but also distribution and trade. All this in turn leads to a decline in the efficiency of production, to a diminished capacity to respond to changes in market conditions, to a fall in the competitiveness on world markets, and to a growth in the scale of the "shadow economy."

4. Raw-Material Orientation and the Worsening Terms of Trade

The limited elasticity in the demand for raw materials leads to major fluctuations in world prices for many of the raw materials being exported from the countries of Central Asia. It is precisely this raw-material orientation of the Central Asian economies that, to a large degree, explains the unstable tendencies in trade and the recent deterioration in the terms of trade. The data show a temporary phase of growth in 1993–95, but then (from the end of 1995) a fall in world prices on the most important forms of commodity exports from Central Asia: petroleum, natural gas, ferrous and nonferrous metals, and cotton. For example, whereas one troy ounce of gold cost approximately 395 to 400 dollars in 1995–96, the price of this commodity had plummeted to 310–318 dollars by

October 1997, and then dropped to 290–295 dollars a year later. And gold is one of the most important articles of export from Uzbekistan and Kyrgyzstan.

In 1997, the countries of Central Asia encountered a deterioration in the conditions of trade because of the falling prices on a whole series of its main export commodities. For example, the average world price of cotton fiber dropped 16 percent in 1996 and a further 14 percent in 1997. Similarly, oil prices fell by nearly 12 percent in 1997.[54]

One must also take into account the fact that the fall in world prices for raw materials is not the only factor affecting trade with the countries of Central Asia. Thus, import is one of the main sources of "capital flight" abroad, for traders can use their own intermediary firms and inflate the prices in import contracts, thereby "legally" sending money to accounts outside the country. Because of the multitude of dealers and prices on world markets (with prices highly differentiated, depending upon the season, volume, and terms of delivery), it is virtually impossible for governments to control and detect any fraudulent inflation in the contracts for importing goods. The deterioration in trade conditions for the countries of Central Asia, with respect to the rise in prices on imports, may reflect not actual price increases, but simply this tactic for evading state restrictions on moving capital abroad.

In addition, it is important to note that the export prices for the majority of commodities from Central Asia are significantly below those prevailing on world markets. That is evident from the data offered in Table 3.3.

Among the various reasons for the sale of export commodities at prices below the prevailing world level (other than such factors as corruption and surreptitious capital flight), one should also take note of objective causes, such as the monopolization of world markets for many categories of raw materials such as nonferrous metals and cotton fibers. Another factor is flaccid (or insufficiently aggressive) marketing, which in turn reflects inexperience and the lack of knowledge about foreign markets.

Because of the financial crisis in East Asia, from 1997 to late 1999 world prices on all the categories of raw materials exported from Central Asia fell significantly. This downturn was especially pronounced in the case of oil and nonferrous metals, but has affected other goods as well. Thus, in 1998 the price of cotton from Uzbekistan dropped by nearly 25 percent; the price of gold has not risen above 300 dollars per troy ounce. The export of some finished goods (e.g., textiles and automobiles from UzDEUavto, the Daewoo plant in Uzbekistan), has also declined sharply

Table 3.3

World Prices and Central Asian Export Prices (1996)

Country	Number of export commodities examined	Number of export commodities sold below the prevailing world price	Percent of export commodities sold below the prevailing world price
Kazakhstan	34	24	70.6
Kyrgyzstan	27	14	51.9
Turkmenistan	30	19	63.3
Uzbekistan	27	18	66.7

Sources: Calculated from data in a study by the Research and Analyst Unit, International Trade Center UNCTAD/WTO, "National Trade Performance and International Demand in the Central Asian Republics" (Fourth Sasakawa Peace Foundation-Issyk-Kul' International Forum, "Central Asia: Economic Development in the Era of Globalization," Tashkent, 1–2 October 1998).

in terms of monetary value. That decline is due partly to the steep decline in world prices and partly to the rising competition that East Asian producers now pose on third-country markets (above all, Russia).

5. Tendency Toward an Import-Substitution Strategy of Development

Numerous statistical and econometric works on countries throughout the world show that an export orientation is far more effective in promoting an increase in jobs, productivity, savings, investment, real incomes, technology transfer, and the development of human capital.[55] However, the countries of Central Asia show a tendency to develop import-substitution lines of production. There are a number of preconditions for this tendency:

(A) High Cost of International Shipping. The countries of Central Asia are located in the center of the continent and lack direct access to the world's oceans, thereby making international shipping both difficult and expensive. The high costs for international freight, compounded by customs duties and other transaction costs, significantly increase the total costs of exporters and thereby reduce the competitiveness of the commodities being exported from Central Asia. That is due to the fact that the determining factor for these countries is precisely this price compe-

tition. In the foreseeable future, there is no reason to expect a significant reduction in freight costs through the opening of new transportation lines or progress in the technology of shipping. It is therefore obviously not efficient to develop assembly plants in the region and to plan on exporting finished goods, since such plants would have to pay double shipping costs—first to import the components and parts, then a second time to ship out the finished goods. Prospects for export from countries in this region are favorable for goods if they are produced mainly from local raw materials, have a high per unit value (in weight and volume), and prove competitive on foreign markets. The best examples of such goods include natural resources and R&D-intensive products (especially information technologies). However, more intensive extraction of many categories of mineral resources has become increasingly costly. In addition, the countries of this region are not so rich in minerals (if measured in per capita terms). Moreover, the processing of these resources requires significant investment and foreign technologies, but—given the fall in world prices on such commodities—transnational corporations are in no hurry to develop the exploitation of such resources. As for R&D-intensive products, development of these branches of industry requires significant investment (including funds for education and science). Nor is it possible to expand these branches without the requisite industrial and economic base. Indeed, the significant scientific potential inherited from the former Soviet Union is now undergoing a rapid degradation.

(B) Overvalued Official Exchange Rate for National Currencies. In recent years, Uzbekistan and Kazakhstan have artificially overvalued the exchange rate for their national currencies, thereby making these countries less competitive. Evidence for this is provided by the low levels of devaluation of national currencies compared to the growth in domestic prices. According to calculations by the authors, in 1995–98 the real exchange rate (for the American dollar) rose approximately 50 percent for the Kazakh tenge and 125 percent for the Uzbek sum.

The high exchange rate and declining competitiveness of exported goods from Kazakhstan are due to the significant influx of foreign investments and credits to extract and export the natural resources. In the economic literature, this phenomenon is known as the "Dutch disease." At the present time, the full efflorescence of this phenomenon is retarded by the problem of limited shipping capacity for Kazakh oil; that barrier has impeded the growth of petroleum exports. However, the completion of two planned pipelines (one through southern Russia to the Black Sea, to be finished by the year 2001, and a second to western China, due to open in 2005) would substantially increase the shipping capacity and the export income of Kazakhstan. This, in turn, would put strong pressure on the exchange rate of the tenge.[56]

Similarly, Turkmenistan also has a high potential for a growth in the real value of its national currency if it opens the alternative natural gas pipeline through Turkey and increases its deliveries of natural gas.

The government of Uzbekistan has deliberately supported an overvalued exchange rate for the sum, thereby causing the demand for hard currency greatly to exceed the supply available. Hence the government has constantly intensified its restrictions on convertibility and its reliance upon administrative methods to distribute foreign currency.

Exporters have suffered most directly and substantially from this overvalued exchange rate of the national currency in Kazakhstan and Uzbekistan. Uzbek exporters, who belong to a system of centralized exports, have endured particularly large losses, since they have been forced to sell their products at domestic state prices—which are below world levels, but even below production costs. This applies, above all, to cotton producers, the mining complex, the fuel and energy complex (especially the natural gas producers), and the textile industry. Apparently, these branches are pure donors in Uzbekistan, a factor that is a disincentive for the production and export of these commodities. Moreover, the country's foreign-currency controls make the decentralized exporters reluctant to exchange part of their foreign earnings for the sum at the official rate. As a result, exporters resort to an alternative strategy: they import goods in high demand, which they then sell at prices based on the black-market rate of exchange. All this only intensifies the pressure on the country's balance of payments. Faced with these circumstances, the government of Uzbekistan attempted to tighten its controls over the import of goods; specifically, it sought to achieve a positive balance of payments by restricting the import of goods. However, these measures not only led to a contraction of imports, but indirectly caused a reduction of exports, since it became more difficult for exporters to conduct a clandestine conversion of foreign-currency earnings through the import and sale of goods on the domestic market. To a large degree, this explains why the exports of Uzbekistan in January–September 1998 fell by 23.4 percent from the same period the previous year.

At the same time, the exchange rate of the Uzbek sum favors imports by those who have access to the official conversion at the high rate on the foreign-currency market. In general, these are enterprises with foreign investment (which alone consume more than half of the total volume of official conversions),[57] trading and importing concerns, and state enterprises representing the large investment projects. In essence, these enterprises receive a kind of subsidy, since they can take into account the unofficial exchange rate for the Uzbek sum when they sell their goods. Moreover, the state budget receives reduced revenues from the earnings obtained from the centralized export of cotton, metals, and the like, since these earnings are converted at the high official rate of exchange. There are also tax losses that could have been assessed from the increased income of exporters, who sell the remaining part of their foreign-currency earnings at the lower exchange rate. Of course, these expenditures can be seen as a kind of unique payment for the accelerated development of manufacturing in Uzbekistan and the further diversification of exports. However, the efficiency of such a redistribution raises certain doubts.

The foreign-currency controls constitute the main protectionist measure in Uzbekistan and create an especially advantageous, monopolistic situation for those who have access to the official market for foreign-currency exchange. The foreign-currency controls have also spawned an unpredictable and volatile "black market" for hard currency, which has a major impact on the general price of goods and adds further uncertainty to trade and the entire macroeconomic situation. In general, the overvalued exchange rate fosters a general import-substitution tendency in the development of the national economy. The foreign-currency controls and the overvalued exchange rate of the Uzbek sum constitute a major obstacle to stable economic growth in the country.

Whereas the overvalued exchange rate of the Kazakh tenge is natural and not deliberately created by the government, in Uzbekistan the exchange rate represents part of a conscious state policy. In essence, the government of Uzbekistan has two main goals: (a) it seeks to transfer to the state treasury part of the income of exporters that the latter obtained mainly from the sale of raw-materials and semi-finished products; and, (b) it aims to facilitate the problem of financing state purchases abroad and servicing the state debt, as well as reducing the cost of imported food products. However, the overvalued exchange rate of the Uzbek currency impedes exports and makes imports cheaper, with negative consequences for domestic producers.

Governments in the countries of Central Asia, in our judgment, fail to realize the importance of an industrialization strategy based on an export orientation and have therefore not taken effective steps to move in this direction. Not a single country of Central Asia has yet made export orientation the strategic basis for development. Therefore, the central banks of Central Asia have not made support for a competitive exchange rate their main task. Exporters, as a rule, receive insufficient tax, customs, and financial privileges, all of which are so essential in the initial stage of moving into foreign markets. Nor does the state afford them adequate administrative and marketing support. In Central Asia, many exporters suffer direct losses precisely because they are exporters.

According to calculations by the present authors (based on the multiplier method of calculating the effect of exports),[58] a 1 percent increase in exports would bring a nominal growth in the GDP of 2.5 percent in Uzbekistan and 4.0 percent in Kazakhstan.

The Role of Government in Managing the Economy

The institutions of the market and the private sector itself are still in the gestation period of development in the countries of Central Asia. Market institutions objectively require an extended development in post-Soviet space and, under these conditions, the efficiency of market forces will not be on a high level. Apparently, private capital will, for a rather long time, remain oriented toward immediate return and speculation, not long-term development. Given the possibilities of long-term disruptions in the market mechanisms of countries with a transition economy, and given the need for large-scale transformation in the economy, the role of state strategy in development and the effectiveness of state management are matters of great significance. It is therefore important to consider some key problems that undermine the effectiveness of the state's role in the economy.

The Soviet Union developed a system of administration where the bureaucratic elite *(nomenklatura)*, while having no right to the personal ownership of capital, nonetheless controlled the production and distribution of the final product. The result was the creation of the so-called bureaucratic bourgeoisie. The method and amount of income depended on the position of a given representative in the bureaucratic hierarchy. The motivation for behavior among members of the state administration rested on a desire to preserve the general conditions of their existence and to achieve a higher rank in this hierarchy, which in turn meant a larger share of the goods produced. For these reasons, in the post-Soviet period the bureaucratic bourgeoisie has taken a keen interest in the private sector and has sought to prevent any significant and especially uncontrolled increase in its economic power. It fears, quite rightly, that the private capital will gain in political influence and threaten its monopoly on political power.[59]

This factor goes a long way toward explaining the slow development of the private sector and the processes of privatization in certain countries of Central Asia. Given the weak development of the private sector and democratic institutions, given the pervasive bureaucratization of economic management, the countries of Central Asia have preserved the system based on a bureaucratic bourgeoisie (at least in part and sometimes in a more fundamental way). All this, in turn, undermines the efficiency of economic mechanisms. The Soviet style and method of controlling economic processes continue to dominate in Tajikistan, Turkmenistan, and Uzbekistan; to a significant degree, they are also still present in the more liberal states of Kyrgyzstan and Kazakhstan. Thus, in speaking about the problems of privatization in Uzbekistan, President Karimov observed in 1995: "The style, methods, and principles of work have remained virtually unchanged. . . . Little has changed in the consciousness of people, in the organization of work, and in the system of incentives."[60] Table 3.4 provides a comparative analysis of the democratic processes in Central Asia.

It bears noting that there is no direct correlation between progress in the sphere of democracy and economic development. Striking evidence for this can be found in the countries of East Asia, which, as a rule, had authoritarian regimes in their first decades after World War II, yet achieved extremely rapid rates of growth and development.[61] Consequently, the problem of democratic rule in the countries of Central Asia, in our judgment, should be seen primarily from this position: to what degree does the contemporary system of state administration contribute to the development of the private sector and technologies—the main locomotives of effective economic growth?

There is a further dimension to the democratization problem: the export orientation of the countries in East Asia provided an important safety device against incorrect state intervention in the economy, since it provided an independent and stern judge in the form of international competition. That exogenous factor was still effective even where the political

Table 3.4

Freedom House Ratings of Central Asian Countries (1997)
(Ranking: Scale of 1–7, with 1 representing the highest and 7 the lowest degree of achievement.)

Country	Political process	Civil society	Independent media	Rule of law	Governance and public administration	Privati- zation	Economy	Private share of the GDP (percent)[a]
Kazakhstan	5.5	5.25	5.25	5.0	5.5	4.25	4.5	40
Kyrgyzstan	5.0	4.5	5.0	4.5	4.25	4	3.5	50
Tajikistan	6.0	5.5	6.25	6.25	7.0	6.25	6.0	20
Turkmenistan	7.0	7.0	7.0	6.75	6.75	6.75	6.0	20
Uzbekistan	6.25	6.5	6.5	6.5	6.0	6.25	6.25	40
For Comparison:								
Albania	4.25	4.25	4.75	4.75	4.75	3.75	4.25	75
Estonia	2.0	2.25	1.75	2.25	2.25	2.25	2.0	70
Russia	3.5	3.75	3.75	4.0	4.0	3.0	4.0	60

Source: Adapted from the conclusions of the Ratings Committee of Freedom House, published in: *Transition: The Newsletter about Reforming Economies* 8, no. 3 (1997): 5. The Committee offered the following explanation of the above categories:

The *political process* section deals with elections and referenda, party configuration, and conditions for political competition in elections. The *civil society* section highlights the degree to which volunteerism, trade unionism, and professional associations exist, and whether civic organizations are influential. Press freedom, public access to a variety of information sources, and the independence of these sources from undue governmental or other influences are covered in the *independent media* section. The *rule of law* section considers judicial and constitutional matters, as well as the legal and de facto status of ethnic minorities. Government decentralization, independence and responsibilities of local and regional governments, and legislative and executive transparency are discussed in the section on *governance and public administration*. The *privatization* section details legislative and actual states of privatization in each country. The *economy* section reviews the development of institutions that form the foundation of a modern capitalist economy—property rights, macroeconomic balance, an independent central bank, and the ability of people to engage in business.

[a]National statistical agencies, as a rule, cite a higher share for the private sector in the GDP. For example, in 1997, Uzbekistan reported that at least 70 percent of the GDP came from the private sector. This higher estimate usually results from the fact that the national statistical agencies regard as "private enterprises" those which have a significant share of state ownership.

regime was far removed from democratic tendencies. The countries of Central Asia encounter significant difficulties in adopting an export-oriented path of development; as yet, not a single country has proclaimed export-orientation as the top priority in its plans for development. In other words, the authoritarian states of Central Asia do not have the "stern judge" who has played an important role in the nondemocratic countries of East Asia. It is therefore much more likely that the countries of Central Asia will make mistakes in their economic development.

The existing model of a "bureaucratic bourgeoisie" in the countries of Central Asia determines the development of the *nomenklatura* elite itself. That is why career success in the civil service of Central Asia depends, to a significant degree, not on actual ability, but on clan ties, hometown connections, and corruption. Experts from the EBRD, on the basis of corruption estimates by a panel of regional analysts, rated all the countries of Central Asia between 7 and 9 on the corruption scale (with 9 being the most corrupt rating possible). In order of increasing corruption, it ranked Kyrgyzstan, Kazakhstan, Turkmenistan, Uzbekistan, and Tajikistan.[62]

In general, corruption wreaks greater harm on investment and economic growth than taxation. On the basis of aggregate data on corruption in seventy countries around the world (in the early 1980s), one researcher demonstrated a substantial statistical correlation between the index of corruption and investments (or the rate of economic growth). His regression analysis "shows that a country that improves its standing on the corruption index from, say, 6 to 8 (0 being the most corrupt, 10 the least) will experience a 4 percentage point increase in its investment rate and a 0.5 percentage point increase in its annual per capita GDP growth rate."[63]

Another negative consequence of retaining the model of a "bureaucratic bourgeoisie" in Central Asia is its role in stimulating capital flight abroad. That exodus of resources, of course, runs contrary to the accumulation of national wealth and its concentration in the hands of indigenous entrepreneurs for further domestic investment. This flight results from the lack of a positive atmosphere and well-organized cooperation, with constant consultations between the private sector and the organs of state administration, where the overriding goal must be to promote general economic development. At present, just the contrary obtains: mutual distrust on the part of both state administrative organs and private business. As a result, the existing system of placing the auxiliary revenues artificially generated by the government (through its protection-ism, various privileges, and special preferences to certain economic agents) serves not to promote the rapid development of industrial poten-tial (as in the countries of East Asia), but the flight of capital abroad.

Yet another manifestation of ineffective government is an excessive monopolization—the so-called Barton gap, so named after its main in-vestigator, Clifford Barton. His research demonstrated how the propen-sity for power, and the potential profit for state officials who set prices, allocate permits, and supply licenses, can lead to the harassment of medium-sized business. The smallest firms largely escaped the harass-ment because they were not sufficiently visible. The largest firms em-ployed specialists to expedite transactions, often with bribes, and had both political connections and influence. In between, the medium-sized firms were too visible to escape the attention of corrupt officials, but lacked the skills and the necessary political connections to defend themselves. Small firms, in fact, may therefore deliberately choose to remain small.[64]

All this explains why small and medium-sized enterprises hold such a small share of the GDP in the countries of Central Asia. Thus, in 1997, small business accounted for only 3 to 8 percent of the GDP in Kazakhstan,[65] and 5 percent in Uzbekistan.

Problems of Science and Education

The countries of Central Asia have a per capita annual income of less than $1,000 and have all the well-known problems characteristic of the least developed countries. However, there are also some special char-acteristics that are due chiefly to the Soviet legacy. One of the positive aspects of this inheritance is the existence of a relatively well-developed scientific knowledge, educational system, and certain R&D branches of industry—elements missing in many countries at a comparable stage of development. The efforts of the former Soviet state created this level of development within the framework of the existing economy and poli-tics. After the onset of liberal market reforms, the majority of such de-veloped spheres have gradually come into alignment with the general level of economic development in these states—in other words, educa-tion, science, and R&D have undergone rather rapid degradation. For example, in recent years in Uzbekistan, the wages of teachers in col-leges and universities as well as scientific and medical personnel are approximately 1.5 times lower than the average wage. Thus, the median income was thirty dollars for professors and twenty dollars for senior researchers at black-market exchange rates. The result is an enormous, and apparently irreversible, exodus of highly skilled personnel from these sectors of the economy. The state has not been in a position to finance these spheres, while the private sector (or, for that matter, the state) has little need for such services, since the problems of the current period are more urgent as far as they are concerned.

The European style of science and scholarship was first established in the countries of Central Asia during the Soviet era. The first university in Central Asia was founded in Tashkent in 1924 by transferring scholars and resources from Russia. Then, on the basis of this first university, the Soviet state built dozens of universities and scientific-research institutes throughout Central Asia. The transfer of ideas, technologies, scholars, skilled personnel, and other resources to increase human capital in Central Asia continued throughout the entire existence of the former Soviet Union. This transfer became especially intense during and after World War II and during the Virgin Lands campaign to expand the arable land in the region.

Many scholars from Central Asia received their education in the leading scientific centers of Russia and Ukraine. During the time of the former Soviet Union, several scientific schools with a worldwide reputation were created in Central Asia. Thus, at the end of the 1980s, the scientific potential of Uzbekistan was regarded as the third highest in the USSR, surpassed only by Russia and Ukraine.

After the breakup of the USSR, the transfer of ideas, scholars, and other resources from other regions of the former Soviet Union to Central Asia not only came to an end, but a reverse process set in. Under conditions of economic crisis, the state budgets of Central Asia were unable to support science, education, and medicine on the earlier level. One of the principal problems has been the inability of graduates from institutions of higher learning (especially technical institutes) to find jobs and to work in their area of specialization. Moreover, because of the extremely low salaries, university faculty and scientific researchers have had to become shuttle traders and traders at bazaars, or to work for the police and military organizations.

The "brain drain"—so typical of many developing countries—has also significantly intensified in Central Asia, with hundreds of thousands of talented scholars and skilled personnel choosing to emigrate from the region. This applies above all to nonindigenous ethnic groups, especially Jews, Germans, Slavs, and Crimean Tatars. Their decision to emigrate is due both to the real deterioration in the economic situation and to their perception of growing nationality problems. This brain drain is the principal reason for the decline in science and hi-tech production in the countries of Central Asia.

These countries have also witnessed the formation of private educational institutions. However, the tuition in these is extremely high when compared with the average salary; hence only a minuscule percentage of the families here can allow themselves to pay such educational fees in private schools and universities. That is all the more true given the almost total lack of opportunities to obtain educational loans at favorable rates.

At the same time, independence has also given rise to new opportunities—above all, the chance for the youth in Central Asian countries to study in the West. But the number of such fortunate youths is exceedingly small (perhaps a few hundred per country); nor is the method by which they are chosen and sponsored an open and transparent process. Moreover, many of them are sent to study social sciences, although it would be more useful for the youth going to the West to study applied sciences and agriculture. For example, the youth from Central Asia who have graduated from a Western university with a degree in "business administration" (the most popular field of concentration) sometimes cannot find any direct application for their knowledge in the poorly developed market systems of Central Asia. Here, the key to success in business is to have personal and clan ties as well as the ability to "make a deal" with government officials and criminal elements. Once such youths return from abroad, they try to find high-paying positions in the branch offices of foreign companies and international organizations, or simply work as translators.

The governments of Central Asian countries have announced plans to make the training of personnel a matter of top priority. Foreign funds and governments are also providing humanitarian assistance to promote the development of science and education. However, the problems of internal economic development do not make it possible, in the immediate future, to create in Central Asia a linkage between "good education" and "high incomes." That is due, above all, to the lack of a government policy to maintain high incomes for educated personnel.

Notes

1. I. A. Karimov, *Po puti uglubleniia ekonomicheskikh reform* (Tashkent 1995), pp. 10–11. Karimov first adumbrated most of these principles in *Uzbekistan: Svoi put' obnovleniia i progressa* (Tashkent, 1992).

2. Cited in *Central Asian Newsfile*, November 1996, p. 6; and in Michael Kaser, "Stabilization and Reform: The Experience of Five Central Asian States" (paper presented at "Challenges to Economies in Transition: Stabilization, Growth, and Governance," an international conference to honor the Kyrgyz som, held 27–28 May 1998 in Bishkek, Kyrgyzstan).

3. J. Sachs and A. Warner, "Economic Reforms and the Process of Global Integration," Brookings Papers on Economic Activity, 1995, no. 1: 118.

4. Kaser, "Stabilization and Reform," pp. 7–8.

5. "Kyrgyz Republic: Recent Economic Developments," IMF Staff Country Report, no. 98/8 (January 1998), pp. 55–56.

6. Ibid.

7. "Republic of Kazakhstan: Recent Economic Developments," IMF Staff Country Report, no. 98/84 (August 1998), p. 94.

8. Zh. Kulekeev and G. Sultanbekova, "Prichiny i puti resheniia problemy neplatezhei v Kazakhstane," *Al'Pari*, 1998, no. 2 (April–June): 9–13.

9. "Turkmenistan: Recent Economic Developments," IMF Staff Country Report, no. 98/81 (August 1998), p. 6.

10. Ibid., pp. 6–7.

11. Ibid., pp. 7, 59–60; Kaser, "Stabilization and Reform," p. 15.

12. "Republic of Tajikistan: Recent Economic Developments," IMF Staff Country Report, no. 98/16 (February 1998), pp. 6–10.

13. "Republic of Uzbekistan: Recent Economic Developments," IMF Staff Country Report, no. 97/98 (October 1997), pp. 18, 100.

14. "Turkmenistan: Recent Economic Developments," IMF Staff Country Report, no. 98/81 (August 1998), p. 12.

15. Ibid., pp. 16–17, 21, 92.

16. "Republic of Kazakhstan: Recent Economic Developments," IMF Staff Country Report, no. 98/84 (August 1998), pp. 11, 23, 35.

17. "Kyrgyz Republic: Recent Economic Developments," IMF Staff Country Report, no. 98/8 (January 1998), p. 10.

18. "Kyrgyz Republic: Enhanced Structural Adjustment Facility," IMF Policy Framework Paper, 1998–2000 (www.imf.org), pp. 5–6.

19. "Republic of Tajikistan: Recent Economic Developments," IMF Staff Country Report, no. 98/16 (February 1998), pp. 15, 17, 29, 55.

20. European Bank for Reconstruction and Development, *Transition Report 1997* (London, 1998), pp. 19, 21, 27, 29, 31.

21. M. Kaser, "Economic Transition in Six Central Asian Economies," *Central Asian Survey* 16 (1997): 5–26. The "sixth" economy here is Mongolia.

22. "Republic of Uzbekistan: Recent Economic Developments," IMF Staff Country Reports, no. 97/98 (October 1997), p. 128.

23. "Republic of Tajikistan: Recent Economic Developments," IMF Staff Country Report, no. 98/16 (February 1998), p. 56.

24. Estimate based on V. Grigoruk, "Agrarnaia reforma," *Al' Pari*, 1998, no. 1 (January–March): 54–57.

25. Ibid.; A. Deberdeev and E. Idrisov, "Sel'skoe khoziaistvo: prichiny krizisa i puti ego preodoleniia," *Al' Pari*, 1997, no. 3 (July–September): 20–24.

26. "Kyrgyz Republic: Recent Economic Developments," IMF Staff Country Reports, no. 98/8 (January 1998), pp. 8, 35, 91.

27. In 1997, to prevent the massive theft of grain from state fields, the government planned to have the security services and militia conduct special measures in rural areas.

28. "Republic of Uzbekistan: Recent Economic Developments," IMF Staff Country Report, no. 97/98 (October 1997), p. 47.

29. Ibid., pp. 56–57.

30. Kaser, "Stabilization and Reform," p. 19.

31. "Kyrgyz Republic: Recent Economic Developments," IMF Staff Country Report, no. 98/8 (January 1998), p. 10.

32. "Republic of Kazakhstan: Recent Economic Developments," IMF Staff Country Report, no. 98/84 (August 1998), p. 27.

33. "Republic of Tajikistan: Recent Economic Developments," IMF Staff Country Report, no. 98/16 (February 1998), p. 56.

34. "Republic of Uzbekistan: Recent Economic Developments," IMF Staff Country Report, no. 98/116 (October 1998), pp. 119–21.

35. "Turkmenistan: Recent Economic Developments," IMF Staff Country Report, no. 98/81 (August 1998), pp. 61–62.

36. D. Hoelscher, "The Banking System Restructuring in Kazakhstan," IMF Working Paper, no. 98/96 (June 1998), pp. 3, 8. 11.

37. K. Omurzakov, "The Kyrgyzstan Economy: Latest Developments and Policies," *Central Asia in Transition*, 1998, no. 61: 2; "The Kyrgyz Republic: Recent Economic Developments," IMF Staff Country Report, no. 98/8 (January 1998), pp. 26–27.

38. "The Republic of Uzbekistan: Recent Economic Developments," IMF Staff Country Report, no. 98/116 (October 1998), pp. 103–7; M. Fuchs, "Reforma finansovogo sektora v Respublike Uzbekistan," *Ekonomicheskoe obozrenie*, 1998, no. 4 (April): 7–11; K. Zhuraeva, "Kommercheskie banki i kreditovanie real'nogo sektora ekonomiki Uzbekistana," *Ekonomicheskoe obozrenie*, 1998, no. 4 (April): 12–16.

39. Kaser, "Stabilization and Reform," p. 20; "Republic of Tajikistan: Recent Economic Developments," IMF Staff Country Report, no. 98/16 (February 1998), p. 57.

40. "Turkmenistan: Recent Economic Developments," IMF Staff Country Report, no. 98/81 (August 1998), pp. 46–47.

41. V. Paramonov, "Analiz nekotorykh tendentsii razvitiia ekonomiki Kazakhstana," *Ekonomika Kazakhstana*, 1997, no. 6 (November–December): 70–76; "Republic of Kazakhstan: Recent Economic Developments," IMF Staff Country Report, no. 98/84 (August 1998), p. 49.

42. "Turkmenistan: Recent Economic Developments," IMF Staff Country Report, no. 98/81 (August 1998), p. 46.

43. "Republic of Uzbekistan: Recent Economic Developments," IMF Staff Country Report, no. 98/116 (October 1998), p. 98.

44. "Kyrgyz Republic: Recent Economic Developments," IMF Staff Country Report, no. 98/8 (January 1998), p. 102.

45. European Bank for Reconstruction and Development, "Transition Report: 1997."

46. "UNCTAD Secretariat Report to the Conference on East Asian Development: Lessons for a New Global Environment," Kuala Lumpur, 29 February 1996, p. 29.

47. International Monetary Fund, *World Economic Outlook* (Washington, DC, 1998), p. 99.

48. S. Chepel, "Ekonomika neplatezhei (makroekonomicheskii analiz i puti preodoleniia)," *Ekonomicheskii vestnik Uzbekistana*, 1998, no. 1 (January): 24.

49. Kulekeev and Sultanbekova, "Prichiny i puti resheniia problemy neplatezhei v Kazakhstane," pp. 9–13.

50. "Turkmenistan: Recent Economic Developments," IMF Staff Country Report, no. 98/81 (August 1998), p. 47.

51. Jean-Claude Berthelemy and A. Varoudakis, *Financial Development Policy and Growth* (Paris, 1996).

52. Ibid.

53. A. Kantarbaeva and U. Shukeev, "Ekonomicheskie reguliatory politiki podderzhki predprinimatel'stva v Kazakhstane," *Al' Pari*, 1998, no. 3: 55–59.

54. *Uzbek Economic Trends: Monthly Update. October 1998* ("TACIS Policy and Legal Advice Programme") (Tashkent, 1998).

55. World Bank, *The World Development Report: 1987* (New York, 1997); A. Kruger, "The Effects of Trade Strategies on Growth," *Finance and Development* 20 (1983): 7; P. Romer, "Capital, Labor, and Productivity," *Brookings Paper on Economic Activity* (Washington, DC: Brookings Institution, 1990), pp. 337–67.

56. "Republic of Kazakhstan: Recent Economic Developments," IMF Staff Country Report, No. 98/84 (August 1998), p. 88.

57. F. Maksudov and I. Anarkulova, "Priamye inostrannye investitsii v ekonomiku Uzbekistana: sostoianie del i perspektivy," *Rynok, den'gi i kredit*, 1997, no. 5 (May): 6–7.

58. W.J. Ethier, *Modern International Economics,* 3rd ed. (New York, 1995), p. 623.

59. V. Rybakov, "'Biurokraticheskaia burzhuaziia' i problemy stanovleniia kapitalizma v Rossii," *Mezhdunarodnaia ekonomika i mezhdunarodnye otnosheniia*, 1996, no. 7 (July): 14–18.

60. I.A. Karimov, "Nashi deti dolzhny byt' luchshe, umnee, mudree i, konechno, schastlivee nas!" *Narodnoe slovo*, 1998, no. 248 (24 December): 1.

61. Tun-jen Cheng, S. Haggard, and D. Kang, "Institutions, Economic Policy, and Growth in the Republic of Korea and Taiwan Province of China," *East Asian Development: Lessons for a New Global Environment*, Study no. 2 (San Diego, 1996).

62. "Survey of Central Asia," *The Economist*, 7 February 1998, p. 15.

63. Mauro Paolo, "Corruption, Consequences, and an Agenda for Further Research," *Finance and Development* 35 (1998): 12.

64. J.S. Hogendorn, *Economic Development,* 3rd ed.; (New York, 1995), pp. 64, 453–54.

65. A. Kanarbaeva and U. Shukeev, "Ekonomicheskie reguliatory politiki podderzhki predpinimatel'stva v Kazakhstane," *Al' Pari*, 1998, no. 3: 59.

4

Adapting to Globalization

Stanislav Zhukov

At the end of the twentieth century, it has become impossible to judge and consider the prospects of individual states apart from the larger global context. The density of international economic, financial, informational, and human contacts is so great that for all the post-Soviet states (without exception) the foreign conditions of development play a determining role with respect to the domestic conditions.

Notwithstanding the critical role of global factors in development, endogamous factors also have an enormous influence on economic growth and its stability. In the case of Central Asian countries, one could cite a number of important internal factors: (1) geographic remoteness from the main centers of the world economy; (2) lack of direct access to the most important trade routes; (3) the small size of the population and its very low level of individual incomes, which in turn predetermine the narrowness of the domestic market; and (4) the exceedingly modest magnitude of domestic savings that might be mobilized for investment.

But the views and ambitions of the ruling elite also have a palpable impact on the concrete trajectories of development in the individual states. Those trajectories, in effect, emerge at the juncture of global and endogamous factors.

Kyrgyzstan: Marginalization

In the first years after the dismantling of the USSR, it was widely believed by the post-Soviet elites that globalization and internationalization would prove to be an unqualified boon for the national economy in each of these newly independent states. However, that is not always the case; not all states have a chance for development in the global economy. Indeed, the fate of many will be that of economic marginalization. It should also be clear that the standardized prescriptions for economic policy do not always ensure that a country will occupy an admirable niche in the world division of labor. On the contrary, these prescriptions, which expose a national economy to global competition, can actually block the development of local productive forces and doom whole states to a vegetable condition. In Central Asia, Kyrgyzstan is in such a condition.

As is well known, this country was the first in the CIS to begin the practical implementation of the package of stabilization measures as formulated in their orthodox variant. It was also the first country to introduce the convertibility of its national currency on current accounts and the first to endorse Article VIII of the IMF Articles of Agreement, which provides for the unification of the exchange rate—a precondition for current accounts convertibility. At first glance, the macroeconomic situation in Kyrgyzstan in 1996–1998 does not appear to be as dismal as it was in the first half of the decade. The profound decrease in GDP and industrial production has given way to growth. Moreover, the rates of growth, when abstracted from their exceedingly low starting point, post very high figures and appear quite impressive. The question is, however, at what cost was this growth achieved?

To answer that question, it is important to analyze the "deficits" that have become so endemic in the economy of Kyrgyzstan. As it turns out, the deficit of the consolidated budgets in 1994–98 never dropped below five percentage points of the GDP; the sole exception was 1997, when the deficit declined to approximately 4 percent of the GDP. The deficit in the trade balance in 1996 was equal to one-fifth of the GDP; the deficit in the balance of payments on current accounts was one-fourth of the GDP.[1] After a substantial improvement of both indicators in 1997 (even if not to a fundamentally safe level), the year 1998 witnessed a deterioration. Namely, the deficit in the trade balance jumped to 16 percent, while the deficit in the balance of payments rose to an estimated 20 percent of the GDP.

Kyrgyzstan has essentially achieved its economic growth by increasing its foreign debt. In 1996, these debts amounted to two-thirds of the GDP, and they continued to rise in the following years. Thus, in 1997 the foreign indebtedness climbed to 80 percent of the GDP and the following year to 90 percent.

The economic policy of the Kyrgyz government assumes that an influx of foreign loans and credits, as well as foreign investment, will stimulate growth in the export branches in the midterm. These future export earnings, in turn, will enable the country not only to pay off the indebtedness accumulated abroad, but also to support a stable exchange rate for the national currency. In this writer's opinion, however, these assumptions are utterly unfounded.

To begin with, there are objective constraints on the opportunities for Kyrgyzstan to diversify and, in any substantial way, increase its exports. Hence future export earnings, or the possibility of increasing them, would appear to be highly problematic. Indeed, these earnings will barely suffice to settle the debts with foreign investors and creditors.

The development of the mineral resources at Kumtor confirms this assessment of the situation. The development of gold-bearing deposits here is the only relatively large-scale project in Kyrgyzstan that has attracted foreign investment. In other words, during the span of nearly a decade, foreign investors have been unable to find any other object worthy of their interest. In accordance with the Kumtor agreements, Kyrgyzstan receives two-thirds of the profit after the gold is sold on world markets. Because of the substantial decline in the price of gold, the profit from the sales of gold has fallen sharply. Moreover, according to some estimates, the current sale price is thirty to forty dollars less than the production costs at the Kumtor site.[2] If so, one cannot exclude the possibility that an expansion in gold mining will not have a positive effect on the Kyrgyz economy. The physical volume of industrial production, as well as the GDP, has of course been growing. Nevertheless, thus far the revenues for the state treasury have remained minimal. According to available estimates, in 1997 the pure profit from the Kumtor project was just 18.9 million dollars.[3] In 1998, the price of gold fell and has since remained at a low level; it is entirely possible that the state budget will even have to subsidize the further extraction of gold.

The economy is thus locked in a vicious circle. By implementing the recommendations of the IMF and conducting an austere anti-inflationary policy, Kyrgyzstan is forced to adhere (even if not openly) to a policy of a fixed nominal rate of exchange. In an open economy with a convertible national currency, an exchange rate for the Kyrgyz som set at an obviously higher rate (relative to the prevailing production costs) has made virtually all domestic branches of production economically non-competitive. A regime of unlimited conversion of hard currency has placed national producers, with their historically based pattern of high production costs, in a position of acute competition with imported goods. It is, simply put, more profitable to meet the domestic demand through imports. Foreign goods, in the great majority of cases, are cheaper than domestic products and, consequently, have been able to conquer the domestic market. After the imported goods are sold, the profits—earned in the Kyrgyz som—can be freely converted to hard currency and taken abroad. Therefore, foreign credits and stabilization funds created to support the national currency are used to pay for imports and, in the final analysis, are recycled from Kyrgyzstan back into the world financial system.

If one excludes gold mining at Kumtor and the production that services this process, the economy of Kyrgyzstan has become mired in a depressed condition. Thus, the country has derived the entire increase in the rate of growth from an expansion in gold mining, which grew from 1.5 tons in 1996 to 17 tons in 1997 and 18.25 tons in 1998.[4] If one excludes all the economic activity associated with the Kumtor development, however, the GDP of Kyrgyzstan increased by just 0.3 percent in 1998 (that is, within the range of statistical error). This growth increases to 1.8 percent, however, if Kumtor is included. A similar picture obtains for industrial production: output in this sector fell by 6 percent (if Kumtor is excluded from the calculation), but rose by 8.3 percent (if it is included).[5]

In recent years, the economy of Kyrgyzstan has thus been forced to operate as part of a vicious circle. There is only one reason it has not collapsed: the influx of new foreign loans and credits.

In the short term, authorities can periodically ease the situation through large, sudden devaluations of the national currency. The government resorted to this step in the fall of 1996, when overnight the som lost nearly a third of its value against the dollar. It repeated this stratagem in the fall of 1998 and again on the eve of 1999. However, that economic policy inevitably reduces the national economy to the level of its export sector and the production of a few basic goods that cannot be imported.

The overwhelming majority of the local population drags out a miserable existence. People have established themselves in all conceivable types of informal, transitional, and quasi-traditional organizations, which proliferated after disintegration of the Soviet planned economy. The goal of those employed in these "dead-end" (in an economic sense) structures is physical survival, not development.

The continuation of the present economic policy is transforming Kyrgyzstan not into a "Central Asian Switzerland," but into a "Central Asian Myanmar." There is growing evidence that Kyrgyzstan has come to occupy a firm niche in the global production and transportation of narcotics.[6] In the absence of alternative opportunities for employment, the population has no choice but to become involved in the cultivation and shipment of narcotic crops. That is all the more likely given the historical preconditions here.[7]

A new decline in the already low level of incomes for the mass of the population in 1998–99 has significantly aggravated social and economic conditions in a country that, at least externally, appears to be tranquil. According to reports of independent observers, however, there has been an intensification of local conflicts over the distribution of land in the overpopulated areas of the Fergana Valley.[8] In February 1999, yet another increase in the taxes on retail traders ignited disorders in the bazaars of Bishkek, as Kyrgyz youths attacked and plundered the trading centers of Russian dealers.[9]

Moreover, the official wage in 1996–98 was approximately 38–39 dollars per month, which, as elsewhere in the CIS, is not even paid on a timely basis. By the beginning of 1999, the aggregate budgetary arrears on wages, pensions, and social assistance amounted to 720 million som (approximately 25 million American dollars at the official exchange rate).[10]

A plethora of other latent conflicts has been developing in the depths of society. These tensions are reflected in the periodic purges conducted by President Akaev—in the government, presidential apparatus, and Central Bank—under the banner of a struggle against corruption. The purges affect the officials of the upper ranks in the presidential administration and various ministries—finance, agriculture, industry, and trade.[11] The regular replacement of top-ranking officials, those who control budget resources and distribute foreign loans and grants, has become an organic element of the current structure of power and property.

However, the powers that be are continuing to follow this same policy. In a situation where local industry has already been demolished, the current ruling class simply does not have any alternative at its disposal. In the fall of 1998, at the height of the Asian and Russian financial crises, only emergency assistance from the IMF saved the economy of Kyrgyzstan from a full-scale meltdown.

In October 1998, Kyrgyzstan joined the World Trade Organization with the status of a developing country. In other words, it agreed to accept the harsh terms and open its domestic market to more foreign competition.[12] Specifically, Kyrgyzstan has had to reduce sharply its import duties (and, for the majority of goods, altogether eliminate them), abolish licenses on export and import operations, and introduce a single set of laws for indigenous and foreign entrepreneurs.[13] Only the future can tell whether these measures hold out good prospects for development, especially in the longer term. In the time frame under review here, Kyrgyzstan continues to demolish and pulverize the economic structure that it inherited from the Soviet era. The most striking evidence that Kyrgyzstan is becoming more and more marginalized is the lack of foreign investment in projects other than the gold-mining complex at Kumtor.

Kazakhstan: Dead-End Dualism

From the macroeconomic perspective, the economy of Kazakhstan appears to be the most balanced in the five Central Asian states. In 1996–98, the deficit of the consolidated state budget did not exceed 3.5 percent of the GDP. Both the balance of trade and, to a lesser degree, the balance of payments have been kept under control. The ratio of foreign indebtedness to the GDP is much lower in Kazakhstan than in the neighboring states of the region.

To be sure, the Kazakh economy is burdened with disproportions of a special kind—something that might be called "transition sores." That term describes a complex variety of arrears, including state arrears on the payment of wages and pensions, but above all, the mutual nonpayment of enterprises, banks, and governmental budgets at various levels. As already demonstrated in Chapter Two, in 1995–1998 the "overdue bills payable" (i.e., past due by more than three months) in Kazakhstan did not drop below 34 percent of the GDP. The presence of such significant imbalances attests to the fact that the economy has accumulated an enormous inflationary potential, which threatens to explode into full view as soon as these monetary overhangs are monetized. Another method for removing the overhang of arrears is to declare a massive bankruptcy of enterprises that are kept afloat by accumulating arrears. But massive bankruptcies would, in turn, lead to a new downward spiral of production and a high rate of unemployment.

As in Kyrgyzstan, Kazakhstan has banked its economic strategy on integration into the world economy at the fastest possible pace. The country faced the threat of a complete disintegration of the inherited industrial structure; it possessed neither the financial resources, nor the technologies, nor the trained personnel to maintain and modernize the existing structure. The government therefore embarked on a large-scale internationalization of its industry. In 1994–97, almost all the lucrative metallurgical, electric power, energy, petroleum, and natural gas enterprises either became the property of foreign companies or came under their management (see Table 4.1).

The national economy is divided into two sectors: export production and all other spheres of production. Foreigners have come to control the plants producing copper, zinc, manganese, lead, aluminum, titanium, uranium, the majority of large electric power stations, coal mines, all petroleum refinery plants, and also some local producers of oil. With a few exceptions, all these producers aim to export their output or to deliver their goods as intermediate inputs to exporters.

The export sector is under the control of foreign capital and operates within the framework of the price and demand constraints of world markets. It is not entirely clear how long-lasting this structure will be. The point is that the monster-like industrial titans of Kazakhstan were created for what was, in principle, a nonmarket economic environment. One cannot fully exclude a possible scenario of events whereby the foreign investors, having drained the expiring enterprises of their last vitality, simply repudiate their announced plans for reconstruction. But even in the most favorable variant, internationalization of the export-oriented and related service sectors will have a profound impact on the national economic structure as a whole.

Indeed, this process of internationalization has already had an impact on Kazakhstan. First, the redistribution of export income to other branches and consumption has sharply contracted, since control over these revenues has shifted into the hands of foreign capital. This is one cause of the increasing degradation of that part of the economic system that has no access to export markets; it has also led to a rapid expansion of poverty in Kazakhstan. Second, the internationalized sector has accelerated the process of bringing domestic prices into line with those on world markets. In turn, the price shock and the shift toward average world price proportions have driven a significant portion of domestic industry and agriculture closer to bankruptcy. Third, the economic development of Kazakhstan has proven to be totally dependent on the price fluctuations of energy resources and metals on world markets.

Table 4.1

Largest Enterprises of Kazakhstan Under Foreign Control[a]

Branch	Enterprise	Foreign partner	Type of control[b]
Electric power and coal	Almatyenergo	Tractebel (Belgium)	EP
	Ekibastuz GRES-2	Independent Power Corp. (UK)	EP
	Karaganda GRES-2	Independent Power Corp. (UK)	EP
	Ust-Kamenogorsk TETs-2	American Electrical Systems (USA)	EP
	Karaganda TETs-2	Ispat-Karmet (UK)	EP
	Ermakovskaia GRES	Japan Chrome Corp.	EP
	Ekibsatuz GRES-1	American Electrical Systems (USA)	EP
	Pavlodar TETs-1	White Swan Ltd (UK)	EP
	Zhezkagan TETs	Samsung (South Korea)	EP
	Zhambyl GRES	Vitol-Munai (Switzerland)	EP
	Coal Mine Maikuben	HTR GmbH (Germany)	EP
	Coal Mine Severnyi	RAO UES and Sverdlovenergo (Russia)	EP
	Coal Mine (Vostochnyi)	Japan Chrome Corp.	EP
	Coal Mine Bogatyr	Access Industries (USA)	EP
Oil and gas	Atyrau Refinery	Telf AG (Switzerland)	EP
	Pavlodar Refinery	CCL Oil (USA)	C
	Shymkentnefteorgsintez	Vitol (Switzerland)	EP
	Iuzhneftegaz	Hurricane Hydrocarbon (Canada)	EP
	Mangistaumunaigaz	Central Asian Petroleum Ltd (Indonesia)	EP
	Aktobemunaigaz	China National Petroleum Corp. (PRC)	EP
	Uzenmunaigaz	China National Petroleum Corp. (PRC)	EP

Ferrous, non-ferrous, and other metals	Shymkent Phosphorous Plant	Donex	GFM
	Zhambyl Phosphorus Plant	IBE Trading	GFM
	Achpolymetall	River International (Switzerland)	GFM
	Kazmarganets	Japan Chrome Corp. (Japan)	EP
	Sokolovsko-Sarbaiskii GOK	Ivedon International Ltd (Iceland)	GFM
	Zhezkazgan Copper Plant	Samsung (South Korea)	EP
	Balkhash Copper Plant	Samsung (South Korea)	EP
	Pavlodar Aluminum Plant	White Swan Ltd (UK)	EP
	Kazzink	Glencore International (Switzerland)	GFM
	Irtysh Copper Plant	Daton Associates (UK)	GFM
	Karaganda Metallurgical Plant	Ispat (UK)	EP
	Ermakovskii Ferroalloys Plant	Japan Chrome Corp.	GFM
	Zheskenskii GOK	Nova Resources (Switzerland)	GFM
	Kazkrom	Japan Chrome Corp.	GFM
	Sary-Arka Polymetal Plant	Nakosta	EP
	Ust-Kamenogorsk Titanium and Magnum Plant	Speciality Metals Co. (Belgium)	EP
	Tsellinnyi Mining and Chemical Plant	Subton Ltd (Israel)	EP
Telecommunications	Kaztelecom	Daewoo (South Korea)	EP
Tobacco and cigarettes	Almaty Cigarettes Factory	Philip Morris (USA)	EP

Sources: Business periodicals of Kazakhstan and Russia, 1994–1999.

[a] Foreign partners and owners of enterprises in Kazakhstan change with incredible speed; the same is true of control. This table serves to illustrate the scope of internationalization of the country's industry, not to identify the current owners of local enterprises. The names of foreign firms, as well as their national affiliation, are given as reported in the local business press.

[b] The following abbreviations are used: EP (equity participation), GFM (contracts for general and financial management), and C (concession).

To be sure, the transfer of economic assets to foreign capital did enable the regime to solve, temporarily, the problems of budgetary financing. In 1993–97, by selling off tasty morsels of industry, the government of Kazakhstan was able to attract more than 1.3 billion dollars in direct foreign investment per year.[14]

This huge influx of resources was immense relative to the scale of the Kazakh economy and had a substantial impact on macroeconomic indicators. When one considers that the GDP of Kazakhstan in 1996–98 was 21 to 22 billion American dollars (at the official exchange rate), each billion dollars from the outside was equal to about 4 to 5 percent of the GDP. The flow of direct foreign investment also helped to stabilize the exchange rate for the Kazakh tenge and, therefore, to keep down inflation. However, even such a massive influx of resources from abroad could not counteract the decline in the Kazakh economy.

The year 1998 demonstrated the fragility of careless calculations based on an export-oriented development. The reduction of world prices on metals and energy resources, together with the contraction of demand on traditional export markets, unleashed a new wave of general economic and industrial decline in Kazakhstan.

As in Kyrgyzstan, the establishment in Kazakhstan has therefore found itself hostage to decisions that it had taken earlier. Having sold off its export producers to foreign companies, the government deprived itself of a source of financial resources that otherwise could have been used to supplement the budget. Nor did its calculations about the growth of tax revenues from export production prove to be entirely substantiated. Not only did the value of exports in 1997–98 fall (thereby reducing the tax base), but the exporters themselves needed state support. In May 1998, the largest exporters already extracted from the government preferential tariffs for electric power and transportation operations.[15]

Thus, a special dead-end variant of the dual economy has taken shape in Kazakhstan. Several dozen export enterprises, which provide jobs for less than one-tenth of the total labor force, have increasingly turned into a separate enclave. At the same time, the contribution from this enclave to the state budget (in the form of taxes and other assessments) has been declining. Indeed, this sector continues to use local electric power and the transportation infrastructure as a subsidized input to its own operations.

In the next few years, such a configuration—in the best-case scenario—will provide a depressed stabilization for the Kazakh economy. In the future, in the event of a favorable change in the world economic situation, the natural resources of Kazakhstan can be redistributed in favor of strategic investors in the form of the leading transnational corporations.

In strategic terms, Kazakhstan banked on becoming a major oil exporter. It is estimated that this country will produce 40 million tons of oil in the year 2000, up to 60 million tons in 2005, and at least 102 million tons in 2010. Exports of total output are estimated to reach 28 million tons in the year 2000, 46 million tons in 2005, and 86 million tons in 2010.[16]

It is widely thought that the principal barrier to the realization of such a rosy scenario is the exceedingly acute geopolitical struggle over the oil and gas reserves in the Caspian Sea. Apart from this factor, however, Kazakhstan also faces problems of a nonpolitical character that are no less complicated. Are the Central Asian oil and gas reserves competitive on a global scale? How will the appearance of new, large-scale exporters of oil and gas affect world prices and the global market as a whole? To which markets and at what point will Central Asia deliver its oil?

In the worst-case scenario, once the fixed capital assets of the metallurgical and petroleum industries have been finally exhausted, exports from Kazakhstan will sharply decrease. That, in turn, will lead to a total collapse of the entire national economy. Such an implosion can easily occur as a result of the unexpected, simultaneous decrease in prices on the other main export goods of Kazakhstan—copper, zinc, lead, aluminum, rolled ferrous metals, and petroleum. In September–December 1998, Kazakhstan was actually close to experiencing such a situation. This catastrophic variant was averted only by emergency assistance from the IMF, which provided a credit of 217 million dollars to supplement the gold and hard-currency reserves of the country (thereby supporting the exchange rate of the tenge). The government also received assistance from the World Bank, which provided a credit of 75 million dollars to finance the state budget.[17]

Kazakhstan is also making enormous efforts to attract foreign capital in branches of the national economy other than oil and metals. Suffice it to say that the banking sector and insurance sphere have been opened up to foreign capital. Nevertheless, the interests of foreign investors have been narrowly concentrated on oil, natural gas, and ferrous and nonferrous metallurgy (a matter that will be explained, in greater detail, in Chapter Five).

One cannot preclude the possibility that, in the event of a new deterioration in the economic situation, the creditors of Kazakhstan and the leading world corporations will take extraordinary measures to save the Kazakh economy. Essentially similar processes unfolded in Mexico in 1994, when the IMF and the American government provided massive financial assistance to the collapsing Mexican economy. If the events in Kazakhstan take an extreme turn, then the largest hydrocarbon reserves could pass over to foreign control—for example, as a result of a deal to trade the oil and gas reserves for emergency financial assistance. That variant, incidentally, had already begun to emerge in the fall of 1998: finding itself in a desperate situation, the government of Kazakhstan surrendered part of its share in the reserves on the Caspian shelf to the Japanese National Oil Company and the American corporation Phillips Petroleum.[18]

A realistic scenario for the next five to ten years cannot envision Kazakhstan turning into a major oil exporter. One can cite a host of problems: the influx of investments is more modest than expected, the development of local reserves poses serious difficulties, the quality of the raw materials is inferior, and the problems of transportation remain unresolved. For all these and other reasons, the fantastic plans to increase the extraction of hydrocarbons are hardly realizable. Under the best of circumstances, the oil exports will reach only 30 to 35 million tons by 2005—which would already be a threefold increase over the current level of exports.

Whatever the scenario, the development of Kazakhstan is almost exclusively dependent on the strategy of the transnational corporations dealing in oil and gas, as well as the economic conditions prevailing on world oil markets. The conception for the development of the country to the year 2030, which has been publicly announced,[19] leaves no doubt that the present elite in Kazakhstan has permitted itself to be drawn along by the flow of events. For the time being, they are not prepared to supplement the "petroleum dreams" (which, no doubt, will in some degree be realized) with urgently needed measures to diversify the economic structure.

Uzbekistan: A Special Path

Notwithstanding certain differences, the paths taken by Kyrgyzstan and Kazakhstan to adapt to globalization are identical in one respect: both countries have relied upon foreign capital, which indeed has emerged as virtually the only agent for development. The state has voluntarily renounced a role in development, and the local private sector is too weak to have any palpable influence on the macroeconomic situation.

At the same time, the deregulation of the exchange rate has drawn Kazakh and Kyrgyz producers into the web of global competition. As a result of the high level of energy consumption, technological backwardness, and breakdown of industrial organization, the local producers in both countries are unable to survive a competitive struggle with cheaper imports.

Uzbekistan, however, has developed a somewhat different trajectory. Two fundamental factors distinguish this country from Kazakhstan and Kyrgyzstan. First, the government of Uzbekistan has remained the main agent of development. In 1995–97, the current revenues of the state budget averaged some 32.5 percent of the GDP (compared with 14.9 percent in Kazakhstan and 15 percent in Kyrgyzstan).[20] By amassing significantly more resources in the state budget, the Uzbek government has considerable freedom for economic maneuvering and also exerts a substantial influence on economic dynamics. Second, Uzbekistan has attempted to protect national producers from global competition by regulating the exchange rate for the national currency.

Uzbekistan proved to be virtually the only country in the CIS that could lay the foundations for what is known as the "nation-state" in the literature on the problems of capitalist development and economic growth. Given the backwardness or underdevelopment of all other basic components, authoritarian rule has been the unifying, integrating element. At the end of the 1980s and early 1990s, this regime was able to avert a breakdown of the national economy.

Several circumstances made a substantial contribution to all this. On the one hand, the establishment of national control over the existing gold and uranium exports enabled Uzbekistan, in a quite rapid manner, to mitigate the negative consequences of a contraction in the influx of financial and physical resources from Russia. On the other hand, cotton is the backbone of agricultural production in Uzbekistan. The country succeeded in reorienting, with relative ease, the export of this industrial crop to world markets. Moreover, the price of cotton on the world market jumped by 24 percent in 1994 and by another 26 percent in 1995.[21] Although one cannot deny the significance of other conditions and sheer accident, one must recognize that both these factors have a significant role. Finally, the main reason for the smaller downturn of production in Uzbekistan (compared with other member states in the CIS) was the targeted, creative efforts of the Uzbek government.

To be sure, from a macroeconomic perspective, the result of all these efforts was to regenerate (or, more precisely, preserve) the imbalance or disequilibrium that prevailed at the end of the Soviet era. There was, of course, one important difference: in that earlier period, the levers of economic control and the resource flows were not in the hands of Uzbek authorities. But Uzbekistan also failed to find an adequate answer to the main challenge—the rapid growth of the population and its economically active segments.

The extreme fragility of the macroeconomic situation in Uzbekistan is explained by the almost complete dependence of the national economy on the demand for cotton on world markets. In 1992–95, cotton provided the lion's share of all export earnings; in 1996–98, it still generated a significant proportion of those earnings. The slightest fluctuations in world prices and demand for raw cotton can deal a devastating blow to the economy of the republic. Nor is the market for uranium any more predictable. Such remains the case despite the fact that, to judge from reports in the world press, Uzbekistan has gained entry to this market by signing a large contract with South Korea in 1996 and another with the United States in 1997.

After halting the decline in production and achieving stabilization in the mid-1990s, Uzbekistan now faces the task of overcoming the disequilibrium and launching itself on a trajectory of positive development. Otherwise, the objectively existing preconditions to unleash dynamic economic growth will have been lost.

In this writer's view, Uzbekistan has a set of preconditions that would allow it to enter upon a trajectory of efficient market development. First, the country has preserved its agrarian periphery. Soviet collectivization distorted the traditional structures of agriculture in Uzbekistan, but did not completely obliterate them—in contrast to Kazakhstan and Kyrgyzstan. Second, Uzbekistan has a mass of relatively cheap labor, which is capable of intensive, monotonous, and unskilled work. Third, for the overwhelming majority of the population, a simple model of consumption still prevails, essentially unaffected by the emergence of international tastes. Moreover, the level of personal consumption is extremely low. Fourth, the population is mentally and psychologically prepared for the rapid development of grassroots capitalism. Significantly, in 1994 (at the crest of the institutional liberalization), 77 percent of the small enterprises in Uzbekistan were private enterprises,[22] not cooperatives (as in the majority of post-Soviet states). Fifth, Uzbekistan has a disciplined bureaucracy, capable of enforcing the implementation of decisions taken by the central leadership of the country.

In a word, Uzbekistan has a series of distinctive characteristics that Alexander Gerschenkron, a pioneer in the study of economic development, once termed the relative advantage of backwardness. By relying upon these comparative advantages, Uzbekistan could preserve its chances to overcome the barriers of its underdevelopment and peripheral status in the world economy.

At the same time, Uzbekistan also inherited from the Soviet past a specific economic system, one with some inherent kinds of special structural traps. To name only three of them:

- Agriculture has an export orientation, but the country must also import a significant part of its foodstuffs. Depending upon the harvest, in 1991–95 the value of grain imports fluctuated between 0.7 and 1.0 billion dollars per year.
- The industrial and agricultural production is energy-intensive, even wasteful, and the country depends upon energy imports.
- The industrial structure has its own special features. If one excludes a small number of enterprises (most of which are small), the manufacturing industry of Uzbekistan has several distinctive characteristics. First, it developed as a second echelon, essentially as an industrial backup for the USSR in the event of war. Second, the industrial structure here is excessively diversified and fragmented. The assortment of manufactured items is excessively differentiated—given the scale of domestic demand or even the demand within the framework of Central Asia and the entire post-Soviet space. Third, the sector of intermediate production received hypertrophic development in the industrial structure; as a rule, that sector represented a link in the production and technological chain of the entire Soviet economy. Thus, the largest industrial enterprise of Uzbekistan and all of Central Asia was the Tashkent Aviation Manufacturing Association; this enterprise obtained parts and components from 1,200 suppliers scattered all across the territory of the former Soviet Union.[23]

From the first years of independence, the economic policy of Uzbekistan aimed at eliminating these structural traps. An obvious achievement of this policy was the breakthrough in the oil and gas branch.

By the end of 1995, Uzbekistan had virtually achieved self-sufficiency in energy and fuels. Oil production rose from 2.8 million tons in 1991 to 7.6 million tons in 1995. During this same period, the production of natural gas increased from 41.9 to 48.6 billion cubic meters.[24]

Simultaneously, the country relied upon foreign loans and credits to reconstruct its oil refinery plant in the Fergana valley. Uzbekistan also built, virtually from scratch, a modern oil refinery in the city of Bukhara.[25] This modernization and development of the petrochemical industry enabled the country to avoid the import of petroleum products. By the beginning of the twenty-first century, Uzbekistan plans to construct in the city of Shurtan the largest natural gas processing and chemical complex in all of Central Asia.[26]

By eliminating the dependence on the import of energy and petroleum products, Uzbekistan was able to improve its trade balance and hence its balance of payments as well. Therefore, in this writer's view, all these efforts should be judged as unqualified positives. However, that optimistic conclusion would only hold if one could disregard the negative experience of the former USSR, as well as dozens of developing countries. In all these cases, countries exhibited impressive results in the initial stages of import-substitution, but in the final analysis found themselves up a blind alley.

Such fears derive from three basic considerations. First, the large-scale projects in the spheres of oil and gas extraction as well as the chemical industry were possible because of foreign loans and credits, not because of direct foreign investment. Consequently, the government gained some improvement in the balance of payments, but at the price of increasing its foreign indebtedness. Second, precious little is known about the real production costs in the extraction of oil and natural gas. Third, once Uzbekistan invested huge amounts of borrowed resources into oil and natural gas processing, it was forced to expand the production of oil and gas at any price—regardless of the real costs of production.

The folly of achieving gross physical volume of production at any price was conclusively discredited by the collapse of the Soviet economy. The strategy of mindless import-substitution has also proven to be a dead end for scores of developing countries.

In theory, the elimination of dependence on the import of energy resources permits a country to construct a national industrial base without regard to external conditions of development. However, one fundamental consequence of globalization is the fact that production costs of individual producers are made comparable with other producers all around the world. Let us suppose that the costs of extracting oil and natural gas in Uzbekistan are quite competitive by world standards, or even that the government—while keeping control over the fuel and energy complex—will subsidize industrial producers in the middle- or long-term perspective (by providing low prices on oil products and electric power). In this event, much will depend on making the right choice in prioritizing branches in the manufacturing sector.

It is essential to concentrate these priorities in the export sector. Otherwise, Uzbekistan will be unable to pay off the loans and credits it has accumulated, or to support the work of the import-dependent fuel and energy complex. However, the current industrial policy of Uzbekistan does not provide an adequate response to this fundamental imperative. Rather, it is designed much in the old Soviet "nonmarket" spirit.

Thus, the most important branch priority of national industry is the manufacture of motor vehicles. In April 1996, the South Korean chaebol Daewoo opened a motor vehicle assembly plant in the city of Asaka; the construction of this plant cost 650 million dollars.[27] In March 1999, another plant began production in Samarkand; it will produce 5,000 automobiles and buses per year. Uzbekistan's partner in this project, Turkey, alone has invested 70 million dollars in this enterprise.[28]

Given the low level of effective domestic demand (which, as already noted in Chapter Two, will remain such in the foreseeable future), the development of the automotive branch in Uzbekistan can only be justified in the event it has a clearly defined export orientation. However, the very modest scales of production at these enterprises already make it clear that not one will be competitive in the global economy. In 1997, the automotive assembly plants in Uzbekistan produced a total of 64,900 vehicles (compared with 25,300 the previous year).[29]

Indirect evidence shows that even the largest automotive plant in Uzbekistan, which was built by Daewoo, has been kept afloat only because investors had access to a preferential mechanism for currency conversion. It is possible that export-significant transactions unconnected with the automotive plant allow Daewoo to earn a profit on the Uzbek market. In a certain sense, the domestic structure of the South Korean chaebols is very similar to the economic organism of contemporary Uzbekistan. Unprofitable transactions coexist with profitable ones; in the extreme case, the aggregate losses are covered by financing obtained from foreign sources. At the same time, the South Korean experience shows that the temporary horizons for the existence of such structures rarely go beyond ten or fifteen years.

Nor are the export prospects good for the branch that produces agricultural machinery, which Uzbek authorities have chosen as a high priority. In 1997–98, Uzbekistan organized a number of joint-venture enterprises to assemble agricultural machinery (with an American partner, Case); its purported goal was to export this production.[30] The annual output at these plants will not exceed a few tens of thousands of units. Case, together with another American manufacturer of agricultural machinery, John Deere, is undertaking analogous projects in Kazakhstan and Russia,[31] which might be seen as potential export markets for the Uzbek producers. Given the fact that these assembly plants operate licensing agreements (with credits from the largest international investment banks), in the final analysis this industrial policy only leads to an increase in the foreign indebtedness of Uzbekistan.

Still more dismal are the prospects for enterprises producing household electronics, a branch upon which Uzbekistan has to some degree been banking. Several examples can be cited here. Daewoo has organized in Uzbekistan the production of computer monitors; in the first stage, the annual output is planned to be 36,000 units per year. Ultimately, imported components are to be replaced by parts that are produced locally.[32] At the same time, Daewoo has also developed the production of video and radio equipment at Uzbek enterprises. Another South Korean chaebol, Samsung, has organized the production of household electronics in Tashkent, with an annual production capacity of 820,000 units.[33] Daewoo has also organized the production of computers in Uzbekistan; it uses imported components and has an annual output of 36,000 units.[34] The Japanese corporation Sony has begun to assemble color televisions at a plant in Tashkent; by the year 2000, its annual production capacity was to be 50,000 units.[35]

The very scale of the planned production, the excessive fragmentation in the assortment, and the total dependence on the import of components—all this shows that the newly created production cannot be competitive on a global scale. The export prospects for the production of these goods are further undermined by the fact that the South Korean chaebols are carrying out analogous projects in neighboring Kazakhstan.[36]

Nor is the choice of other branch priorities understandable. Among the most absurd examples is the international concern "C-Pro": in a country rich in agricultural raw materials, this company is organizing the production of powders for instant drinks, dried breakfasts, broth, coffee, and other instant foods.

Of course, if so inclined, one might prefer to regard all these projects as a test by transnational corporations to determine whether Uzbekistan is suitable as a future export platform for the assembly of manufactured goods. However, the fact that the country is isolated from world markets does not speak in favor of such a view. Apparently, faced with a dearth of investment resources, Uzbekistan is prepared to undertake practically any project that is proposed by foreign investors.

At what price did these experiments become possible? They draw upon resources from two channels. On the one hand, Uzbekistan subsidizes industrial producers by setting low prices on energy resources and electric power. The fuel and energy complex operates as a donor for the other branches of the economy. On the other hand, a significant portion of these projects (which, for a variety of reasons, cannot become competitive on a global scale of production) is apparently being realized within the framework of multilateral barter deals. In other words, while exporting raw materials and semi-finished goods, in exchange Uzbekistan does not receive real money, but components to assembly a limited number of finished goods. In addition, the government has created for such projects an exceptionally preferential tax rate, and often even finances them from centralized resources. This approach has an obvious analogue in Soviet industrial policy. This system of cooperation is extremely advantageous for foreign corporations, something that cannot be said about the side receiving the investments.[37]

How does this mesh with the tendencies of globalization? The global economy has many layers and offers a niche for virtually every model of development. The world has a considerable number of countries that pursue an inefficient industrial and structural policy: namely, they finance import-substitution at the expense of the export of their own natural resources and agricultural raw materials. That model of development is viable so long as the influx of export earnings is sufficient to sustain, at a certain critical level, mass consumption and to purchase abroad the components (or other intermediate products) for that production created in the process of import-substitution. Moreover, it rather quickly becomes clear that by reducing the dependence of finished goods on the foreign markets, a country finds itself in an analogous or even more perceptible dependence on the import of intermediate and investment goods. Sooner or later this leads to a breakdown in the balance of payments.

The most striking example of this pattern was the collapse of the Soviet economy, which was temporarily sustained by the surge in world oil prices, but then overwhelmed by the growth in foreign loans. Despite the obvious lessons of a failed economic experiment, the experience of others is rarely taken into consideration when a strategy of national development is being formulated. As a result, other states repeat the same typical errors.

In contrast to the Soviet Union, which for a long time could allow itself to ignore the costs of such a development strategy, not one of the post-Soviet states can do the same. Because of their critical dependence on the influx of foreign resources and because of their inclusion into international economic relations, these post-Soviet regimes simply do not have a reserve of time at their disposal.

Uzbekistan had to pay for its inefficient import-substitution with a hard-currency and financial crisis that commenced in the fall of 1996 and has persisted ever since. The external manifestations of this crisis included a significant budget deficit (as is attested by independent sources), a profound and growing gap between the official and black-market exchange rates on the Uzbek sum, a high rate of inflation, and a rapid increase in the foreign debt.

The economic policy of Uzbekistan has other defects. The investment policy is creating new structural traps without eliminating the old ones. The available statistics on capital investment attest that the lion's share of new investment is aimed at the fuel and energy complex, the infrastructure, and construction for nonproduction purposes. While the significant investments in the energy branches are at least partly justified, the same cannot be said of the other targets of investment.

The nonproduction sphere and infrastructure consume more than half of all investments in fixed capital. This policy also reflects an inertia left over from the Soviet era. To be sure, both the social sphere and the infrastructure are critically important for the economic development of the country. However, two key facts must be taken into account: the very low level of incomes of the population (which, incidentally, are not expected to increase in the near future), as well as the limited amount of resources at the disposal of the government. Given these constraints, Uzbekistan cannot devote, as it currently does, such significant resources (in relative terms) to construction for nonproduction purposes.

These facts, along with many other circumstances, lead to the conclusion that the economic policy currently pursued by Uzbekistan will not launch this country onto a trajectory of self-sustained growth. On the contrary, current strategy is preparing the ground for economic collapse. It is entirely possible that within the span of a few years Uzbekistan will be seen as a "country of missed opportunities."

In this author's judgment, the inadequacy of Uzbekistan's economic policy lies in the following. First, agriculture is still used as a donor for other branches (a point that will be elaborated below, in Chapter Eight). Second, the industrial policy still relies chiefly on import-substitution, not exports. Third, the excessive emphasis on authoritarian power impedes the development of grassroots capitalism. Despite the clear massive inclination toward entrepreneurial activity, in 1996 small enterprises employed fewer than 240,000 people (just 2.8 percent of the total labor force).[38] Nor has the situation fundamentally improved in the interim. For purposes of comparison, it should be pointed out that on 1 April 1998 the small enterprises of Kazakhstan employed 950,000 people (15 percent of the total workforce).[39]

Paradoxical as it might appear, Uzbekistan—in the event that it reestablishes full-scale cooperation with the IMF and World Bank—can count on a fresh flow of funds to continue these experiments. It is well known that the World Bank is rather active in financing infrastructure projects. Moreover, the experience of neighboring Kyrgyzstan and Russia attest to the fact that the Bretton Woods institutions exercise virtually no control over funds once they are disbursed.

Moreover, a large devaluation of the sum (which is inevitable in the event that the exchange rate is deregulated) will further aggravate the lack of competitiveness among domestic producers. Uzbekistan has officially announced that in 2000 it will introduce the convertibility of its national currency and accept Article VIII of the IMF. The more the production created under this policy of import-substitution, the more difficult it will become to realize this intention without provoking serious downturns in the industrial sector.

Conclusion

In the post-Soviet space, factors of a global order prevail over specific local conditions. At the same time, each of the Central Asian countries has offered its own response to the challenge of globalization. Kyrgyzstan and Kazakhstan have attempted to establish a grip on the global economy by counting on their own natural resources. The economy in these countries has been stratified into two sectors: *an export sector* (the dynamics of which depend entirely on the situation in world markets if only because export consists mainly of raw materials and goods with a low level of processing) and *all other branches of production.*

The export sector of Kyrgyzstan is too small to sustain the national economy on its own. Therefore, this country represents a case of marginalization. In Kazakhstan, the export earnings are incomparably higher than in Kyrgyzstan—both in absolute and in per capita terms. Moreover, although Kazakhstan has few chances to realize the hopes for "an oil miracle," in the next five to ten years this country will be able to increase its oil exports to world markets.

Uzbekistan is endeavoring to find its own niche in the agrarian, raw-material, and industrial structures of the modern world. Given the special features of its economic mechanism, Uzbekistan has not experienced the bifurcation of the economy into two sectors, as happened in Kyrgyzstan and Kazakhstan. The Uzbek economy continues to function as a single unit where administrative methods determine the allocation of resources and financial flows among sectors and enterprises. Resources obtained through the export of cotton, uranium, gold, and several non-ferrous metals are poured into the development of industry. That strategy is successful only in the event that the resulting industrial production is competitive on a global scale. If this production cannot compete on world markets, then the result will be an economy with fully ruined agrarian and raw-material sectors and inefficient industry. In other words, it would be a small-scale replica of the former Soviet and current Russian situation. Therefore, at the present time, it makes sense to talk about an intermediate niche for Uzbekistan.

Against the background of the marginalization of Kyrgyzstan and the continuing free-fall in Kazakhstan, the situation in Uzbekistan at the end of the 1990s seems preferable. If, at the beginning of the decade, Uzbekistan conducted a liberalization like that in Kyrgyzstan or even Kazakhstan, it would have been fated to suffer a marginalization no less acute than that now overtaking Kyrgyzstan.

For states developing in the system of objective limitations noted at the beginning of this chapter, the active intervention of the state into the economic process is an absolute necessity. There is apparently no alternative to the large-scale redistribution of resources and profits among different sectors of the economy; only a government can carry out this task. The experience of Kazakhstan and especially Kyrgyzstan demonstrates that blind adherence to the principles of laissez-faire does not hold out good prospects. But it is another matter when the resources that the Uzbek government succeeded in mobilizing are not distributed in the optimal fashion.

As the rich experience of the world demonstrates, the point is not that import-substitution as a strategy of development is inherently on the decline in comparison with an export-oriented approach to development. Rather, the problem is that, under conditions of globalization of the world economy (because of the free conversion of national currencies), competition based on production costs has also become global. If this circumstance is taken into account, the branch priorities that Uzbekistan has identified as strategic are the wrong ones. The domestic market here is extremely small; the prospects for exporting motor vehicles and household electronic appliances are highly dubious.

The choice of branch priorities corresponds poorly to the real potential of the country. That potential, above all, lies in the sphere of agrobusiness as well as light and textile industries. Moreover, the inefficient import-substitution in Uzbekistan is realized at the expense of foreign loans and credits, which then give rise to the question of paying off these foreign obligations. In this author's view, Uzbekistan will not be able to adhere to the present economic policy for any extended period of time.

Notes

1. For the sources of data on these and other indicators characterizing the profound imbalances in the mutual relations between the Kyrgyz and the world economies, see below, Table 5.5.

2. Iu. Razguliaev, "Dast li pribyl' kirgizskoe zoloto?" *Aziia. Ekonomika i zhizn'*, no. 6 (February 1998): 5.

3. A. Evplanov, "Kirgizskoe evrobondy budut obespecheny zolotym zapasom strany," *Finansovye izvestiia* (Moscow), no. 39 (4 June 1998): iii.

4. Iu. Razguliaev, "Zoloto ne sdelalo ikh bogatymi," *Aziia. Ekonomika i zhizn'* (Almaty), 1998, no. 5 (February): 13; V. Garmash, "Strany Sodruzhestva vybiraiutsia iz krizisa," *Finansovye izvestiia*, no. 20 (24 March 1998): v; "CAMECO Announces 1998 Financial Results and Subsequent Developments," *The Almaty Herald*, no. 155 (11–17 February 1999): 9.

5. "Sotsial'no-ekonomicheskoe polozhenie Kyrgyzskoi Respubliki v ianvare-dekabre 1998," *Bankir* (Bishkek), no. 2 (27 January 1999): 4. See also Table 2.1.

6. See G. Voskresenskii, "Vol'nyi rynok narkotikov," *Vek* (Moscow), no. 16 (17–23 April 1998): 6; Iu. Razguliaev, "Narkoticheskii aisberg," *Kazakhstanskaia pravda*, 20 November 1997, p. 4.

7. On the involvement of the Turkestan region (including the territories of modern Kyrgyzstan) in the international network of production and commerce in narcotics, see B. Kalachev and A. Barinov, "Organizovannaia, prestupnaia. . . ," *Segodnia*, 16 October 1997, p. 7.

8. Iu. Razguliaev, "Prizraki Oshksoi tragedii v kirgizskom parlamente," *Vremia-MN* (Moscow), 10 March 1999, p. 6.

9. V. Berezovskii, "Bishkek: pogromy na bazarakh," *Rossiiskaia gazeta*, 11 February 1999, p. 7.

10. Iu. Razguliaev, "Askar Akaev obnaruzhil sabotazhnikov," *Vremia-MN*, 15 January 1999, p. 6.

11. M. Gerasimov, "Prezident Akaev boretsia s korruptsionerami," *Nezavisimaia gazeta*, 22 December 1998, p. 5.

12. I. Sedykh, "Ekonomicheskuiu politiku Rossii budet diktovat' Kirgiziia," *Segodnia*, 19 October 1998, p. 1.

13. Iu. Razguliaev, "Kirgiziia vstupila v VTO," *Vremia MN* (Moscow), 24 September 1998, p. 1.

14. Calculated from *Tendentsii razvitiia ekonomiki Kazakhstana*, November 1998, Table 9.7.5.

15. M. Khasanova, "Itogi vneshneekonomicheskoi deiatel'nosti Respubliki Kazakhstan v 1998 g. i prognoz na blizhaishuiu perspektivu," *Al' Pari*, 1998, no. 4: 11.

16. *Panorama*, no. 41 (23 October 1998): 8.

17. N. Absaliamova, "Finansovye donory doveriaiut Kazakhstanu," *Kazakhstanskaia pravda*, 24 December 1998, p. 2.

18. See Chapter Seven, by O. Reznikova, in this volume.

19. N.A. Nazarbaev, "Kazakhstan-2030," *Kazakhstanskaia pravda*, 11 October 1997.

20. Calculated on the basis of data from the World Bank.

21. *Uzbek Economic Trends. Monthly Update*, July 1998 (TACIS, European Expert Service), p. 1.

22. D. Isamiddinova and N. Sirazhiddinov, "Usloviia funktsionirovaniia malykh predpriiatii v postsovetskikh stranakh (na primere Uzbekistana i Rossii)," *Ekonomicheskoe obozrenie* (Tashkent), 1998, no. 1 (January): 45.

23. D. Aliaev and L. Zavarskii, "V Tashkente neletniaia pogoda," *Kommersant-Daily* (Moscow), 27 April 1996, p. 11.

24. See Interstate Statistical Committee, *Commonwealth of Independent States in 1998. A Digest of Provisional Statistical Results* (Moscow, 1999), pp. 56–57.

25. *National Corporation Uzbekneftegaz* (Tashkent, 1998), p. 49; *Delovoi mir* (Moscow), no. 32 (22–25 August 1997), p. 4.

26. *National Corporation Uzbekneftegaz*, pp. 45, 49.

27. *Central European Economic Review*, 1996, no. 3: 7.

28. *Izvestiia* (Moscow), 18 March 1999, p. 4.

29. *Commonwealth of Independent States in 1998*, p. 61.

30. G. Chernogaeva and N. Ivanov, "Amerikanskie traktora rvutsia na prostory SNG," *Kommersant-Daily* (Moscow), 2 June 1998, p. 11; *Russkii telegraf*, 27 May 1998, p. 7.

31. I. Gidaspov and A. Sinitskii, "Kulikovo pole," *Finansovye izvestiia* (Moscow), no. 27 (18 May 1999): iii.

32. *Aziia. Ekonomika i zhizn,'* no. 36 (September 1997), p. 2.

33. *Russkii telegraf,* 5 June 1998, p. 7.

34. *Kommersant-Daily,* 15 August 1997, p. 8.

35. *Finansovye izvestiia,* no. 55 (29 July 1997): 1.

36. A. Petrovskii, "Prezident otkryl televizionnyi zavod," *Kazakhstanskaia pravda,* 29 May 1998, p. 2.

37. *Aziia. Ekonomika i zhizn,'* no. 35 (September 1997), p. 2.

38. Isamiddinova and Sirazhiddinov, "Usloviia funktsionirovaniia," p. 48; *Commonwealth of Independent States in 1998,* p. 291. According to Uzbek law, a "small enterprise" is defined as one with fewer than fifty employees in industry and construction, twenty-five in agriculture, ten in science and scientific services, and five in trade.

39. A. Tukaev, "Analiz razvitiia malogo biznesa v Kazakhstane," *Al'Pari* (Almaty), no. 2 (April–July 1998): 69.

5

Foreign Trade and Investment

Stanislav Zhukov

For many reasons, foreign factors play a decisive role in determining internal development in all the countries of Central Asia. There are no exceptions. To an increasing degree, the world market determines the general direction, type, and rhythm of economic development, as well as the structure of growth in Central Asia.

An important positive factor for all the Central Asian economies was not only the expansion of exports, but also foreign assistance and the influx of direct foreign investment. The combination of these factors varied from one state to the next. Kyrgyzstan, Turkmenistan, and especially Tajikistan are kept afloat mainly because of foreign loans and assistance. In Kazakhstan and Uzbekistan, which have an export potential that is incomparably greater, economic growth has relied mainly on foreign trade. In Kazakhstan, moreover, direct foreign investment has played an important role in economic development.

To what degree are these foreign economic relations of the Central Asian states properly balanced? Have they retained reserves for the further expansion of exports? What kind of economic structure is being formed in this region under the influence of exogenous factors? These and other related questions are the focus of the present chapter.

Problems of Sustaining Stable Growth in an "Open Economy"

As a result of the breakup of the USSR, all the post-Soviet economies almost instantaneously began to turn into essentially "open economies."

The transformation from autarky to openness occurred almost automatically; it represents probably the central structural change in the process of the transition to a market economy. In 1995–1998, export and import quotas (which are accepted as a measurement of openness) constituted no less than 30 to 40 percent of the GDP in all the states of Central Asia (see Table 5.1).

The shift to openness resulted from the combined action of four basic factors. First, there was a change in absolute and relative prices. In the Soviet economy, the prices of raw materials were substantially lower than the average world levels. During the process of liberalization, the prices for raw material commodities rose at high rates. Second, all post-Soviet states (including those in Central Asia) sought to reorient, to the maximum possible degree, their raw material flows and commodity deliveries toward world markets if they enjoyed any export demand. Third, the production in raw-material and export branches decreased less than those branches producing finished goods and those servicing domestic demand. Moreover, a number of countries even expanded the physical volume of production for such commodities as oil, natural gas, gold, silver, and some other raw materials. Fourth, the relations between enterprises located in different states now assumed the form of foreign economic ties.

In Kazakhstan and Kyrgyzstan, exports in 1993–97 increased by 1.9 times, reaching 6.4 billion dollars for Kazakhstan and 580 million dollars for Kyrgyzstan. The exports of Uzbekistan also significantly increased, rising to approximately 4.5 billion dollars in 1997.

The reorientation toward exports was predetermined by structural peculiarities of local economies that had already been established in the Soviet era. On the one hand, within the framework of the division of labor in the former USSR, the Central Asian republics shipped significant volumes of commodities to the other Soviet republics. On the other hand, the Central Asian states (to one degree or another) received subsidies from the central Soviet budget. The collapse of a single economic complex in 1991 drove the Central Asian states to seek access to world markets. The contraction of demand in Russia, which was due to the special features of that country's economic policy, suddenly deprived Central Asia of its traditional markets and forced these states to find third-country markets for their goods. This reorientation was all the more necessary since Central Asia could no longer rely on the delivery of critically important products from Russia and the other republics. Those

Table 5.1

Export and Import Shares of GDP in Central Asia, 1995–1998[a]

Country	Indicator	1995	1996	1997	1998
Kazakhstan	Export as percent of GDP	39.0	32.0	32.2	26.6
	Export as percent of goods sector production	90.5	82.8	85.1	75.3
	Import as percent of GDP	43.5	33.9	35.0	34.6
Kyrgyzstan	Export as percent of GDP	27.5	27.6	34.2	33.2
	Export as percent of goods sector production	43.3	40.5	55.0	55.6
	Import as percent of GDP	35.2	45.9	40.2	50.5
Tajikistan	Export as percent of GDP	115.4	73.1	80.6	45.7
	Export as percent of goods sector production	177.5			
	Import as percent of GDP	124.8	63.4	81.1	58.8
Turkmenistan	Export as percent of GDP	48.2	89.1	31.0	
	Export as percent of goods sector production	70.3	115.3		
	Import as percent of GDP	35.0	69.1	47.1	
Uzbekistan[b]	Export as percent of GDP	38.0 (41.0)	33.0 (52.1)	29.5 (66.4)	24.7 (59.2)
	Export as percent of goods sector production	24.2	27.5	30.9	35.0
	Import as percent of GDP	38.4 (41.4)	33.9 (53.6)	30.4 (68.5)	23.0 (55.2)

Sources: Calculated from the following: Interstate Statistical Committee, *Commonwealth of Independent States in 1998* (Moscow, 1999), p. 37; *Commonwealth of Independent States in 1997* (Moscow 1998), p. 37; *Sotsial'no-ekonomicheskoe polozhenie Respubliki Kazakhstan* (Almaty), 1999, no. 1 : 5; Natsional'nyi institut statistiki i prognozirovaniia, *Statisticheskii ezhegodnik Turkmenistana. 1996*, vol. 1 (Ashgabat, 1998): 8–9; World Bank, *Statistical Handbook 1996. States of the Former USSR* (Washington, DC, 1996), p. 416; data supplied by the Ministry of Macroeconomics and Statistics of the Republic of Uzbekistan; and the sources cited above in Table 2.6.
[a]Due to recent changes in the methodology of calculation, figures for different years are not strictly comparable.
[b]Calculations in parentheses are based on the black-market exchange rate.

goods had been essential to the operation of the local economies, and new suppliers had to be found. As a result, the only way that the Central Asian states could ensure the uninterrupted operation of their economies was to obtain imports from new sources outside the CIS. And the only way to finance such imports was to secure new export earnings.

The foreign trade turnover averages about 60 percent of the GDP in Kazakhstan, 80 percent in Kyrgyzstan, and approximately 90 percent in Turkmenistan. In Tajikistan, because of the special conditions obtaining in its transition economy, the aggregate exports and imports exceed the GDP. Uzbekistan, according to calculations based on the official exchange rate, is less dependent on foreign economic ties. However, if the black-market exchange rate is used, the aggregate export and import quotas exceed the size of the GDP.

Without hyperbole, one can say that the Central Asian economies exist only through their inclusion in the international division of labor. If cut off from the channels of international trade, they would immediately atrophy and wither away.

The critical dependency on exports is particularly evident if one compares the export quotas not with the total GDP, but only with the production of goods (excluding services). In this case, the ratio between the commodity exports and the production of goods amounts to 75–85 percent in Kazakhstan and 55 percent in Kyrgyzstan. In Uzbekistan, this indicator for 1998 was 35 percent.

Whole branches of local economies are oriented almost exclusively toward export demands. That is particularly characteristic of Kazakhstan: exports accounted for 57.7 percent of the total output of oil and gas condensate in 1997, and then 72.1 percent in the first five months of 1998. Still higher are the corresponding figures for oxides and aluminum hydroxide (108.8 percent in 1997 and 88.6 percent in January–May 1998), ferrous alloys (72.1 and 82.6 percent, respectively), rolled ferrous metals (94.6 and 91.7 percent), and copper (95.1 and 91.8 percent).[1]

Given this critical dependence on foreign trade, all the countries of Central Asia—without exception—are distinguished by an extremely unfavorable branch structure and (in some cases) geographic distribution of their exports.

Oil, natural gas, electric power, raw cotton and cotton fiber, ferrous and nonferrous metals, gold, and uranium account for more than four-fifths of the aggregate exports from this region. Table 5.2 shows the total structure of exports from the countries of Central Asia. Thus, in the

Table 5.2

Industry Breakdown of Export Earnings (in percent)

Industrial branch	Kazakhstan 1996	Kazakhstan 1997	Kazakhstan 1998	Kyrgyzstan 1996	Kyrgyzstan 1997	Kyrgyzstan 1998	Tajikistan 1996	Tajikistan 1997	Tajikistan 1998	Turkmenistan 1996	Turkmenistan 1997	Uzbekistan 1996	Uzbekistan 1997	Uzbekistan 1998
Total exports														
Food products	11.5	11.9	8.6	34.4	19.6	20.5	13.6	4.9	6.5	0.3	0.5	4.9	4.1	3.5
Oil, gas, electricity	36.9	38.4	44.1	16.5	18.4	9.4	24.3	21.3	20.4	76.8	82.4	6.7	13.1	8.7
Ferrous and nonferrous metals	32.3	33.3	32.9	8.3	5.7	4.0	36.9	34.9	42.2	0.2	1.1	3.8	5.0	5.6
Chemicals	9.2	6.7	5.1	7.3	3.3	4.2	0.5	0.2	0.9	0.5	0.5	2.6	1.9	1.6
Cotton and textiles	2.4	1.7	1.3	14.0	8.7	6.4	23.9	28.2	22.1	21.5	15.2	41.4	39.3	42.2
Machinery, equipment, transport vehicles	5.1	3.9	2.2	10.0	8.4	10.9	0.6	2.1	2.6	0.1	0.1	3.2	6.7	4.6
Other	2.6	4.1	5.8	9.5	35.9	44.6	0.2	8.4	5.3	0.6	0.2	37.4	29.9	33.8
Exports outside the CIS														
Food products	2.4	2.2	2.7	9.1	3.7	4.9	2.6	0.1	0.3			0.3	0.3	0.2
Oil, gas, electricity	27.2	30.5	31.7	0.2	0.4	0.3	2.5	0.2	0.2			0.6	0.4	0.4
Ferrous and nonferrous metals	55.9	55.0	51.4	21.1	7.6	3.5	58.0	51.8	60.9			3.8	5.5	5.8
Chemicals	6.7	3.0	2.9	16.1	3.6	4.8	0.8	0.1	0.0			2.0	1.2	0.8
Cotton and textiles	3.4	2.9	1.8	31.8	11.2	6.9	35.9	39.9	30.9			48.6	51.2	52.9
Machinery, equipment, transport vehicles	0.7	0.4	0.7	6.8	4.2	4.9	0.1	0.2	0.3			2.0	2.7	0.4
Other	3.7	6.0	8.8	14.9	69.3	74.7	0.1	7.7	7.4			42.7	38.7	39.5

case of Kazakhstan, the data in this table show that in 1998 oil, gas, and metals accounted for 77 percent of national export revenues and 83.1 percent of its exports to markets outside the CIS. In Kyrgyzstan that same year, gold (subsumed under the category of "other") accounted for about one-half of all exports and three-quarters of all exports to markets outside the CIS. For Tajikistan in 1998, electric power, aluminum, and cotton accounted for 84.7 percent of total exports; aluminum and cotton provided 91.8 percent of all shipments to markets outside the CIS. In the case of Turkmenistan, natural gas and cotton were the source for about 97 percent of all export earnings in 1997. In Uzbekistan in 1998, cotton, gold, and uranium (the gold and uranium listed under the category of "other") generated 76 percent of all export earnings and more than 90 percent of export revenues from markets outside the CIS.

Moreover, this critical dependency on the export of a limited assortment of goods did not diminish in the 1990s but, on the contrary, actually increased. The relative significance of such items as machine-building, equipment, transportation vehicles, and chemical products declined in virtually every country. This was abetted by the continuing reorientation of export flows from the Central Asian states to markets outside the former Soviet Union. The dynamics of the structure of exports show more starkly than any other indicator the fact that in the global economy Central Asia has assumed the role as a supplier of mineral and agricultural raw materials.

The de-industrialization of exports proceeded with particular speed in the largest states of Central Asia. Thus, in the case of Kazakhstan, the proportion of machinery, equipment, and transportation vehicles in aggregate exports fell from 5.1 percent in 1996 to 2.2 percent in 1998. For exports to countries outside the CIS, this proportion remained at the same low level. In Uzbekistan, the proportion of machinery, equipment, and transportation vehicles in exports to countries outside the CIS dropped from 2.0 percent in 1996 to just 0.4 percent in 1998.

This raw-material orientation of exports from the Central Asian states has also given rise to a further problem: the region has become precariously tethered to a small number of foreign markets. Thus, in 1996–98, *the top trading partner* received one-third or more of all the exports from the states in this region; the only exception here was Uzbekistan (see Table 5.3). Or, measured by another indicator, the *three leading export markets* devoured 50–60 percent of the exports from Turkmenistan and Kazakhstan and 60–70 percent of the exports from Kyrgyzstan and

Table 5.3

Geographic Distribution of Exports (in percent)

Country	Indicator	1996	1997	1998
Kazakhstan	Leading partner[a]	44.5	33.9	28.9
	Three leading partners	57.1	49.5	47.1
	Five leading partners	64.2	59.8	60.4
	CIS	56.0	48.0	42.0
	Non-CIS	44.0	52.0	58.0
Kyrgyzstan	Leading partner[b]	25.3	26.9	37.8[c]
	Three leading partners	68.3	60.1	70.3[c]
	Five leading partners	80.5	79.7	81.9[c]
	CIS	78.0	53.0	46.0
	Non-CIS	22.0	47.0	54.0
Tajikistan	Leading partner[d]	28.3	30.8	
	Three leading partners	63.8	72.8	
	Five leading partners	77.3	83.3	
	CIS	43.0	37.0	35.0
	Non-CIS	57.0	63.0	65.0
Turkmenistan	Leading partner[e]	41.3	29.7	
	Three leading partners	60.5	53.6	
	Five leading partners	73.1	67.8	
	CIS	67.0	64.0	
	Non-CIS	33.0	36.0	
Uzbekistan	Leading partner[f]		11.6	
	Three leading partners	26.8		
	Five leading partners	38.8		
	CIS	23.0	34.0	26.0
	Non-CIS	77.0	66.0	74.0

Sources: Sodruzhestvo nezavisimykh gosudarstv v 1997 godu (Moscow, 1998), pp. 66–67; *Sodruzhestvo nezavisimykh gosudarstv v 1996 godu*, pp. 66–67; Natsional'nyi Bank, *Platezhnyi balans Kyrgyzskoi Respubliki. Deviat' mesiatsev 1998* (Bishkek, 1999), p. 23; data from the customs statistics of Kazakhstan and the Ministry of Macroeconomics and Statistics of the Republic of Uzbekistan.

[a]Kazakhstan's leading partner in 1996–1998 was Russia.

[b]Kyrgyzstan's leading partner was Russia (1996), Switzerland (1997), and Germany (1998).

[c]Data for January–September 1998.

[d]Tajikistan's leading partner in 1996–1997 was the Netherlands.

[e]Turkmenistan's leading partner in 1996–1997 was Ukraine.

[f]Uzbekistan's leading partner in 1997 was Russia.

Tajikistan. Exports from Uzbekistan (for which comparable data are not available for different years) appear to be more geographically balanced. However, that impression may be misleading; it may simply be due to the peculiarities of Uzbek statistics, which assiduously "conceal" foreign trade transactions involving gold and uranium.

The high degree of branch and geographic concentration in exports has also facilitated the process whereby foreign shocks are easily transmitted to local economies. An unfavorable dynamic in just two or three raw-material markets, or turbulence in a few key countries (including Russia, Ukraine, China, and Turkey), has an immediate impact on the economic situation in Central Asia.

The only way to reduce the negative impact of external turmoil is to diversify exports and, thereby, diminish the overweening dependence on a few commodities and a few markets. Unfortunately, however, the Central Asian economies are currently moving in precisely the opposite direction. Not only is the process of turning this region into a raw-material appendage to the world economy moving full speed ahead, but the national strategies of development are essentially oriented toward consolidating this role in the foreseeable future. Inter alia, this means that the economic growth of Central Asia will become still more dependent on foreign factors.

The Raw Materials Bias of Foreign Investment

Foreign factors are exerting a growing influence on the economic development of the Central Asian states through not only trade, but also investment. Indeed, foreign investment has become the most important factor in the economic growth of post-Soviet states.

In Kazakhstan, the proportion of foreign sources for financing investment in fixed capital increased from 13 percent in 1996 to 22 percent in 1997 and then to 26.3 percent in 1998.[2] In Uzbekistan, the foreign share of capital investment also increased: 16 percent in 1996, 18 percent in 1997, and 23.4 percent in 1998.[3] In Kyrgyzstan, foreign sources accounted for 71 percent of investment in 1996 and 76 percent in 1997.[4] In the midterm perspective, the significance of foreign investment in all the countries of this region will increase further.

Thus, not only the current production process, but also the prospective structure of the economies in the Central Asian states is, to a significant degree, being determined by external factors.

What kind of structure is emerging in this region under the active (and sometimes determining) influence of foreign capital? To answer this question, it is helpful to analyze the detailed statistical information available for Kazakhstan. The choice of Kazakhstan is not accidental: this country has devoured the lion's share of direct foreign investment in the region from 1991 to 1998. According to estimates by international financial agencies, the net influx (total investment minus withdrawals) in the Kazakh economy amounted to 4.2 billion dollars, or approximately 80 percent of all direct investment to the region during this period.[5]

Table 5.4 shows the branch structure of direct foreign investments in the Kazakh economy from 1993 to 1998. The data here show that 46.3 percent of the investment flows went to oil and natural gas, and another 25.1 percent to nonferrous metallurgy. Moreover, the surge of interest among foreign investors in nonferrous and, to a lesser degree, ferrous metallurgy came during 1995–97. It was precisely in this period that the government of Kazakhstan, at an accelerated rate, transferred the largest metallurgical enterprises to foreign control (see Chapter Three). If these years are excluded, oil and natural gas accounted for 70–80 percent of all direct foreign investment in the country.

As these data clearly indicate, interest in other sectors and branches of the Kazakh economy has been minimal. Suffice it to say that the aggregate direct foreign investment in the food-processing industry during nearly six years amounted to 261.2 million dollars (3.5 percent of the total influx of direct foreign investment). Branches producing mass consumer goods absorbed still more modest funds.

An analogous situation is also characteristic of the other countries of Central Asia. In Kyrgyzstan, the great bulk of foreign investment went to develop the Kumtor gold-mining deposits. In Uzbekistan in 1996–97, the oil and gas sector consumed 43–55 percent of all foreign investment (including credits and loans).[6] No less than one-fourth to one-third of the investment in the Uzbek economy was also channeled into gold mining and the development of other mineral resources.

As a result, the specific targets of foreign investment in Central Asia have served to reinforce this region's role as a raw-material supplier for the world economy. For the present, therefore, one cannot seriously count on foreign investment to promote a diversification of local productive structures.

Unbalanced Relations with the World Economy

Thus, all the Central Asian economies find themselves in a critical dependency on the behavior of external factors. That dependency cannot fail to have an impact on economic dynamics in the region.

Table 5.4

Direct Foreign Investment in Kazakhstan: Industry Breakdown

Industrial Branch	Investment	1993–94	1994–95	1996	1997	1998[a]	1993–98[a]
Oil and gas	Millions of dollars	1,519.8	315.1	387.1	718.0	519.8	3,459.8
	Percent of total	78.7	32.0	23.1	34.1	67.2	46.3
Other mining	Millions of dollars	0.0	0.0	118.6	67.7	0.0	186.3
	Percent of total	0.0	0.0	7.1	3.2	0.0	2.5
Energy and electricity	Millions of dollars	0.0	0.0	126.0	128.3	74.6	328.9
	Percent of total	0.0	0.0	7.5	6.1	9.6	4.4
Ferrous metallurgy	Millions of dollars	0.0	102.1	122.9	110.6	0.0	335.6
	Percent of total	0.0	10.4	7.3	5.2	0.0	4.5
Nonferrous metallurgy	Millions of dollars	17.9	344.5	706.5	761.3	41.8	1,872.0
	Percent of total	0.9	35.0	42.2	36.1	5.6	25.1
Food processing	Millions of dollars	86.5	38.5	41.7	70.5	24.0	261.2
	Percent of total	4.5	3.9	2.5	3.3	6.2	3.5

Telecommunications	Millions of dollars	27.8	34.9	20.4	126.4	4.5	214.0
	Percent of total	1.4	3.5	1.2	6.0	0.6	2.9
Mass consumer goods	Millions of dollars	0.0	0.0	56.1	12.1	14.4	82.6
	Percent of total	0.0	0.0	3.4	0.6	1.9	1.1
Financial sector	Millions of dollars	19.0	11.9	3.4	25.9	37.5	97.7
	Percent of total	1.0	1.2	0.2	1.2	4.8	1.3
Other	Millions of dollars	260.1	137.3	91.0	86.2	57.0	631.6
	Percent of Total	13.5	13.9	5.4	4.1	14.7	8.4
Total	Millions of dollars	1,931.1	984.3	1,673.7	2,107.0	773.7	7,469.8

Source: TACIS/European Expertise Service, *Kazakhstan Economic Trends*, November 1998, table 9.7.4.

[a]Data for January–September 1998.

In 1998, after several years of uninterrupted growth, the export earnings of Kazakhstan fell by 17 percent. The same year, the value of exports declined by 11 percent in Kyrgyzstan and 20 percent in Uzbekistan and Tajikistan.[7] For the Central Asian economies and their high export quotas, the negative foreign-trade shock was the main reason economic activity contracted and the rates of growth fell.

Thus, the GDP of Kazakhstan dropped in 1998 by 2.5 percent. If one is to believe official statistics, the growth rate remained positive in both Uzbekistan and Tajikistan. However, in Uzbekistan the dollar value of the per capita GDP (even if calculated on the basis of the overvalued official rate of exchange) fell from 630 dollars in 1997 to 600 dollars in 1998. The dollar value of the GDP also declined in Kyrgyzstan. As a result, the per capita GDP shrank from 385 dollars in 1997 to 345 dollars in 1998.

At the same time, the aggregate value of imports to Kyrgyzstan rose by 15 percent, with a particularly large increase (43 percent) on imports from countries outside the CIS.[8] As a result, Kyrgyzstan's imports amounted to more than 50 percent of the GDP. The economic growth of Kyrgyzstan in 1998 therefore was propelled by imports. An analogous situation obtained in Tajikistan, where an insignificant increase in imports (3 percent) produced a 5.3 percent growth in the GDP. Such a high rate of growth in the GDP is explained by the very low starting point of economic activity.

The phenomenon of economic growth in Uzbekistan does not lend itself to rational explanation. Given export and import quotas amounting to a quarter of the GDP in 1998 (with each quota amounting to more than half the GDP if black-market exchange rates are used), how did Uzbekistan succeed in maintaining a 4.4 percent rate of growth? That growth is all the more puzzling since exports fell by one-fifth and imports by 27.3 percent. In short, the mysterious growth in Uzbekistan is simply inexplicable.

Apart from trade, foreign investment also can function as an instrument for transferring external shocks. In Kyrgyzstan, direct foreign investment decreased by 71 percent, falling from 350.3 million dollars in 1996 to 100.7 million in 1997.[9] In Kazakhstan, after a record investment of 2.107 billion dollars in 1997, the flow of investment in 1998 decreased by half (according to preliminary calculations). In 1999, Kazakhstan expects to attract no more than 1.2 to 1.5 billion dollars in direct foreign investments.[10]

Apart from a negative impact on the level of production (which is triggered by the contraction in export demand and investment activity), foreign shocks also exert an indirect influence on the Central Asian economies. The fall in export incomes and the influx of hard currency (as direct investments) reduce the capacity of monetary authorities to ensure a predictable behavior in the exchange rate for the national currency. As a result, in April 1999 the authorities in Kazakhstan were forced to resort to a large, single devaluation of the tenge. Simultaneously, the soft regime for setting the exchange rate of the national currency within the framework of a previously announced hard-currency corridor was replaced by a free-floating policy. In Kyrgyzstan, the next wave of devaluation came in the fall and winter of 1998—after the Asian crisis and, especially, the Russian financial catastrophe. In September 1998, the nominal rate of the som to the dollar dropped by 8.9 percent; it fell a further 7.5 percent in October, 21.5 percent in November, and 4.4 percent in December. Altogether, in the second half of 1998, the som lost 51.7 percent of its value.[11] In the spring of 1999, a new wave of devaluations began, this time caused by the collapse of the Kazakh tenge.

In Uzbekistan in the spring of 1999, the gap between the official and the free exchange rate of the national currency increased to a factor of 3.1 (compared to 2.4 in 1997 and 2.25 in 1996). This dynamic points to the inevitability of a devaluation of the Uzbek sum in the near future. An analogous fate most likely awaits the Tajik ruble and the Turkmen manat.

Such a strong dependency on foreign factors imposes certain imperative limitations on the quality and character of the economic policy that each country can elect to follow. Certainly one of their principal imperatives should be to achieve and maintain a foreign balance in the national economy.

At the same time, by the end of the 1990s all the Central Asian economies, without exception, are nowhere close to achieving this goal. In this regard, the economies of Kyrgyzstan and Tajikistan are in the most depressing condition (see Table 5.5). In 1995–1998, the foreign debt of Kyrgyzstan increased from 51 to 89 percent of the GDP; the ratio of foreign debt to exports rose from 170 to 247 percent. These data demonstrate that both the relative macroeconomic stability and the resumption of positive rates of growth in Kyrgyzstan were due solely to the accelerated growth of the foreign debt.

The same considerations also apply to Tajikistan, where the foreign debt has reached 80 to 90 percent of the GDP and is more than one and

Table 5.5

Foreign Debt, Trade, and Current Accounts
(as percent of GDP and exports)[a]

Country	Indicator	1996	1997	1998
Kazakhstan	Foreign debt as percent of GDP	20.2	26.5	30.0[b]
	Foreign debt as percent of exports	60.4	78.2	96.8[b]
	Current account as percent of GDP	−3.6	−4.1	−10.5[c]
	Foreign trade account as percent of GDP	−1.9	−2.8	−8.0
Kyrgyzstan	Foreign debt as percent of GDP	66.6	79.5	89.4[b]
	Foreign debt as percent of exports	204.6	200.7	246.6[b]
	Current account as percent of GDP	−24.6	−8.1	−14.0[b]
	Foreign trade account as percent of GDP	−18.3	−6.0	−16.3
Tajikistan	Foreign debt as percent of GDP	66.6	97.9	85[c]
	Foreign debt as percent of exports	90.9	120.7	165[c]
	Current account as percent of GDP	−7.3	−5.4	−15[c]
	Foreign trade account as percent of GDP	9.7	−0.5	−13.1

Turkmenistan			
Foreign debt as percent of GDP	42.4	73.5	
Foreign debt as percent of exports	44.4	237.1	
Current account as percent of GDP	2.3	−32.5	
Foreign trade account as percent of GDP	20.0	−14.0	
Uzbekistan			
Foreign trade as percent of GDP[d]	17.0 (26.8)	18.5 (41.8)	20 (48)[c]
Foreign debt as percent of exports	51.5	62.9	87[c]
Current account as percent of GDP[d]	−7.0 (−11.0)	−3.9 (−8.8)	−3.6 (−8.6)
Foreign trade account as percent of GDP	−0.9	−0.9	1.7

Sources: Calculated from: *Platezhnyi balans Kyrgyzskoi Respubliki*, pp. 12–13; *Biulleten' Natsional' nogo Banka Kyrgyzskoi Respubliki*, no. 12 (1998): 70; TACIS/European Expertise Service, *Kazakhstan Economic Trends*, November 1998, tables 9.6.2 and 9.71; sources cited in Table 5.1; database of the World Bank.

[a]Data on Kazakhstan and Kyrgyzstan are compiled from national statistical sources; data on Tajikistan, Turkmenistan, and Uzbekistan come from the database of the World Bank. It is important to take into account the fact that international statistics substantially underestimate the foreign indebtedness of the post-Soviet states.

[b]January–September 1998.

[c]Estimates by the author.

[d]The Uzbek GDP in parentheses is calculated at the black-market exchange rate.

one-half times the volume of export earnings. Kyrgyzstan and Tajikistan, in terms of their level of development, belong to the ranks of the least developed countries in the world; it is highly probable that their debts will be written off by the donor countries. One cannot exclude the possibility that in the future the international financial organizations will have to help keep the Kyrgyz and (to a lesser degree) the Tajik economies afloat by making additional loans and credits. The third world offers a plethora of examples of how, for decades on end, a country can be propped up by the infusion of such foreign assistance.

At the same time, both Kyrgyzstan and Tajikistan are far from achieving an equilibrium in their trade and payment balances. With a negative balance in current accounts (equal to 15 percent of the GDP), it makes no sense whatsoever to talk about a "stabilization" of the national economy. At this level of disequilibrium in relations with the world economy, any kind of sensible industrial policy, or a predictable policy in the exchange rate, is inherently impossible.

Given that Kyrgyzstan is unable to increase its export earnings in any substantial way, the only realistic method to achieve a better foreign balance is to reduce imports. This can be achieved by a sharp devaluation of the som. In turn, a devaluation will lead to a further reduction in the dollar value of the GDP and the corresponding per capita indicators. However, the more quickly Kyrgyzstan balances its current account and foreign trade, the better. Only then will the economic authorities have an objective basis for reading the economic data and laying the foundations for a long-term economic strategy appropriate to the country's potential.

To be sure, until the fall of 1998 the high exchange rate on the som (which was sustained by increasing foreign indebtedness) provided a powerful stimulus for imports. As a result, the imbalance in the interaction of the Kyrgyz and world economies was constantly increasing.

Tajikistan faces analogous tasks. In recent years, Tajik exports have fluctuated in the range of 600 to 750 million dollars, and the prospects for them to increase, as in Kyrgyzstan, are highly limited. Thus, sooner or later, Tajikistan will have to resort to a substantial reduction in its imports; that, in turn, will trigger a decrease in economic activity and reduction in the per capita indicators for the GDP.

In Turkmenistan, achieving a balance in foreign economic relations lies beyond the realm of economics. Until Turkmenistan renounced barter exchanges of natural gas for Ukrainian goods in 1997, the net in its export-import transactions was a significant positive balance. Nor were creditors troubled about the solvency of this country, which exported in 1990–1993 approximately 50 to 70 billion cubic meters of natural gas per year.[12] With the contraction of gas exports, the indicators for the balance in foreign economic relations sharply deteriorated. However, in the event Turkmenistan resumes its deliveries to Ukraine or expands its exports of natural gas to Iran, these indicators would quickly jump back to their former level.

From the perspective of foreign indebtedness, the Kazakh and Uzbek economies are more balanced than is the case in Kyrgyzstan and Tajikistan. In Kazakhstan, the foreign debt represents about one-third of the GDP; in Uzbekistan, depending upon the exchange rate used, the foreign debt was 20 or 48 percent of the GDP in 1998. Moreover, one must take into account that a major devaluation of the Uzbek som (which is entirely probable) and the devaluation already undertaken against the Kazakh tenge will mean an increase in the proportion of foreign indebtedness vis-à-vis the GDP in these two countries.

The situation with respect to foreign indebtedness appears substantially more urgent if one compares the debt to export earnings. In both Kazakhstan and Uzbekistan, the foreign indebtedness is growing at a markedly faster rate than are exports. Should this tendency persist, both countries in the next few years will encounter definite problems in fulfilling the foreign obligations. This is all the more likely since the calculations included in Table 5.5 are based on aggregate exports. In fact, however, the latter include considerable barter and clearing deliveries. Therefore, the ratio of indebtedness to hard-currency exports in all these countries is 20 to 30 percent higher than the aggregate figures presented in this table. In addition, one must also bear in mind that export deliveries in Kazakhstan in 1998 decreased, and in Uzbekistan the value of exports fell in both 1997 and 1998. Nor can either government really count on writing off this foreign indebtedness.

Less balanced are the relations between the largest Central Asian states and the world economy in terms of current accounts. In Kazakhstan, because of the sharp deterioration in the balance of trade in 1998, the negative balance in current accounts rose to approximately 10 percent of the GDP (compared to 4.1 percent one year earlier). In Uzbekistan, the maximum magnitude of the negative balance of payments (relative to the GDP) came in 1996. Since then, this negative balance has steadily declined. However, if one calculates this indicator using the black-market exchange rate, in 1998 this "hole" in the current account amounted to approximately 9 percent of the GDP.

It is possible to achieve greater balance by reducing imports. Uzbekistan was forced to use measures to repress imports in 1997 and, especially, in 1998. A large-scale devaluation of the Kazakh tenge in April 1999 should also lead to a reduction of imports. In contrast to Uzbekistan, which restricts the flow of imports by administrative measures, Kazakhstan relies on market instruments.

Conclusion

At the dawn of the new century, international conditions appear to be unfavorable for the development of the Central Asian states. For all the diverse fluctuations, the prices of the basic export goods from this region—energy, metals, and cotton—demonstrate a distinct, long-term tendency to fall. Because of the contraction of production in the main export markets of the Central Asian countries (viz., Russia and East Asia), the demand for its goods has fallen accordingly.

Given the fact that raw materials dominate exports, the Central Asian countries themselves cannot control the dynamics of their export earnings. That is to say, they cannot resort to such standard levers as a devaluation of the national currency or a reduction of wages.

However, the most counterproductive reaction to this situation would be a return, even a partial one, to the more autarchical strategy of development. In addition, to judge from all the available data, the instability on world markets will only increase; so far as Central Asia is concerned, this region has no alternative except to submit to the logic of global development. The top-priority goal of national states consists in reducing the negative current account of the balance of payments.

Notes

1. Zh. Alekeshova, "Kon´iunktura vazhneishikh eksportnykh tovarov Respubliki Kazakhstan," *Al' Pari* (Almaty), 1998, no. 3: 90.

2. Natsstatagentstvo, *Sotsial'no-ekonomicheskoe razvitie Respubliki Kazakhstan. Ianvar'-dekabr' 1998* (Almaty, 1999), p. 37; Statkomitet SNG, *Statisticheskii biulleten'. No. 23* (Moscow), December 1998, pp. 37–39.

3. *Statisticheskii biulleten'. No. 23*, pp. 37–39; data from the Ministry of Macroeconomics and Statistics of the Republic of Uzbekistan.

4. *Statisticheskii biulleten'. No.23*, pp. 37–39.

5. International Monetary Fund, *World Economic Outlook. May 1997* (Washington, DC, 1997), p. 107; database of the World Bank.

6. *National Corporation Uzbekneftegaz* (Tashkent, 1998), p. 50, and information obtained from the Ministry of Macroeconomics and Statistics of the Republic of Uzbekistan.

7. *Commonwealth of Independent States in 1998*, p. 37, and data from the Ministry of Macroeconomics and Statistics of the Republic of Uzbekistan.

8. Interstate Statistical Committee, *Commonwealth of Independent States in 1998* (Moscow, 1999), p. 37.

9. "Sotsial'no-ekonomicheskoe razvitie za 1993–1997 gg.," *Bankir* (Bishkek), no. 48 (2 December 1998), p. 5.

10. *Panorama* (Almaty), no. 42 (18 December 1998), p. 2.

11. Calculated from: "Sotsial'no-ekonomicheskoe polozhenie Kirgizskoi Respubliki v ianvare-dekabre 1998," *Bankir*, no. 2 (27 January 1999), p. 4.

12. K. Dittman, H. Engerer, and C. Hirschhausen, "Much Ado About . . . Little?" *Kazakhstan Economic Trends*, November 1998, p. 36.

6

Kazakhstan and Uzbekistan: The Economic Consequences of Membership in the World Trade Organization

Eskender Trushin and Eshref Trushin

The states of Central Asia occupy different positions with respect to joining the World Trade Organization (WTO). Kyrgyzstan became a member at the end of 1998. Turkmenistan and Tajikistan, for the present, have not applied to enter and do not even have the status of observer in this organization. In the course of the last few years, both Kazakhstan and Uzbekistan have conducted a dialogue about the terms upon which they might become members.

A working group to accept Kazakhstan into the WTO was organized in February 1996 and held two meetings in 1997 and 1998. During this period, Kazakhstan made considerable progress in the negotiations and achieved a significant liberalization of its foreign trade. However, there are still definite discrepancies between its Agreement on WTO and the economic policy of Kazakhstan. The most important include: (1) the customs system; (2) the system of standardization; (3) lack of transparency of laws and shortcomings in applying legislation; and (4) rights of intellectual property.

The working group for accepting Uzbekistan into the WTO was established in December 1994. In September 1998, the government of that country sent the WTO a "Memorandum on the Foreign Trade Regime." The export-import rules of Uzbekistan do not comply with the requirements of the WTO. Although the government of Uzbekistan continues to carry out reforms in its trade policy, the discrepancies between its policies and WTO requirements remain significant. Among other things, they include: (1) a substantial share of trade belongs to the government (for cotton, metals, and other goods); (2) the state sets many key prices (e.g., cotton, grain, and energy resources); (3) import contracts must be "registered," a requirement that can be used to raise nontariff barriers to imports; (4) hard currency regulation—i.e., a bureaucratic distribution of foreign currency and limits on the convertibility of the national currency; (5) the existence of substantial state budgetary subsidies in the economy, which were estimated by the EBRD in 1997 at 3.2 percent of the GDP; (6) a list of products that are banned from export; (7) preferential tax treatment for national exporters of certain goods; and (8) shortcomings in the legislation and its application with respect to intellectual property.

These obstacles notwithstanding, there are several long-term factors that make it essential for Kazakhstan and Uzbekistan to join the WTO.

First, the growth of exports from the manufacturing branch can encounter the problem of trade barriers in other countries. If members of the WTO (especially the developed countries) raise nontariff barriers against non-WTO members, this can cause serious problems in the future trade of Kazakhstan and Uzbekistan. This is especially true for agricultural products, leather, textiles, chemicals, and metals. At the present time, the countries of Central Asia (except Kyrgyzstan), like many other countries with a transition economy, continue to be classified as having "nonmarket economies" and fall under the sway of individual rules that are often established, in an arbitrary fashion, by the importer states.[1] As long as Kazakhstan and Uzbekistan export raw materials, other countries are not interested in trade barriers, since these would only increase their own costs and reduce the competitiveness of domestic producers (especially if these countries lack their own sources of these raw materials). However, this situation can change if Kazakhstan and Uzbekistan increase the share of exports from the manufacturing branch. In these circumstances, their foreign trade interests are best defended by membership in the World Trade Organization (WTO). Trade partners who belong to the WTO are limited by contractual obligations against taking measures to limit exports from each other. The threat of antidumping measures (which, incidentally, have already been applied by a number of developed countries against Uzbek and Kazakh imports) is the most important aspect. Membership in the WTO affords some protection, even if it is not perfect. States that do not belong to the WTO are clearly in a much worse position if they do not have significant countermeasures at their disposal (and neither Kazakhstan nor Uzbekistan has these). Antidumping and other defensive measures applied to countries with a nonmarket economy are more severe and less transparent than measures against countries with a market economy. Upon becoming members of the WTO, Kazakhstan and Uzbekistan would shed the stigma of having "nonmarket economies" and could thereby eliminate any discriminatory practices against them.

Second, membership in the WTO will raise and strengthen their reputations as reliable trading partners. Thus, the sooner they become members of the WTO, the sooner they will enjoy the benefits of greater confidence on the part of foreign investors.

Third, exports from Kazakhstan and Uzbekistan will be guaranteed access to the markets of other WTO member states. The latter countries, which either denied most-favored nation (MFN) status to Kazakhstan and Uzbekistan, or granted this status provisionally (with a mandatory annual review), will have to grant this status on a permanent basis. That is, there will be no conditions and no need to sign numerous bilateral agreements.

Fourth, as a result of the reduction in transaction costs and the increase in incentives for national exporters in Kazakhstan and Uzbekistan, there will be an increase in the flow of investment resources to domestic producers. This capital will go to those enterprises that have the strongest actual and potential comparative advantages and that will help to make the utilization of national resources more efficient. For Kazakhstan and Uzbekistan, this means that the turnover of international trade will increase. The favorable preconditions for the growth of exports will create conditions to accelerate economic growth.

Fifth, once Kazakhstan and Uzbekistan join the WTO, they will be able to conduct consultations with all the members of this organization on the creation of a legal mechanism that would regulate 90 percent of the total volume of world trade. This will help Kazakhstan and Uzbekistan to find potential partners and new markets to sell domestic goods. Both countries will gain access to operational international commercial information; to the requisite information regarding foreign economic policies and laws; and to intentions of governments from the WTO member states. All this will enable Kazakhstan and Uzbekistan to formulate an effective trade and economic policy. They can then ensure greater flexibility in trade and increase their potential capacity to prevent and ameliorate external shocks.

Sixth, membership will help reduce the role of the shadow economy and corruption in the two countries. This positive gain will result from a dismantling of trade barriers as well as the simplification and guarantee of transparency of procedures in export-import transactions. At the present time, according to expert estimates, the share of the shadow economy in these countries (not including the criminal economy) constitutes at least one-third of the GDP.

Seventh, upon entering the WTO, Kazakhstan and Uzbekistan will receive the guaranteed freedom of transit across the territory of any other member of the WTO. This is especially important for these landlocked states. This provision (Article V of the WTO rules) is especially important for Uzbekistan in its relations with the surrounding countries of Asia and Europe, which now have an oligopoly on transit services. Of these countries, Russia and China are particularly important. If, as expected, these two countries become members of WTO, the situation for Uzbekistan will improve significantly.

Eighth, participation in the WTO will not only ensure legal protection for exports, but also provide an incentive to raise the competitiveness of the economy as a whole and to undertake fundamental structural reform. The process of joining the WTO offers a unique opportunity for the presidents of Uzbekistan and Kazakhstan to use this process as political "cover" in order to undertake a basic transformation of the economy. Such changes at the present time have encountered covert resistance from influential clan groups and opponents of reform. It is also important to consolidate the results of reform in law in order to prevent any retreats in the future.

Ninth, by joining the WTO, Uzbekistan and Kazakhstan can ensure the removal of the existing barriers and problems to the economic integration of Kyrgyzstan, Uzbekistan, and Kazakhstan. In particular, it will enable them to harmonize differing state regulations (e.g., for customs, tariffs, taxes, and hard currency), to ensure free cargo transit, and to resolve various other differences.

Upon entry into the WTO, the export-oriented branches will profit from the liberalization of foreign trade, since they will have advantages in international trade. In Kazakhstan, this concerns above all the extractive sector (oil as well as ferrous and nonferrous metals). In Uzbekistan, this primarily concerns branches of agriculture (cotton, silk, fruits, and vegetables) as well as the extractive industries.

However, in Kazakhstan the main export sector for the extraction of mineral resources is already almost completely privatized. It has been divided up among foreign transnational corporations, which have much experience and adequate knowledge of world markets. Therefore, the export of mineral resources from Kazakhstan does not particularly need preferential treatment on the part of developed countries. Moreover, Kazakhstan has already moved significantly forward in its preparation for membership in the WTO; to a significant degree, it has already deregulated its foreign trade. Thus, in the near future, Kazakhstan will apparently join the WTO.[2] It will probably accomplish this sooner than Uzbekistan. Consequently, in the short-term perspective, Kazakhstan is not likely to experience a major effect from the increase of exports, since its reserves for expanding the raw-material exports in the short term are nearly exhausted.[3] Moreover, the export of mineral resources will have a direct impact on the incomes of only 3 to 4 percent of the population. At the same time, the cost of labor in Kazakhstan is higher than in Uzbekistan and other countries of Central Asia. Therefore, one should not expect a significant influx of foreign investment in Kazakhstan to develop labor-intensive branches of production. However, Kazakhstan has at its disposal potentially significant comparative advantages for the development of metallurgy and metalworking as well as the chemical and petrochemical industries.

In Uzbekistan, by contrast, in the short- and middle-range perspective, the advantages of joining the WTO and liberalizing foreign trade are significant. That is because Uzbekistan did not sell off the main export sector to foreign enterprises and retained all profits for the republic. Moreover, the majority of the population will obtain the advantages from liberalizing the agrarian sector.

Uzbekistan also has the opportunity to receive significant long-term advantages from joining the WTO. These advantages result from the fact that after progress in negotiations on agriculture, textiles, and garments within the framework of WTO in the first years of the next century, the agro-industrial complex of Uzbekistan will receive additional opportunities to gain advantages from the export of agricultural products, food processing, and light industry, but also from the development of allied branches of industry.

Common to both Kazakhstan and Uzbekistan will be the creation of favorable conditions to increase the volumes of export and to sustain stable economic growth.

It is still not precisely known how the reform program required for WTO membership will affect Uzbekistan and Kazakhstan. That is because the specific obligations and terms of membership have not yet become known. At this point, it is only possible to discuss the potential consequences that membership, and the mandatory reforms, might have for these two states.

The main economic goal of the governments of Uzbekistan and Kazakhstan is a high, stable rate of real economic growth, and to accomplish this on the basis of structural changes. The specific targets include the stabilization of domestic prices, an increase in exports, improvements in the infrastructure, the creation of new jobs, the elimination of poverty, a reduction of the inequality in incomes, and steps to ensure development that is ecologically safe for the environment. Here the authors will attempt to judge whether the impending changes and reforms required for WTO membership actually correspond to the long-range goals of these two governments for social and economic development in their respective countries.

Structural Improvements and Economic Growth

The economic reforms that the WTO requires before it can accept Kazakhstan and Uzbekistan will contribute to progressive structural changes, economic growth, and a higher standard of living for the population. The reforms will accomplish these changes in two principal ways.

First, they will stimulate an influx of resources to those branches and enterprises that have the greatest current and potential comparative advantages in international trade. This will lead to the formation of an economic structure that can ensure the maximum income by exploiting the relative advantages of specialization in the these two countries.

Second, the reforms will reduce the likelihood of mistakes and uncertainties in conducting economic reform and complying with the demands for the progressive trade regime. Since WTO conditions have been accepted through international agreements, this assurance will raise the confidence of foreign investors in the economies of both countries. By extension, this will also increase the rate at which new technologies, knowledge, and skills of business organization flow into the two countries.

The impending reforms will allow Kazakhstan and Uzbekistan to embark on an export-oriented path of industrialization and development. It will enable them to adapt the structure of their countries so as to receive the maximum benefit from the new opportunities that WTO membership can offer.

The more that Uzbekistan and Kazakhstan improve the economic incentives for producers and consumers, and the more they provide a transparent and stable environment, then so much the faster will be their rate of economic growth (all other things being equal). In particular, the less that the two countries squander scarce resources to sustain noncompetitive import-substitution branches, the less that they discriminate against branches with current and potential competitive advantages, the greater will be their rate of economic growth. After the implementation of reform, economic resources will be allocated primarily in accordance with the dynamic of comparative advantages and specialization in the two countries.

Security of Food Supplies

It bears pointing out that the GATT agreement did not address the question of agriculture. Only in the Uruguay Round in 1994 were these issues put on the agenda and made part of the agreements within the framework of the WTO.

The agreement on agriculture at the Uruguay Round provides for a reduction in export subsidies on foodstuffs produced by the developed countries. This change could lead to a rise in the world prices on food products in the short term.[4] As a result, one can conclude that those countries of Central Asia that currently depend upon foreign foodstuffs to a significant degree will suffer negative consequences—a higher cost for food imports. Indeed, the problem of fluctuations in the price of foodstuffs on the international market is one of the principal reasons these countries regard security in food supplies a vital necessity and why they have been encouraged to increase the domestic production of grain. Table 6.1 shows the degree to which the individual countries of Central Asia depend on the import of foodstuffs.

As the data in this table demonstrate, in most cases the food products comprise about one-fifth of the total volume of imported goods. The table also shows that virtually all the countries of Central Asia (with the exception of Kazakhstan) are net importers of food products; the annual

Table 6.1

Dependence of Central Asia on Imported Foodstuffs

Country	Imported foodstuffs (as percent of total imported commodities)	Net import of food products (import minus export, as percent of total volume of imports)
Kazakhstan[a]	11.3	0.4
Kyrgyzstan[b]	21.6	7.4
Turkmenistan[a]	21.0	20.9
Uzbekistan[a]	23.2	19.3
Average[c]	19.3	12.0

Source: Calculated from the database of the World Bank.
[a]Averages for 1995–1997.
[b]Averages for 1995–1996.
[c]Unweighted.

net import of foodstuffs constitutes an average of 12 percent of total imports in the countries of Central Asia. Thus, an increase in the world prices on food products by 1 or 2 percent will raise the costs of imports to the countries of Central Asia by less than 0.24 percent. This amount is insignificant when compared with the usual annual fluctuation of world prices on food and can be offset by the oscillating prices on other items in the balance of payments. More important, realization of the Agreement on Agriculture from the Uruguay Round includes only a very moderate liberalization of agriculture in developed countries. As a result, it will not have a significant impact in reducing the fluctuations of world prices on food products in the next few years.

However, with the liberalization of trade policy and the intensification of agrarian reforms, Uzbekistan and the other countries of Central Asia can rather quickly change from net importers of food products into net exporters. This possibility takes into account the significant potential for an increase in the yields and efficiency of agriculture. It also recognizes the opportunities, in the middle- or long-range perspective, to increase access to the food markets of developed and developing countries. In the short term, if Uzbekistan abolishes export taxes on cotton and other forms of economic discrimination against private farmers (if the cotton production is transferred to farmers), it can raise substantially the yields, reduce the land area devoted to cotton cultivation, expand the area sown to food products, and accordingly increase substantially the production of foodstuffs. In general, if the government of Uzbekistan (under the appropriate regulation) gives the private sector the freedom to choose the structure of crop cultivation and to engage in the mass production of food, not only on private plots but also on kolkhoz land, this will significantly strengthen the country's security with respect to food products.

In other words, to obtain the advantages created by the Uruguay agreement and the future rounds of negotiations within the framework of the WTO, the countries of Central Asia need to accelerate structural reform in the economy. For that very reason, the reform of trade policy will enable Uzbekistan and the other Central Asian countries to increase the volume of production in agriculture. All things being equal, the security of food supplies in these countries will definitely improve.

Of course, certain food products (such as wheat and rice) could face stiffer competition from imports. However, the supply of food products through imports does not, in itself, necessarily reduce the security of provisioning if one considers the fact that the Central Asian states can create grain reserves to deal with any import problems. They are currently building up such reserves and can use them both to supply consumers and to provide farmers with seed grain.

The Creation of Jobs and Distribution of Income

It is clear that a certain part of those employed in the most protected branches of industry (for example, oil refining, the manufacture of motor vehicles, and household electronics in Uzbekistan) could lose their jobs once protectionist barriers are dismantled and the imports in these sectors increase. At the same time, branches that have potential competitive advantages will develop more quickly since they will become more profitable. This applies especially to agriculture and the associated branches of manufacturing industry as well as many extractive branches of the economy. If the structure of domestic prices in these countries is corrected, they will move still closer to world levels. That in turn will bring some redistribution of incomes among different branches of the economy and different groups of the population.

First, in Kazakhstan and especially in Uzbekistan, additional jobs will be created not only in rural areas, but also in cities. It is quite possible that the growth of these new jobs will proceed at a somewhat faster rate than had been the case prior to these countries joining the WTO. This growth in employment could result from the strong development in those branches of industry linked to the delivery of resources for agriculture and the processing of agricultural products (food processing, leather and shoes, chemicals, and certain branches of light industry).

Second, a new impulse for the creation of jobs in these countries will come from accelerated development in the extractive branches of industry and in the branches of primary processing of mineral resources (ferrous and nonferrous metallurgy, fuel, chemical, and petrochemical industries). This growth is all the more likely because direct foreign investment will increase once these two countries become WTO members.

Third, with the growth of incomes and the increased demand (on the part of agriculture, the extractive industries, and the associated branches of manufacturing), the sphere of producer and consumer services will also exhibit a dynamic pace of development.

One can expect that the share of agriculture and the extractive industries in the GDP will initially show some increase, but thereafter a gradual decrease. That turnaround will naturally ensue as incomes are diverted from the primary branches to the manufacturing and service spheres.

As a result of the liberalization of foreign trade, wages, and profits in the export branches will also increase. Consumer prices will decline on the domestic market as a result of the lower price of imports and the reduction in the costs of domestic production.

State Budget Revenues

There is a widespread—and mistaken—view that the liberalization of trade will automatically reduce revenues to the state budget. Such a decline is supposed to ensue from the reduction in export duties and import tariffs.

First, the lowering of export and import duties, on the contrary, will help to expand the trade turnover. It is well known that the tax rates (overt and hidden) on exports and imports to Uzbekistan, Kazakhstan, and the other countries of Central Asia (with the exception of Kyrgyzstan) are so high that once these have been reduced, the volume of export-import transactions will increase. Hence the revenues of the state budgets in Central Asia in fact could become larger, despite the lowering of per unit duty rates on commodities.

Second, the reduction of official duties on import-export operations will diminish the incentives to use unofficial channels for the distribution and sale of goods. As a result, more goods will be shifted from the channels of the shadow economy into official trade channels. As a result, the tax levies and incomes for the state budgets in these countries will increase.

Third, at the present time, the countries of Central Asia (except Kyrgyzstan) have retained a plethora of restrictions on both exports and imports in the form of "nontariff" barriers. As a result of such restrictions, these countries have suffered significant damages, which are known as "losses from dead cargoes." That is to say, this is an absolute loss of net income for all of society, since no one—neither the state, nor entrepreneurs, nor consumers, nor representatives of the black market—received these earnings. The transformation of nontariff restriction into tariffs, in fact, will increase the revenues of state budgets in Central Asia. That is especially true when one considers the reduced corruption in the state apparatus as a result of the elimination of nontariff barriers.

As a whole, the transformation of nontariff barriers into tariffs and the reduction in the high level of export and import duties can significantly increase the revenues of the state budgets in Uzbekistan and Kazakhstan. A simplification of this structure and the standardization of the tariff levels will reduce administrative costs and discourage corruption at customs. It will also lower the general level of domestic prices and, thereby, cut inflation and generally make the utilization of economic resources more efficient. That higher efficiency will extend both to import-substitution and to export-oriented sectors of the economy.

Nevertheless, it should be noted that the liberalization of cotton prices in Uzbekistan will entail certain unfavorable consequences for the state budget. Namely, in the short term the budget will forfeit a significant income from the natural "time gap": that is, between the time when it adopts the reform measures in trade policy in agriculture, and the time when it reaps the full gains from these changes. To be sure, it is impossible to avoid reducing budgetary expenditures at least during the two to three years of price reforms. At the same time, the growth in the income of the rural inhabitants (who constitute 60 percent of the population in Uzbekistan) will lead to a reduction in those items of expenditure in the state budget devoted to social needs. In all likelihood, the budget revenues will be restored through a moderate direct tax on agriculture after two to four years. That will be feasible because of the increased volumes of agricultural production.

Nevertheless, Uzbekistan could anticipate a potential increase in its budget deficit, which of course is fraught with a variety of attendant negative consequences (e.g., contraction in public investment and a higher inflation rate). A budget shock is inevitable because the liberalization of prices on agricultural goods must be carried out in one decisive step, not gradually, if it is to elicit the maximum possible response from producers. Nevertheless, it is preferable that the budgetary allocations for agriculture *not* be reduced; likewise, it is desirable that the government continue to give a preferential tax treatment to agricultural enterprises. For these goals, it is perhaps necessary to establish a stabilization fund, created with the assistance of loans from the World Bank and other international organizations. Such resources would be specifically allocated and stipulated for resolving the problem of stabilization during the transition period. According to preliminary estimates, this fund will require approximately 170 million American dollars per year.[5]

The Impact of WTO Membership on Industrialization

There is a fear that certain developments, in the short term, could have a negative impact on the development of import-substitution industries as well as the R&D branches of industry in Uzbekistan and Kazakhstan. The developments that appear to pose the principal threat are threefold: (a) the reduction of tariff protection; (b) the creation of equal conditions for the sale of domestic and imported goods on domestic markets; and (c) the abolition of state subsidies and other privileges given to domestic enterprises. The development of assembly production (e.g., the motor vehicle and household electronic plants in Uzbekistan) is becoming increasingly problematic because of the growing competition on domestic markets. However, in our view, one cannot say categorically that entry into the WTO will necessarily increase the difficulties of industrialization.

In reality, as a result of the rapid liberalization of imports, the existing import-substitution branches encountered stiff competition from the imports of motor vehicles and electronic goods. However, one should keep in mind the fact that the reduction of import tariffs in Uzbekistan and Kazakhstan is bilateral: in exchange, the trade partners in the WTO must also lower their barriers on imports from Uzbekistan and Kazakhstan. As a result, the latter two countries will gain an additional advantage. This advantage for export-oriented producers can be significantly greater than the losses incurred by the domestic import-substitution producers. Thus, as a result of the liberalization of trade in Uzbekistan and Kazakhstan, the long-term perspective envisions a net profit because of the transition to an export-oriented industrialization. Moreover, the majority of the population in Uzbekistan, in the short term, could profit from the liberalization of foreign trade. That is because of the dominance of agriculture, which, along with related branches and the service sphere, has obvious comparative advantages.

Moreover, with the rapid development of agriculture, the extractive industries, and associated branches of industry and service branches, Uzbekistan and Kazakhstan could substantially increase the purchasing power of their populations. Under these conditions, the domestic import-substitution enterprises will nonetheless have a chance for survival and development if the consumer preferences of the Uzbek and Kazakh populations are on the side of domestic producers. In other words, if the population of these countries will buy mainly domestic goods, this will create conditions favorable for the successful development of import-substitution branches of machine-building and the chemical industry.

World practice, in particular the experience of successful industrial policy among the countries of East Asia,[6] shows that an export-oriented policy can resolve the structural contradiction between the need for a rapid development of manufacturing and, simultaneously, the retention of incomes from primary sectors. An export-oriented policy contributes to the dynamic transfer of resources from sectors with relatively low productivity (such as the primary sector) to sectors with higher productivity (manufacturing branches). Moreover, this can be done without reducing the returns on investment in the primary sectors.

To ensure long-term success, it is essential to adapt the industrial policy to new conditions. The government and private sector in the countries of Central Asia must direct all their actions toward the development of export-oriented industrialization. Above all, they must do this on the basis of the manufacturing branch. In this respect, they should give special attention to training the workforce and to organizing the "production of capital goods" on a competitive basis within the countries of Central Asia. The limited amount of investment resources dictates the need to choose strategic branches or so-called "growth points," which should be the focus of labor and material resources. The development of these strategic branches will give an impulse to the whole economy and make it possible to find a stable place in the world market for manufactured goods.

In the case of Uzbekistan, the greatest potential in the short- and middle-term perspective is to be found in the following branches of industry:

- Labor and resource-intensive branches of manufacturing that can use the domestic material resources and that have sufficient qualified labor resources (which are relatively inexpensive). These include textiles, metal fabrication, chemicals (especially oil and gas, fertilizers, and ceramics), and food processing.
- Various R&D branches that require a specific design for each investment project. These include the following branches: biochemicals (pharmaceuticals, especially those using domestic raw materials); the production of various goods of industrial electronics that have significant scientific and productive potential (photo and solar elements, special lighting instruments, etc.); commercial applications of nuclear physics; a number of areas of medical research.

The stable development of primary branches (agriculture, energy, and mining) provides the best foundation for solid development in both the secondary (manufacturing and construction) and tertiary (service) branches of the national economies of all the countries of Central Asia. In this regard, special attention should be given to agriculture, since this sector employs the larger number of people in all the countries of the region (except Kazakhstan).

These considerations also support the view that, in the initial stage, fundamental agrarian reform must serve as the basis for rapid and stable growth in the region. Reform in this sector can ensure a substantial increase in productivity, which, in turn, can have a strong impact on the successful development of both manufacturing and the general macroeconomic situation. There are several reasons why this is so. First, cotton, as the main product of agriculture in this region, can ensure a significant volume of hard currency for macroeconomic stabilization and the import of foreign capital goods. Second, agricultural development can guarantee a supply of cheaper food products for cities and therefore further reduce the cost of labor. Third, the reforms can liberate a substantial share of the rural population, thereby providing additional, cheap labor for rapid industrialization. Finally, the growth of savings among the rural population is an indispensable precondition for the development of domestic private investment, including the banking sector and the sphere of financial services.

It would be unduly optimistic to hope that, in the short term, the industrial sector will provide sufficient export earnings to cover the costs of importing foodstuffs into the countries of Central Asia. In Uzbekistan, the diversion of resources from agriculture to finance the costly import-substitution projects in industry cannot ensure steady economic growth. It might be possible for such redistribution to occur in the event of a low price elasticity for the supply of agricultural products. For example, despite the rather low state procurement prices on cotton and grain in Uzbekistan, the yield of these crops is almost constant. However, this low yield has not been increasing. It is necessary to take into account the potential opportunity losses in the volume of production that can be ascribed to this system of prices and distribution of incomes.

As world practice has demonstrated, an increase in the price of agricultural products naturally leads to an increase in the volume of production. Such is the case if there is a sufficiently developed infrastructure, that is, good roads, supplies of water irrigation, and other essential services (as in the countries of Central Asia). The production of cotton and grain in Uzbekistan can increase, at a minimum, by 1.2 to 1.5-fold, if the domestic procurement prices are raised by 100 percent (that is, to 80–90 percent of world price levels). According to the estimates of experts,[7] an increase in the agricultural yield can be achieved through higher labor intensity of the peasants (by giving them a material incentive for increasing harvests). This increase can be achieved without taking any capital-intensive measures—for example, by more meticulous care of the plants and by providing timely and high-quality performance of the whole complex of measures involved in production. In other words, it can be done without taking into account the savings achieved by eliminating losses incurred during storage or transportation.

The countries of Central Asia have certain comparative advantages in light industry. These include the following factors:

- the workforce here is skilled, low-paid, and relatively abundant;
- the region's main raw material is cotton, which at the present time is not widely utilized within the countries of Central Asia;
- the chemical industry is relatively well developed and has enormous reserves of hydrocarbon raw materials for the production of synthetic fibers;
- the necessary infrastructure and factories, although with somewhat outdated machinery and equipment, already exist.

The development of textile production in Uzbekistan and other countries of Central Asia will also be aided by a number of other factors.

These include the growth in the world consumption of textiles, the tendency to shift the world textile production closer to the source of the raw materials, and also the creation of favorable conditions for foreign investors once the countries of Central Asia become members of the WTO.

The world textile markets have very stiff competition and a multitude of protectionist barriers (in both developed and developing countries) that are not easily overcome. Some developing countries with relatively extensive experience in the production of textiles (China, Pakistan, India, Indonesia, and the like) have literally flooded the world market with cheap but high-quality products. In addition, the Asian financial crisis of 1997 came amidst a sharp decline of world prices on many goods, including textiles. This tendency will not change in the next few years.

Nevertheless, given the renewal of negotiations on textiles and clothing in 2005 (within the framework of the WTO), and given the significant potential of light industry and the prospects of possible impulses for economic growth in the countries of Central Asia, it is absolutely essential to give special attention to the production of textiles for export. And not only textiles. As Rasulev has correctly pointed out,[8] the weakest link in the countries of Central Asia is the presence of a large number of lines of production with a partial technological cycle. Precisely these areas offer enormous opportunities for an expansion of export potential. For example, upon the application of the appropriate technologies, it is possible to obtain from the natural gas currently being produced a broad assortment of polymers, nitrolaquer acids, and other materials that enjoy a high demand. In addition, it suffices here to make a relatively small investment, to apply new technologies, and to complete the technological cycle to obtain a significant effect.

At the present time, light industry in the countries of Central Asia is in difficult straits. For example, according to data assembled by the Committee on the Affairs of Insolvent Enterprises (a subdivision of the State Property Committee of Uzbekistan), at the beginning of 1998 the association "Uzbeklegprom" (Uzbek Light Industry) included 143 enterprises; of this total, no fewer than 124 showed signs of economic difficulties. Moreover, the rapid increase in domestic prices on raw cotton (as a result of the liberalization of trade policy in Uzbekistan) can undermine Uzbek light industry, since cotton had been the principal raw material. Consequently, before the deregulation of prices on raw cotton, a fundamental restructuring and privatization should be carried out in light industry. This restructuring requires state support as well as the concentration and mobilization of all resources, for these branches of industry can be defined as strategically important for the initial development. In any case, the domestic price on cotton fibers should be lower than the world price by an amount sufficient to cover its transportation and other costs for delivery abroad. This is an important factor in ensuring the competitiveness of national producers of textiles.

The textile industry has played a leading role in the industrialization of many countries.[9] There are several reasons. First, this branch requires relatively small amounts of start-up capital and also provides a quick return on investment; these characteristics thus make it easy to initiate production in this branch. Moreover, this branch is very labor-intensive, a characteristic that makes it appropriate for creating a mass of new jobs quickly. Second, the textile industry begins with the usual weaving of cloth, which does not require any advanced technologies. The materials and technologies can also be very easily adapted to other lines of production that use cotton and synthetic fibers. For example, the textile industry on Taiwan has developed more quickly than the manufacturing branch as a whole.[10]

The Problem of Transportation

A substantial impediment to the opportunities for an export-oriented development in the countries of Central Asia is their remoteness from the main trading partners and their lack of direct access to the world's oceans. Moreover, 1994–96 witnessed a significant increase in the charges for railway cargo, which increases the costs of exporting goods. That is all the more important in Central Asia, which ships up to 90 percent of its freight by rail.[11] For the countries of this region, the reduction of international freight charges is a question of the greatest importance. For example, the average cost of delivering a 20-foot container weighing 10 tons from Tashkent to Western Europe is approximately 3,000 to 4,000 dollars. The cost of shipping such a container from Tashkent to Milan is 3,000 dollars (via Chop, but 4,000 dollars via Riga); from Tashkent to Paris the cost is 3,100 dollars (via Brest, but 3,800 dollars via Riga). The cost of shipping the same container is 2,000 dollars to Riga or Brest, and 2,300 dollars to the Iranian port of Bandar-Abbas. It costs 3,500 dollars to ship a fifty-ton railway car to Brest or Riga.[12] The high rates of international shipping increase significantly the costs of production and, therefore, reduce the competitiveness of domestic goods.

Thus, for all of Central Asia, the high cost of transportation constitutes one of the key problems, and it severely weakens the capacity of domestic goods to compete on world markets. As has been noted earlier,[13] an inadequately developed infrastructure begins to impede and sometimes simply to suppress the development of commercial ties, thereby dimming the prospects for achieving general economic growth. In essence, this problem creates an additional transportation tax on all export-import transactions and undercuts the incentives for production.

The communications problem once more underscores the acuteness of the problem of technological development in Central Asia. That is precisely because R&D goods have the highest value per unit of price and size, and therefore are the cheapest from the perspective of shipping costs. This is yet another argument in favor of the need to adopt a strategic approach to development and the export of products from technology-intensive lines of production.

In the long-term perspective, stable economic growth is impossible without a diversification of exports, whereby the proportion of raw materials would decrease and the share of finished goods would increase. World market conditions will promote such tendencies: the share of agricultural products and raw materials in world trade turnover is declining, and indeed it will continue to do so in the foreseeable future. Moreover, the prices on raw materials are more volatile than those on manufactured goods. Uzbekistan, Kazakhstan, and the other developing countries have encountered a declining demand for raw-material exports and, therefore, have had to cope with changes in the terms of trade. There are good grounds to assume that the price fluctuations for raw-material commodities on average are significantly greater than the prices for goods from the manufacturing branch. Changes in the world prices on raw materials can have a multiplier effect on the entire macroeconomic situation of developing countries that export such goods.

Still another argument in favor of joining the WTO is the possibility of attracting more foreign investment, which can then be used to create new production capacities and to promote technological progress. To be sure, one must bear in mind the growing competition around the world for foreign investment and the consequences of the world financial crisis. Because of these factors, one cannot count on a very large influx of such investments in the countries of Central Asia. However, the countries of Central Asia can create conditions to obtain the maximum benefit from those foreign investments that do come to the region. For this, it is above all necessary to understand that foreign investment is oriented toward import-substitution production on the domestic markets of individual countries in Central Asia. That is why these investments cannot in principle be very substantial, since these markets are too small to sustain the large-scale production of many industrial products. As a result, it is possible to attract large-scale capital investments here, but only for the export-oriented industries. To expand these exports, however, it is necessary to liberalize foreign trade and join the WTO.

One must also take into account the fact that, as a rule, foreign investment does not come to countries with an inadequate development of national private enterprises. In developed states and in the majority of successfully developing countries, it is precisely the export-oriented development (above all, by domestic private firms) that ensures economic growth, which in turn can attract foreign investors. The WTO agreement requires that member countries not discriminate against foreign investors; in other words, they must establish terms that are no worse for foreign investors than for domestic enterprises. In fact, however, many countries of Central Asia grant foreign investors a more advantageous regime than that established for domestic investors. One of the challenges for the governments of Central Asia is to build economic growth on domestic (above all private) investment. For this to happen, it is essential that these states give domestic investors the same favorable conditions already granted to foreign investors. Strange as that might sound, this policy will also promote an increase in foreign investment.

Reduced Opportunities for Government Economic Management

The process of deregulation restricts the choice of instruments that the governments of Kazakhstan and Uzbekistan can employ for conducting economic policy. The rules of the World Trade Organization foresee limits on the use of import tariffs and licenses, the elimination of export subsidies and licenses, a ban on the uncompensated copying of foreign technology, the disestablishment of barriers for investment activity, and so forth. The loss of autonomy, however, is not only due to the fact that Kazakhstan and Uzbekistan assume certain obligations on the basis of agreements: market forces are also at play. Thus, openness of trade will reduce the capacity of Uzbekistan and Kazakhstan to plan such indicators as the volume of production, or the level of employment and inflation. At the present time, it has already become impossible to expand production in isolation from foreign demand or to avoid the import of inflation from countries that are trading partners.

However, one must take into account the fact that the governments of Kazakhstan and Uzbekistan do not always conduct the optimal economic policy. That is especially evident if one judges the final results: disproportions in the economies are still enormous, many reforms are progressing at a snail's pace (and sometimes implemented with clear mistakes), and the quality of macroeconomic regulation and management of the economy leaves much to be desired. Therefore, the liberalization of the real production sectors and the deregulation of foreign trade by entering the WTO will signify the elimination of the main macroeconomic disproportions and a reduction in the negative consequences of possible errors (from voluntarism in economic management). This will all mean a higher efficiency in the economy as a whole.

Conclusions

This article has argued that liberalization in the real production sector and in foreign trade (to comply with the letter and the spirit of the WTO) corresponds well with the final goals that the governments of Uzbekistan and Kazakhstan have set for the social and economic development of their countries.

Uzbekistan and Kazakhstan now must face the following challenge: can the governments sacrifice the narrow commercial interests of certain clan factions or false state interests in sustaining inefficient import substitution in order to satisfy the real interests of the majority of the people? The question is to what degree the governments of Uzbekistan and Kazakhstan, with the assistance of exporters who derive benefits from membership in the WTO, can persuade those who fear losing their income as a result of greater openness. It is also a question of how clearly the governments of Uzbekistan and Kazakhstan understand their long-term strategic trade interests, and whether they still wish to become integrated into the world economy. They must also decide whether they are prepared to become aggressive exporters, within open and export-oriented economies, and whether they wish to find an opportunity to expand their access to the markets of other countries. In addition, they must determine whether they are ready to seek and define their interests within the framework of the agenda of the WTO.

As is well known, participation in the WTO not only gives rights, but also imposes certain obligations.[14] Thus Kazakstan and Uzbekistan are required to convert their nontariff barriers to imports into tariffs and to reduce the general level of customs duties. They are also obliged to deregulate trade services, to strengthen and enforce laws on the rights of intellectual property, to refrain from subsidizing exports, to limit and reduce subsidies to enterprises, and to avoid any bilateral trade that infringes on the rights of a third country. They also must give importers and exporters, whether citizens or foreigners, the right to protest official measures that impinge upon trade. Additionally, they are bound to apply the same criteria and standards to imported as to domestic goods, and not to employ such measures to restrict imports.

In principle, Kazakhstan and Uzbekistan can join the WTO while taking into account their special conditions, with reservations and privileges that correspond to the special characteristics of these countries. Both countries are also obliged to convert nontariff barriers on agricultural imports to tariffs and to fix these. In principle, the members of the WTO can demand that the highest tariffs be reduced. At the present time, Uzbekistan and Kazakhstan do not subsidize their agricultural exports and therefore the most that the WTO members can demand is that they not do so in the future.

It is probable that Uzbekistan will need to reform its monopolistic "state-commercial" trading organizations for the procurement of cotton and cereal, to subject them to demonopolization and privatization, and to remove any kind of state financial support for these organizations. It will also have to eliminate all the restrictions on the export of agricultural products, including the nontransparent procedures for granting export permissions and licenses.

It is, as before, still unclear just how radical the reforms in Uzbekistan's trade policy and state trading organizations must be to accommodate the demands of WTO members for admission to that organization. However, it is already clear that these reforms will not be superficial. Therefore, to obtain the maximum advantage from membership in the WTO, it is desirable that Uzbekistan accelerate and intensify reforms in agriculture to create an efficient institutional structure. That means the creation of a system of family farmer enterprises in crop cultivation and the formation, on the basis of such farms, of a broad network of cooperatives in the sphere of agribusiness, trade, and services.

The scale and pace of progress in Uzbekistan and Kazakhstan along the path toward reform in its trade policy and for acceptance in the WTO (along with the associated rights of intellectual property and the service sphere) will depend on the degree to which these governments are prepared to carry out the requisite measures and to assume the necessary expenditures to adapt to a new trade regime.

For Uzbekistan and Kazakhstan, it would be premature at this point to assume obligations associated with the immediate liberalization of financial services. The experience of most East Asian states and many other countries shows that to receive advantages from the admission of foreign financial organizations to the domestic market, the country should first deregulate national financial institutions and create a competitive environment on domestic financial markets. Under conditions where interest rates are artificially low or in real terms actually negative, where the state provides credits for enterprises, and where barriers restrict competition among domestic financial organizations, the admission of foreign financial organizations to the domestic market can only ensure that foreign financial agencies more quickly gain a monopolistic dominance, not the creation of a competitive environment and an improvement in the efficiency of financial services. In an unprepared domestic financial environment, the unrestricted access of foreign banks can end in the bankruptcy of all the national banks, which have high costs of service and which are incapable of competing with foreign banks. Under the conditions prevailing in Kazakhstan and Uzbekistan, where the markets are not yet fully liberalized, and where a full restructuring of the banking system has not been carried out, the admission of foreign banks and other financial institutions to the domestic markets (for purposes of raising the efficiency of financial services) can be advantageous for these countries only if they introduce certain restrictions. The purpose of such restrictions is to avert a decline in the efficiency of domestic banks. To be sure, these limits must be temporary; they should remain in place only until the national financial institutions can become competitive with the foreign banking institutions.

The financial crisis in East Asia, along with contemporary research on the link between the development of the financial sector and economic growth, shows that the liberalization of the financial sector, if conducted prematurely (i.e., in the absence of a sufficiently developed national financial system and reliable financial institutions) can lead to a fall in economic growth. Therefore, liberalization of the financial sector (in contrast to the liberalization of trade) carries greater risk and demands a more cautious approach and a longer transition period.

The best approach to the liberalization of the financial sector in Kazakhstan and Uzbekistan, in the judgment of these authors, is the following. First, this process should be made dependent on the level of development of financial institutions of these countries. In other words, it is important to link the financial liberalization to the development of financial institutions. Second, it is necessary to raise the level in this sphere by drawing upon technical assistance from the IMF, WTO, and developed countries. That should be done within the framework of a seven-year transition period, foreseen by the WTO for countries with a transition economy.

Prior to entry into the WTO, Uzbekistan and Kazakhstan should carry out the following basic, preparatory measures:

- Kazakhstan and Uzbekistan began their negotiations for entering the WTO without sufficient research and consultation with experts. In 1998, to be sure, Kazakhstan did prepare estimates on the elasticity of imports.[15] It is necessary to make a detailed study to determine the sensitivity of different branches of the economy to specific protectionist measures (quotas, tariffs, and the like) and to the abolition of such policies. The goal is to determine the "freedom of maneuver" available to the governments of these countries in their negotiations with the WTO.

- For acceptance into the WTO, it will naturally be demanded that each country accept Article VIII of the IMF agreement on the convertibility of national currencies for current accounts. After all, failure to observe this article contradicts the nondiscriminatory rules of trade (for example, the WTO rules in the "Agreement on Investment Measures Pertaining to Trade"). However, it is precisely hard-currency controls that, at the present time, represent the principal nontariff measure to protect the markets of Uzbekistan. Therefore, with the liberalization of hard currency policy, it is essential, simultaneously, to raise the level of tariffs on imports from the current most widespread rate of approximately 30 percent to 40 percent. The goal here is to compensate for the reduced protection of the domestic market. And precisely this level of tariffs can be accepted as the starting point in negotiations for the entry of Uzbekistan into the WTO.

- The rules of the WTO forbid export subsidies. However, without these, it will be rather difficult for Kazakhstan and Uzbekistan to expand exports in the middle-range perspective by increasing the production of finished goods from the manufacturing branch. Therefore, it is essential to examine carefully the acceptable time for Kazakhstan and Uzbekistan to enter the WTO. Moreover, it is also necessary to review the question of the possible increase in export subsidies, since the member countries of WTO, if they are in the process of transition to a market economy, should cease export subsidies only in the course of seven years from the date that the agreement with the WTO takes effect.

Thus, the foregoing suggests that Kazakhstan and Uzbekistan have no alternative but to joint the WTO, at least in the long run.

Notes

1. R. Pomfret, "Torgovaia politika dlia perekhodnoi ekonomiki syr'evogo kharaktera" (paper presented to the international conference on "Economic Policy of the Republic of Uzbekistan after the Acquisition of Independence," Tashkent, 30–31 January 1997), pp. 2–8.

2. M. Khasanova, "Kazakhstan: Foreign Trade Policy," in *Central Asia: The Challenge of Independence*, ed. Boris Rumer and Stanislav Zhukov (Armonk, NY, 1998), pp. 202–3.

3. M. Khasanova, M. Esergepova, S. Akisheva, G. Shurabekova, Zh. Alekeshova, and B. Kabenov, "Problemy vstupleniia Kazakhstana v VTO: tarifnye mery i zashchita otechestvennykh proizvoditelei," *Al' Pari*, 1998, no. 3: 32.

4. M. Khor, "Macroeconomic Policies That Affect the South's Agriculture," Third World Network (http://www.twnside.org.sg/south/twn/title/macrocn.htm).

5. According to IMF data ("Republic of Uzbekistan: Recent Economic Developments," IMF Staff Country Report, no. 98/116 [October 1998], table 15, p. 53), in 1997 the state budget of Uzbekistan received a net income from the low procurement prices on cotton and cereals in the range of 1.8 percent of the GDP. That income constituted 6 percent of all revenues coming into the state budget. If one considers that subsidies to agriculture in the form of lower taxation (with a GDP in Uzbekistan of approximately 9.6 billion dollars, based on a hypothetical exchange rate in 1997 of 100 sum to 1 dollar), then this 1.8 percent of the GDP (or 6 percent of the state budget) amounts to 170 million dollars. These funds are needed for the state during the period of complete liberalization of prices on cotton and cereals if the state does not reduce its expenditures.

6. H. Park, "Industrialization and Trade," in *Handbook of Development Economics*, ed. H. Chenery and T. Srinivasan (Amsterdam, 1987).

7. E. Trushin, "Rol' agrarnogo sektora v dostizhenii ustoichevogo ekono-

micheskogo rosta," in: *Makroekonomicheskie problemy perekhodnogo perioda v Uzbekistane* (Tashkent, 1998), p. 315.

8. A. Rasulev, "Vneshneekonomicheskaia deiatel′nost′ Uzbekistana: sostoianie, problemy i perspektivy," *Rynok, den′gi i kredit,* 1997, no. 6: 8–12.

9. Onoda Kinya, "Japan's Synthetic Fiber Industry: From Development to Industrial Adjustment," in *Industrial Policy in East Asia* (Tokyo, 1993), pp. 30, 37–38.

10. Yamagata Tatsufumi, "Taiwan's Textile Industry: From Industry Promotion to Trade Friction," in *Industrial Policy in East Asia* (Tokyo, 1993), p. 90.

11. A.A. Adylov, "Opyt vneshnei ekonomicheskoi politiki i osnovnye orientiry razvitiia" (paper presented to the international conference on "The Economic Policy of the Republic of Uzbekistan after the Acquisition of Independence," Tashkent, 30–31 January 1997), pp. 9–10.

12. "Sistemy multimodal′nykh ekspeditorskikh perevozok," Proekt doklada TACIS (Tashkent, 1997), p. 158.

13. "V poiskakh vykhoda," *Biznes–Vestnik Vostoka,* 1997, no. 7 (February): 22.

14. A.B. Terekhov, *Svoboda torgovli: analiz opyta zarubezhnykh stran* (Moscow, 1991), p. 190; K. Anderson, *LAO Economic Reform and WTO Accession: Implications for Agriculture and Rural Development* (Singapore, 1999), pp. 10–16.

15. Khasanova, "Problemy vstupleniia Kazakhstan v VTO," pp. 202–3.

7

Central Asia and the Asian-Pacific Region

Oksana Reznikova

From the very day that the states of Central Asia were formed, they found themselves within the powerful fields of gravity of the modern world. The economic leaders of the Asian-Pacific region exert a growing influence on the economic situation in Central Asia. This chapter will examine the scale and thrust of economic interaction between the Central Asian states and the Asian-Pacific region, as well as the mid- and long-term prospects for their mutual relations. The reorientation of the five Central Asian states toward the Asian-Pacific region is moving at a rather rapid pace; the future of the five states depends, to a critical degree, on how successful they are in finding a niche in the division of labor in this dynamic region of the world economy.

Foreign Trade Ties

For all five Central Asian countries, without exception, the basic form of participation in the world economy is trade. The export and import flows in Central Asia significantly surpass, in terms of volume, the foreign credits and loans, not to mention the infusion of direct foreign investment in the region. In 1995, trade with Asia accounted for 14 percent of the aggregate export of the Central Asian states. Of the Asian markets, the largest consisted of China (26.3 percent of Asian trade), Turkey

(21.9 percent), and South Korea (10.4 percent). Of the imports from Asia, these same three countries supplied 5.0 percent (China), 28.8 percent (Turkey), and 33.3 percent (South Korea).[1] The states of the Asian-Pacific region rank third in significance as a foreign trade partner (after Russia and Europe). The volume of trade with the Asian-Pacific countries substantially exceeds the turnover with neighboring countries, such as Turkey and especially Iran (see Table 7.1). Only in the case of Turkmenistan are the economic ties with Turkey more significant than the trade with the Asian-Pacific region.

Moreover, for the Central Asian region as a whole, China has become the second most important export market after Russia. This is true for both Kazakhstan and Kyrgyzstan, which have an extended common border with China. The main exports from Kazakhstan to China consist of coal, petroleum, aluminum, ferrous alloys, copper, mineral fertilizer, nickle, and ferrous metal (both in rolled and scrap forms). Kyrgyzstan exports to the People's Republic of China (PRC) consist primarily of cotton fiber, wool, and antimony. In return, these two Central Asian states receive foodstuffs, clothing, footwear, and electronic consumer goods. In other words, raw materials with a low degree of processing are exchanged for the most elementary types of mass consumer goods (Table 7.2).

Whereas this trade with Central Asia is marginal for China (representing less than 1 percent of its total trade turnover), several Chinese provinces have oriented their trade flows toward the Central Asian republics. In 1996, the Xinjiang-Uigur Autonomous Region (XUAR) obtained 43.3 percent of its imports from Kazakhstan and 14 percent from Kyrgyzstan; of the total exports from this Chinese territory, 15.8 percent went to Kazakhstan and 12.9 percent to Kyrgyzstan.[2] In short, so far as the contiguous regions of China are concerned, Kyrgyzstan and especially Kazakhstan have become their principal trade partners, even surpassing Hong Kong.

To stimulate trade with Kazakhstan and Kyrgyzstan, the Chinese cities of Jeminay, Tacheng, Turugart, and Huocheng were given the status of "cities open for border trade."[3] The Kyrgyz city of Naryn´ on the border with China was similarly pronounced a "free trade zone."[4]

The informal "shuttle" trade between Kyrgyzstan and XUAR has also reached a significant scale. Each year, Kyrgyz and Kazakh shuttle traders import the most rudimentary consumer goods from China (worth tens of millions of dollars). Such a large-scale trade turnover is based on close personal connections. The ethnic Kyrgyz in XUAR are estimated

Table 7.1

Central Asia: Geographic Structure of Exports and Imports
(as percent of total exports and imports)

Country	Kazakhstan			Uzbekistan		Kyrgyzstan			Turkmenistan			Tajikistan		
	1995	1996	1997	1995	1996	1995	1996	1997	1995	1996	1997	1995	1996	1997
Recipients of Central Asian exports														
Russia	42.3	44.5	33.9	15.5	11.6	25.7	26.7	16.4	3.6	2.0	7.5	12.7	10.2	8.5
Turkey	1.4	0.8	1.6	3.8	1.0	0.8	1.0	1.3	8.0	4.7	6.8	1.1	0.2	1.1
Iran	1.0	1.0	1.3	0.02	0.5	1.0	1.2	1.0	0.6	1.0	16.4	0.1	0.2	0.5
China	5.9	7.4	6.9	1.2	2.8	16.7	7.2	5.2	0.4	0.1	0.3	0.7	0.8	1.8
S. Korea	1.8	2.9	2.0	5.1	5.8	0.2	0.0	0.0	0.2	0.0	0.1	1.2	3.2	0.4
Japan	0.9	1.4	1.7	0.1	0.2	0.1	0.2	0.2	0.01	0.0	0.0	1.1	0.0	0.0
Sources of Central Asian imports														
Russia	49.0	55.0	46.0	26.2	21.0	21.8	20.8	26.9	7.0	11.8	13.4	17.0	11.1	15.3
Turkey	3.3	3.6	4.1	3.0	7.6	7.3	5.7	6.2	11.8	9.2	12.5	0.5	0.8	0.7
Iran	0.4	0.1	0.2	0.1	1.1	0.4	0.4	0.8	2.7	3.4	3.2	0.1	1.6	1.6
China	0.9	0.8	1.1	0.9	0.7	1.2	0.9	4.6	0.6	0.9	0.6	0.05	0.2	0.2
S. Korea	1.1	2.1	3.0	15.8	6.9	0.5	0.6	0.7	0.05	0.06	0.05	0.0	1.1	0.7
Japan	0.2	0.4	0.7	1.6	1.2	1.4	1.5	0.4	0.6	0.6	0.6	0.0	0.2	0.0

Sources: Goskomstat Turkmenistan, *Eksport i import Turkmenistan za ianvar'-dekabr' 1996 goda* (Ashgabad, 1997), pp. 2–7; Natsional'noe statisticheskoe agentstvo Respubliki Kazakhstan, *Statisticheskii biulleten'*, *no. 4* (Almaty, 1997), pp. 47–54; World Bank, *Statistical Handbook 1996. States of the Former USSR* (Washington, DC, 1996), pp. 249, 424, 454, 521; *Sodruzhestvo nezavisimykh gosudarstv v 1995 godu* (Moscow, 1996), pp. 64–66; *Sodruzhestvo nezavisimykh gosudarstv v 1996 godu* (Moscow, 1997), pp. 66–67; *Sodruzhestvo nezavisimykh gosudarstv v 1997 godu* (Moscow, 1998), pp. 66–67; estimates by the national statistical services in the states of Central Asia.

to number more than 130,000 people, and these people have maintained close ties with their historic homeland.[5]

For Central Asia, South Korea has become another very important trade partner from the Asian-Pacific region. Indeed, in the case of Uzbekistan, South Korea is now its main export market in the Asian-Pacific region. Moreover, whereas China primarily buys products from Central Asia, South Korea itself has been expanding export deliveries to this region. The key point is that, in 1994–97, South Korean corporations chose to make Uzbekistan a test site for investment. A group of companies, united around the chaebol Daewoo, constructed several assembly plants here that, by local standards, are rather large. The delivery of equipment and components for this production, carried out primarily on the basis of trade credits and barter deals, is also reflected in the trade statistics.

Exports from South Korea to Uzbekistan amounted to 436 million dollars in 1995, but declined to 326 million dollars in 1996 (see Table 7.3). Until the production of subassemblies and components is shifted to Uzbek enterprises, the import of intermediate products and parts to produce goods on the basis of assembly-line technology will remain relatively high.

South Korea also has actively expanded its foreign trade with Kazakhstan. In 1996, the volume of trade turnover between these countries doubled over the previous year and amounted to 266 million dollars. A serious impulse to the development of South Korean trade with Kazakhstan and Uzbekistan came from the presence in both countries of a Korean diaspora, which has successfully incorporated itself into the process of market changes. In 1938, in the course of the "relocation of peoples," tens of thousands of ethnic Koreans were moved from areas of the Soviet Far East to Central Asia. According to the last census (1989), the Korean population included 183,000 in Uzbekistan and 103,000 in Kazakhstan.[6]

Against the background of dynamic expansion of trade between the Central Asian states and China and South Korea, the trade turnover with Japan has increased at a slower tempo. In 1996, the aggregate export of the region to the land of the rising sun amounted to approximately 100 million dollars. Japanese exports to Central Asia were on roughly the same level (see Table 7.4).

At the same time, after a perceptible growth in the first half of the 1990s, in 1996–97 the trade volume between the Central Asian states

Table 7.2

Dynamics of Trade: Central Asian States and China, 1992–1997
(in millions of dollars)

	Country	1992	1993	1994	1995	1996	1997
Exports	Kazakhstan	229	166	149	294	461	442
	Kyrgyzstan	28	59	56	69	36	32
	Tajikistan	0.8	0.4	0.9	6	6	13
	Turkmenistan		4.5	1.5	7	2	2
	Uzbekistan	40	36	77	35	127	
Imports	Kazakhstan	205	72	70	34	36	47
	Kyrgyzstan	16	19	11	6	9	32
	Tajikistan	0.4	0.3	5	0.4	1	2
	Turkmenistan		3	5	8	11	7
	Uzbekistan	68	35	88	23	32	

Sources: Statkomitet SNG, *Ekonomika Sodruzhestva nezavisimykh gosudarstv (kratkii spravochnik)* (Moscow, 1993), pp. 78–81; Statkomitet SNG, *Vneshneekonomicheskaia deiatel'nost' gosudarstv Sodruzhestva v 1994 godu* (Moscow, 1995), pp. 211–12, 223, 316–17, 331–32, 342–43; Statkomitet SNG, *Statisticheskii ezhegodnik* (Moscow, 1995), pp. 56–57.

Table 7.3

Dynamics of Trade: Central Asian States and South Korea, 1992–1997
(in millions of dollars)

	Country	1992	1993	1994	1995	1996	1997
Exports	Kazakhstan	13	42	60	92	178	130
	Kyrgyzstan	0	0.5	0.5	0.8	0.1	0.1
	Tajikistan		1.4	1.6	9	25	3
	Turkmenistan		4	0	3.5	0	0.6
	Uzbekistan	13	55	40	147	267	
Imports	Kazakhstan	0.2	8	67	43	88	129
	Kyrgyzstan	0.7	0.2	4	3	5	5
	Tajikistan		0.4	1	0.1	7	5
	Turkmenistan		2	3	0.6	0.7	0.5
	Uzbekistan	0.4	9	26	436	326	

Sources: Statkomitet SNG, *Ekonomika Sodruzhestva nezavisimykh gosudarstv (kratkii spravochnik)* (Moscow, 1993), pp. 78–81; *Statkomitet SNG, Vneshneekonomicheskaia deiatel'nost' gosudarstv Sodruzhestva v 1994 godu* (Moscow, 1995), pp. 211–12, 223, 316–17, 331–32, 342–43; Statkomitet SNG, *Statisticheskii ezhegodnik* (Moscow, 1995), pp. 56–57.

Table 7.4

Dynamics of Trade: Central Asian States and Japan, 1992–1997
(in millions of dollars)

	Country	1992	1993	1994	1995	1996	1997
Exports	Kazakhstan	48	36	27	45	87	108
	Kyrgyzstan	0	0	0	1	1	1
	Tajikistan		22	11	8	0.2	0
	Turkmenistan		0.7	0	0.2	0	0.1
	Uzbekistan	5	3	5	2	9	
Imports	Kazakhstan	4	3	53	8	18	29
	Kyrgyzstan	0	0.1	3	7	12	3
	Tajikistan		2	0	0	1	0.3
	Turkmenistan		4	7	7	8	7
	Uzbekistan	6	24	24	45	55	

Sources: Statkomitet SNG, *Ekonomika Sodruzhestva nezavisimykh gosudarstv (kratkii spravochnik)* (Moscow, 1993), pp. 78–81; Statkomitet SNG, *Vneshneekonomicheskaia deiatel' nost' gosudarstv Sodruzhestva v 1994 godu* (Moscow, 1995), pp. 211–12, 223, 316–17, 331–32, 342–43; Statkomitet SNG, *Statisticheskii ezhegodnik* (Moscow, 1995), pp. 56–57.

and the Asian-Pacific region has leveled off and stabilized. For example, Kazakhstan's exports to China have stagnated at the level of approximately 450 million dollars and its imports at 40 to 50 million dollars (see Table 7.2). The flow of goods between Central Asia and the XUAR has also stabilized.[7] In the coming years, it seems highly unlikely that there will be a substantial growth in the exchange of goods between the Central Asian states and the countries in the Asian-Pacific region. And it is not simply a matter whereby the newly independent states have exhausted the possibilities for the extensive expansion of exports by reorienting domestic producers from the internal market to foreign markets.

All the states of Central Asia belong to the category of "land-locked countries," that is, countries that lack direct access to the world's oceans and therefore find themselves cut off from the main trade routes. The obvious result is a contradiction that defies easy resolution. Unless the region is integrated into the global economic space, the prospects for all five countries are at best problematic; however, that very integration is blocked by the sheer facts of geography. In this case, the idea of a "Silk Route" of the twenty-first century has acquired growing popularity, for the restoration of that earlier silk route is supposed to enable Central Asia to overcome its geographic isolation and to open it to the world economy.

The Silk Route of the Twenty-First Century

Geography has given Central Asia the potential role of serving as a transit bridge between Europe and the Asian-Pacific region. During the times of the Roman Empire, this territory was transected by trade routes linking Rome with Shanghai. Later, the silk route declined in importance. Since the time when Central Asia was incorporated into the Russian Empire, the territory of Siberia provided the land communications between Europe and Asia.

In this new context, it is not a matter of reestablishing a historical transportation route between Asia and Europe, but of the economic opening of the landlocked territory of Central Asia. Not geography and trade, but the natural resources of the region constitute the basis of the vision of a great silk route of the twenty-first century.

Under contemporary conditions, it is proposed to construct the new silk route on three main foundations: energy, a transcontinental transportation system, and telecommunications. The backbone of this project (which unites global, regional, and local interests) is to exploit the natural resources of the region—above all, the huge reserves of oil and natural gas. The realization of the raw-material potential of Central Asia will make it possible to give the necessary dynamism to local economies and, simultaneously, to provide the large importers of hydrocarbons with stable deliveries of raw materials. This presupposes and stimulates the integration of the region into the global system of transportation and informational communications. A developed transportation infrastructure will make it possible to cut the cost of shipping cargoes between the Asian-Pacific region and Europe.

Oil, Gas, and Energy Bridges

There are reasons to suppose that in the twenty-first century Asia will turn into one of the important suppliers of energy on the world market. The known reserves in Kazakhstan amount to 2.2 billion tons of petroleum and 2.5 trillion cubic meters of natural gas. Turkmenistan has natural gas reserves of 2.89 trillion cubic meters, and Uzbekistan another 1.9 trillion cubic meters.[8] The predicted reserves in Kazakhstan, including the deposits on the shelf of the Caspian Sea and the basin of the Aral Sea, could total more than 13 billion tons of oil and 6 trillion cubic meters of natural gas. The estimated reserves for Turkmenistan amount to 6.3 billion tons of oil and 15.5 trillion cubic meters of natural gas; Uzbekistan is predicted to have 0.3 billion tons of oil and 2.0 trillion cubic meters of natural gas.[9]

Even in the distant perspective, Central Asia has no serious chance of overshadowing the Persian Gulf as the main supplier of oil and natural gas on the world market.[10] Nevertheless, the Caspian region (primarily Kazakhstan and Turkmenistan, along with Azerbaijan) is entirely capable of occupying a share of the market similar to that held, at the present time, by the Norwegian Sea.

A host of circumstances, however, impedes the inclusion of the Central Asian states in the international division of labor, with the role of large-scale suppliers of oil and natural gas. It is often thought that the main obstacle here is the acute geopolitical struggle for control over the resources of the region and the transportation of hydrocarbons to world markets. That view appears to be one-sided, however. The main obstacles to transforming Kazakhstan and Turkmenistan into major exporters of oil and natural gas are economic, not geopolitical.

In the middle of 1996, the first vice-president of the Italian company Agip (which is firmly ensconced in the world oil and natural gas business) posed a rhetorical question: "Why, given the enormous resource potential, do the projects in the [Central Asian] region develop so slowly?" He then gave an exhaustive answer to this question: "Realization of large-scale oil and gas projects leads to a surplus of oil, for which one must first identify the appropriate markets."[11] Ever since, the development of events in the oil and gas market has only intensified the urgency of the question of selling Central Asian hydrocarbons.

The potential exporters themselves have not adduced any serious research on the prospects for selling Kazakh oil and Turkmen gas. This writer is aware of only one such study, which was conducted by specialists in the Russian Federation. Their hypothetical calculations suggest that the only realistic, large-scale market for Central Asian oil and natural gas in the middle- and long-term perspective is in the countries of the Asian-Pacific region.[12] Reference here, in the first instance, is to China. According to some calculations, the proportion of net imports (imports minus exports) in the aggregate use of oil in China amounted to 12 percent in 1995, but will grow to 45 percent in the year 2000.[13] Moreover, the prospect is for the significance of the Chinese market to grow both because of the rapid growth of this continental economy, and because of the restructuring of its energy balance in favor of oil and natural gas. Japan is also extremely interested in diversifying the sources for its own hydrocarbons as well.

The oil and natural gas companies of these countries are actively penetrating the Kazakh market. The pace of privatization of the main producers of hydrocarbons was so fast in Kazakhstan that, by the middle of 1997, all the hydrocarbon deposits of any magnitude were already under direct or indirect foreign control. Asian companies did not stand aside during this process (see Table 7.5). The companies of Asian-Pacific states are also active in Turkmenistan, where they entered as participants in virtually all the major projects for the transportation of natural gas to world markets.

Huge capital investments are needed to realize the raw-material potential of this region. The sum of investments planned for the development of the oil and gas resources of Central Asia cannot be precisely calculated. Many of the projects prepared at the present time appear to be rather exotic. However, if events develop in a favorable way, investments could amount to tens of billions of dollars. A substantial part of these will be mobilized in the countries of the Asian-Pacific region. Thus, China has announced plans to invest approximately 9.5 billion dollars to develop Kazakh oil production over the next five to six years.[14]

In the competition for Central Asian oil and gas, China relies upon a number of advantages, the most important of which include the territorial proximity to the region and the rapidly growing demand for energy resources. Certainly another competitive advantage for the PRC is the similar geological structure of the mineral deposits of Western Kazakhstan and the largest Chinese deposits in the northeastern Tarim Basin; hence the characteristics of crude oil from both areas are similar.[15] As the president of the Kazakh oil company Uzen'munaigaz points out, the Chinese specialists have accumulated significant experience in working with the initial unprocessed oil, which has a large quantity of paraffin, and that should substantially increase the yield of petroleum at the Kazakh deposits.[16]

The export of oil to the east is the most advantageous route for Kazakhstan itself. In this case, the pipeline will cross virtually the entire territory of this country, and hence the tariffs on pumping the oil will go to the treasury of Kazakhstan, not neighboring states.

There is growing evidence that the PRC is close to finishing the preparation of a complex program to develop its own oil and gas holdings as well as the transportation network. As an organic element in this strat-

228

Table 7.5

Oil and Gas Projects in Central Asia with the Participation of Countries from the Asian-Pacific Region

Country	Foreign Participant[a]	Form of Partnership[a]	Investment Plans
Exploration and extraction of oil and natural gas			
Kazakhstan (Aktobemunaigaz, oil and gas company)	CNPC[b] (China)	60% of stock in Aktobemunaigaz	Develop three oil deposits; total investment of $1.1 billion in 1997–2017 (including $585 million in 1998–2003)
Kazakhstan (Uzen'munaigaz, oil and gas company)	CNPC[b] (China)	60% of stock in Uzen'munaigaz	Develop the Uzen' deposits ($4 billion in 1998–2010)
Kazakhstan (Mangistaumunaigaz, oil and gas company)	Central Asian Petroleum (Indonesia)	60% of stock in Mangistaumunaigaz	Explore and extract oil from 15 deposits in Mangistau Oblast ($4.1 billion in 1998–2030)
Kazakhstan	JNOC[c] (Japan), Japan JIT Oil (Kazakhstan)[d]	Japanese side conducts the project alone	Complex project to explore and extract oil and gas in the northwestern area of the Aral Sea, on the Tereken Basin (Aktiubinsk oblast). Aggregate investment of $1.358 billion by the year 2025
Kazakhstan	JNOC[c] (Japan)	Japanese side conducts the project alone	Complex project to explore oil and gas deposits in the Aral Sea area (near the city of Aral'sk). Investment: $90 million by 1999

Kazakhstan	Mobil (USA) and Sumitomo (Japan)	n.a.	Oil exploration in western Kazakhstan
Kazakhstan	INOC[e]	Indian side conducts the project alone	n.a.
Turkmenistan	Petronas (Malaysia)	n.a.	Exploration and extraction of oil on the shelf zone of the Caspian Sea
	Chinese Oil Engineering-Construction Corporation (China)	n.a.	Reconstruction of oil well at the Koturdepe deposit

Oil and gas pipeline

Kazakhstan	CNPC[b] (China)	Handle construction and seek financing	Oil pipeline of 3,000 km (Aktiubinsk oblast to the border of XUAR, then on to Karamai). Investment: $3.5 billion
Kazakhstan	CNPC[b] (China) and Iranian companies	Handle construction and seek financing	Oil pipeline of 250 km (from Uzen' deposit to Iran). Investment: approximately $1 billion
Turkmenistan	National Engineering-Construction Company of Iran	Construction of natural gas pipeline in exchange for future gas deliveries	Gas pipeline Koperdzhe (western Turkmenistan)-Iran, 200 km. Investment: $195 million, plus another $70 million to construct gas processing plant
Turkmenistan	Unocal (USA), Delta (Saudi Arabia), Hyundai (S. Korea), Itochu (Japan), Impex (Japan)	n.a.	Gas pipeline Dauvletabad and Sovetabad (eastern Turkmenistan)-Afghanistan-Pakistan, 1,270–1,464 km, with possible extension to New Delhi. Investment: $2 to 2.5 billion

(continued)

Table 7.5 *(continued)*

Country	Foreign Participant[a]	Form of Partnership[a]	Investment Plans
Turkmenistan	CNPC[b] (China), Mitsubishi (Japan)	n.a.	Gas pipeline Turkmenistan-Uzbekistan-Kazakhstan-China (northern part of Tarim Basin in Lianyungang), 6,200 km. The project then has several variants for further extension.[f] Investment: $7.13 billion

Sources: Kazakhstanskaia pravda, 3 December 1997, p. 2; Ibid., 5 June 1997, p. 1; Ibid., 5 April 1997, p. 1; *Panorama* (Almaty), no. 37 (26 September 1997), p. 2; no. 19 (16 May 1997), p. 8; no. 14 (11 April 1997), p. 6; no. 27 (10 July 1997), p. 1; *Izvestiia* (Moscow), 28 October 1997, p. 3; *Rossiiskaia gazeta* (Moscow), 26 October 1996, p. 7; *Nezavisimaia gazeta* (Moscow), 18 September 1997, p. 3; Ibid., 4 September 1998, p. 5; *Biulleten' inostrannoi kommercheskoi informatsii* (Moscow), no. 36, (28 March 1998), pp. 10–11.

[a]The names of companies and terms of agreements are given as they appear in the sources.

[b]CNPC is China National Petroleum Corporation.

[c]JNOC is Japanese National Oil Company.

[d]Created by three Japanese companies: Teikoku Oil Company Ltd, Japanese Petroleum Exploration Company Ltd, and Indonesia Petroleum Ltd.

[e]INOC is Indian National Oil Company.

[f]The four variants for further shipment to Japan include the following possibilities:
1. Lyanyungang (China)–Nantung (China)–Kitakiusiu (Japan). 880 km;
2. Lyanyungang (China)–Mokpo (S. Korea)–Kitakiusiu (Japan). 1,162 km;
3. Lyanyungang (China)–Mokpo (S. Korea)–Tsupuga (Japan). 1,730 km;
4. Lyanyungang (China)–Mokpo (S. Korea)–Niigata (Japan). 2,307 km.

egy, China also intends to develop the oil deposits in Central Asia, with the subsequent shipping of this raw material across the territory of China. In a March 1998 meeting of the All-Chinese Assembly of People's Deputies, the head of the Xinjiang Oil Administration declared that, in the near future, China will begin to lay an oil pipeline in the northwestern part of the country. This pipeline will combine into a single network all the oil fields and petrochemical bases located in the central and western provinces of the PRC. This general network will include the oil pipeline linking the city of Karamai (XUAR) with the Aktiubinsk oil fields in Kazakhstan. The plan is to complete this construction in the course of eight years. China expects this pipeline to provide 25 million tons of crude oil per year.[17]

These plans naturally led to a search for the requisite financing. In October 1997, the largest bank in Hong Kong (but now in the PRC), the Bank of Hong Kong, opened a branch office in Kazakhstan.[18] This bank is part of the HSBC group, which has aggregate assets that exceed 257 billion dollars.[19] Apparently, this bank will realize the financing of the multi-billion-dollar projects. Moreover, for this purpose the Bank of Hong Kong can mobilize not so much the resources of continental China, as the capital of the rich Chinese diaspora—the so-called "Huaqiao." As is well known, up to the present time more than 90 percent of the direct foreign investment in China is concentrated in the twelve southern provinces of the country, chiefly in Guangdong, with which the Huaqiao has close kinship and linguistic ties.[20]

At the same time, a series of factors could push back the timing for the development of the Kazakh hydrocarbons by the China National Petroleum Corporation (CNPC). First of all, one limitation here is the fact that the oil pipeline from the central areas of China, which pass through XUAR, at the present time breaks off at the city of Shanshan. Therefore, to deliver the Xinjiang and Kazakh oil to consumers in the central and southern provinces, it is necessary to transfer the oil to railway tank cars, which substantially increases the shipping costs. No less important is the fact that the construction of the main oil pipeline from Xinjiang Uigur Autonomous Region to the central and southern provinces of China is economically feasible only in the case that the deposits in XUAR themselves produce at a level of at least 20 million tons of crude oil per year. In turn, the time for beginning the construction of the oil pipeline from XUAR to western Kazakhstan depends on how quickly the Kazakh companies (Uzen´munaigaz and Aktobemunaigaz), which are controlled by CNPC, raise production to 20 to 25 million tons.[21] If neither of these conditions is met, then China will have to provide substantial subsidies to pump oil through the pipeline.

Second, the XUAR lacks the capacity to process large volumes of oil. The aggregate productivity of the three existing oil refineries here amounts to approximately 20 million tons per annum. A new plant currently under construction will make it possible to increase the refinery capacity by just 2.5 million tons.[22] However, in the Xinjiang Uigur Autonomous Region itself, by the year 2000 it is planned to increase output to 17 to 20 million tons (from the current level of 15 million tons).[23] This schedule simply leaves no room for the refining of Kazakh oil.

Third, the relatively low prices of oil also are blocking the construction of the oil pipeline. Even before the large drop in oil prices on world markets, Chinese experts had already pointed out that one can seriously consider the prospects for an oil pipeline from Kazakhstan to China only if the price on oil rises. Given the low world prices on oil, and given the current tariff on shipping one ton of oil ($1.5 per 100 km), this project has no real prospects of becoming profitable.[24]

Fourth, at the present time, the government subsidizes the prices on oil for the end users in China.[25] It is not entirely clear for how long and on what scale the government is prepared to subsidize a rising import. Its refusal to provide subsidies will inevitably reduce the general consumption of hydrocarbons; that is all the more probable because of the intensive reconstruction of large enterprises in the state sector of the PRC that Chinese authorities have planned for the next few years.

Finally, one should not overlook the fact that powerful lobbyist groups in China have a vested interest in directing capital investment to projects at home, not abroad. Given the high level of unemployment and the future restructuring of inefficient industrial enterprises in the state sector (which inescapably will cause additional stress on the labor market), it will be no simple matter for China to divert enormous resources for investment in projects outside its own territory.

The quality of the oil from the Mangyshlak oil fields (Kazakhstan) is likewise the source of many problems. To transport this oil, the Soviet Union built the only "hot" (i.e., heated) oil pipeline in the world, which runs from Uzen′ to Samara; that pipeline, of course, weighs like a heavy yoke on the product cost of the raw material.[26] It simply makes no economic sense to pipe oil in this impure state over thousands of kilometers. Consequently, major capital investment will be required to purify the oil of paraffin at the production site in order to make its shipping cost-effective.

Nevertheless, in the long-term perspective, a shift toward the development of the oil and gas resources in the XUAR and contiguous areas of Kazakhstan is inevitable. That is because the northwestern areas of China contain up to one-third of that country's total oil reserves, which should be tapped in order to support the high rates of economic growth.[27] One must also bear in mind that ownership of the main deposits of hydrocarbons in the area of the South China Sea is contested by several states, thereby creating difficulties for their development.[28] Even *The Economist*, which is skeptical about Kazakhstani-Chinese oil collaboration, nonetheless concedes that, if China deems an oil pipeline to Central Asia as strategically necessary, it can realize the project without regard to commercial considerations.[29]

Until recently, Central Asia Petroleum (an Indonesian company and a subsidiary of the Medco Energy Corporation) planned to make huge investments in oil extraction in Kazakhstan. These plans can suffer from the economic collapse of the Indonesian economy. At the same time, the Panigoro family that owns the Medco Group, like the majority of business families in Indonesia, apparently has widespread contacts in the Chinese ethnic diaspora.[30] One cannot exclude the possibility that the investments of Central Asia Petroleum were originally oriented toward China; hence the crisis in Indonesia does not pose a threat. If one takes into account the close cooperation of the Indonesian family conglomerates with the leading Japanese corporations and banks, it is fair to assume that the interests and resources of Japanese capital also stand behind the deal of Central Asia Petroleum.[31]

Japan is capable of substantially increasing the construction of oil and gas pipelines that, in turn, can give the Central Asian region access to this highly profitable markets. Indeed, Japan is even more interested than China in gaining access to the Central Asian hydrocarbons; Japan's main advantage in the competition for Central Asian hydrocarbon resources is its aggregate economic power. Revealingly, Japan is the largest creditor for Kazakhstan, Turkmenistan, and Kyrgyzstan. For example, in 1992–96, Japan extended bilateral credits to Kyrgyzstan worth 144.5 million dollars; that is comparable to the loans of the IMF (153 million dollars) and the Asian Development Bank (160 million dollars).[32] On 1 October 1998, Japan was the only large creditor of the Kazakh government in bilateral arrangements.[33] It is therefore not surprising that the majority of international conferences by Kazakhstan's donors are held in Tokyo.

In addition to operating as a major stockholder in international financial institutions, Japan unquestionably has a major influence on their credit policies. That power is especially evident in the case of the Asian Development Bank. Above all, because of lobbying efforts by Japan, all five states of Central Asia have received the status of developing countries, which has given them access to the preferential lines of assistance and credits.[34]

Japan's interest in hydrocarbon riches in this region is so great that, beginning in April 1994, the Japanese National Oil Company (JNOC) conducted, free of charge, geological and geophysical work in the coastal zones of the northwestern part of the Aral Sea. The president of JNOC also announced the willingness of his company to extend the geological exploratory work to the basin of the Caspian Sea.[35] In April 1997, JNOC (in collaboration with three corporations of the private sector) signed a large-scale agreement with the government of Kazakhstan for the geological exploration and sharing of future output.

Somewhat earlier, in the fall of 1996, the Japanese National Oil Company signed a major agreement on the exploration for oil near the city of Aral'sk. According to this contract, the company will receive certain advantages in future agreements pertaining to the extraction and export of oil. The oil reserves in the Kazakh portion of the Aral Sea are estimated at 100 million tons.[36]

Japan does not have a contiguous border with Central Asia, and it is also more dependent on the import of hydrocarbons than the other leading states. It is, therefore, keenly interested in the most rapid possible opening up of Central Asia under any of the possible routes—whether through the PRC, Turkey, Iran, or Afghanistan and Pakistan. In the modern world, which is thickly covered by the network of the global communication systems, geography is subordinate to geo-economics. Japan can import oil and liquefied gas from any open and especially equipped seaport. It is therefore not surprising that Japanese capital is even active in Romania, a country that at first glance might well seem to be remote from Central Asia. The point is that the Romanian port of Constanta (which has been declared a free trade zone) can, under a favorable sequence of events, be transformed into the most important staging post in the "Silk Road-Northern Europe" route.[37]

Japan is interested in creating several alternative routes for the export of hydrocarbons from Central Asia. This would enable Japan to reduce its critical dependence on any single route. Japan's position here is shared by the European Union, which officially supports the construction of oil and natural gas pipelines through the territories of any country, including Iran.[38] In contrast to the United States, Japan does not suffer from an anti-Iranian allergy. In part, that is due to the fact that Japanese corporations officially are in close cooperation with this Middle Eastern state. Nor does China raise objections to unblocking the Iranian route.

In the opinion of many specialists, the shipping of Central Asian hydrocarbons through the Iranian port of Bandar-Abbas is the optimal, shortest route for gaining access to world markets. One fundamental rule of the pipeline business stipulates that the fewer the national borders, the better. However, the Iranian route has, until recently, been blocked by well-known American sanctions.

Some analysts argue that the natural gas from Turkmenistan can also cross through the territory of Iran to reach China.[39] The uncertainties with respect to the routes for shipping Central Asian oil and gas create the greatest possible opportunity for speculation. Hypothetically speaking, the system of oil and natural gas pipelines linking China and Central Asia can also be used to ship oil from other sources. As the well-informed magazine *The Economist* points out, in the case of an unforeseen military conflict in the South China Sea (and, at the present time, the PRC imports oil primarily by sea) the Central Asian pipelines could be switched over to pump oil from the Near East.[40]

Kazakhstan is well endowed not only with hydrocarbons, but also with electric power. In 1990, it produced 87.4 billion kilowatt-hours of electricity. However, in 1998 (because of the acute economic crisis), the production of electricity fell by 43 percent (to 49.8 billion kilowatt-hours).[41] The massive insolvency of the end users is contributing to the further contraction of demand on electric power.

A special situation has emerged in Pavlodar oblast. The aggregate capacity of electric power stations in this oblast, which use mainly coals from the Ekibastuz Basin, amounts to 8,300 megawatts, but in fact is being used at only one-third capacity.[42] Such a palpable surplus of generator capacities, in principle, allows Kazakhstan to export electricity to the markets of neighboring states. One such potential market is China. For this purpose, experts of the two countries are exploring the possibility of erecting a high-voltage line from Ekibastuz to Chuguchak (Tacheng).[43]

The likelihood of realizing this electric power bridge is increasing, because it is strongly supported by Western corporations. The American company AES is active on both sides of the Kazakh-Chinese border. In Pavlodar oblast, it bought the largest electric power plant in Kazakhstan—the Ekibastuz State District Power Station no. 1, which has a capacity of 4,000 megawatts. Simultaneously, in partnership with the Israeli company Sun Tree AES, it obtained a concession to operate the Ust'-Kamenogorsk State Power Station (with a capacity of 322 megawatts), the Shul'binsk State Power Station (702 megawatts), the Ust'-Kamenogorsk thermal power station (240 megawatts), and a number of smaller electric power plants. With the participation of AES, China realized eight projects in the sphere of electric power. In June 1997, Sun Tree AES opened finances for the Chinese energy company Yangchang International Power, which declared its readiness to construct and manage the largest thermal power stations in China.[44]

Transportation Corridors

The second pillar of the new Silk Route should be a transcontinental transportation system. Its task is to intensify the integration of Central Asia into the global exchange of commodities and also to provide access to the raw material resources of this region.

The main shipments are by rail. Right up to the beginning of the 1990s, railway freight between the East and West of the Eurasian continent flowed through the Trans-Siberian route. However, in the first half of the 1990s, the Trans-Siberian route encountered a new competitor in the form of the Trans-Asian railway. In September 1990, in the area of the junctions at Druzhba-Ala, the railway lines of Kazakhstan and China came together.[45] In addition, the People's Republic of China substantially modernized that segment of its own railway system contiguous to Central Asia. In May 1996, construction was completed on the segment Mashhad-Tedzhen, which linked the railroad system of Turkmenistan and Iran. Simultaneously, Iran provided a connection between its railways and the seaports on the Persian Gulf.[46] As a result, the Asian countries have integrated their railroads into a single network.

In March 1993, the European Union, the five states of Central Asia, and three governments in the Trans-Caucasus adopted a declaration for a project called TRASECA ("the Transport-Corridor Europe-Caucasus-Central Asia).[47] In fact, the new silk route was intended to be joined to the European transportation infrastructure through the corridor of "Istanbul-Western Europe." The TRACEKA project includes seventeen huge super-projects for the reconstruction and construction of new highways and railroad lines, the reconstruction of seaports, and the creation of an infrastructure to service this transportation main line.[48]

The length of these transportation routes from the Pacific Ocean ports of China and Japan through Central Asia to Istanbul is much shorter than the Trans-Siberian line. Thus, compared with the Trans-Siberian Russian route, the route Tianjin-Istanbul is shorter by 1,286 km, Lianyungang-Istanbul by 2,350 km, Shanghai-Istanbul by 2,320 km, Hong Kong-Istanbul by 3,545 km, and Yokohama-Istanbul by 2,350 km.[49]

A shorter distance, in combination with competitive shipping rates on cargoes, can in principle promote the reorientation of freight movements between Asia and Europe from the Trans-Siberian to the Trans-Asian route.[50] To be sure, at the present time up to 98 percent of this cargo flow (estimated at 580 billion dollars) goes by sea because of the relative cheapness of oceanic transportation.[51] However, on average the shipment of cargo by sea requires 56 days; a shift to rail shipping would reduce this transit time to 11 or 12 days.[52]

As a result of the formation of the pan-Asian railway network, Central Asia obtained direct access to the markets of countries in the Asian-Pacific region. Kazakhstan and China have already signed special transportation agreements on the use of the port at Lianyungang for the transit of Kazakh cargoes to states in the Asian-Pacific region.[53] The linkage of the Turkmen and Iranian railroads enables Central Asia, through the port at Bandar-Abbas, to access the markets of the Persian Gulf. The third direction (Almaty-Bishkek-Naryn´-Kashgar-Karakorum Highway-Islamabad-Karachi), which gives Central Asia access to ports on the coast of the Indian Ocean, will enable both truck and rail transportation. For Kazakhstan, this is an even shorter access to the ocean than the route through the Iranian port at Bandar-Abbas.[54] In tandem with the Kazakh-Kyrgyz route to the ports of Pakistan, an Uzbek-Kyrgyz route may also open that would use the road Andizhan-Osh-Kashgar,[55] but also the Tajik-Chinese route of "Gornyi Pamir-Karakorum highway."[56]

Local transportation is closely integrated with the shipping projects of global and regional significance. Virtually all of the projects being carried out in Central Asia to develop the transportation networks are financed by Japan and the Asian Development Bank (which, to a considerable degree, is under Japanese control). Top priority is accorded to railway transportation. First, in shipping at great distances, railway transportation is more economical than trucking. Second (and most important), only a rail line into Central Asia can carry the heavy-tonnage equipment and pipes needed to realize the oil and gas contracts and to construct the oil and natural gas pipelines. Japanese credits are being used to reconstruct the railway junction at Druzhba-Lan (Kazakhstan-China), to modernize the railway system of Turkmenistan, and to rebuild the rail car depot at Almaty (Kazakhstan) and Ashgabat (Turkmenistan) into repair plants.[57]

Simultaneously, the construction of motor vehicle roads and bridges is also being financed. In 1997, the Japanese government extended to Semipalatinsk (Kazakhstan) a low-interest credit of 260 million dollars for a thirty-year term to construct a new bridge over the Irtysh River, since the old bridge was in a state of dangerous dilapidation.[58] A Japanese firm Isikawadzimi Harima had the winning tender in bids to perform the construction work.[59] This bridge will carry the main transit line linking China, the states of Central Asia, and Russia. The Bishkek-Osh highway in Kyrgyzstan, which is of critical importance for internal and inter-regional communication, is an all-weather thoroughfare; it has been virtually rebuilt through credits from the Japanese government (viz., its Fund for Foreign Economic Cooperation) and the Asian Development Bank.[60] At the same time, the Asian Development Bank is financing the reconstruction of the highway Almaty-Karaganda-Astana-Borovoe.[61]

In the formation of modern transportation communications, Japan approaches Central Asia as a single unit that, in turn, should be incorporated into the Eurasian macroregion. In the spring of 1998, the Japanese corporation Sumitomo proposed an initiative to create in Central Asia the nucleus of an integrated logistical complex. Until very recently, all cargoes were shipped solely through the railroads of the former USSR. After the division of a single railway complex, there arose the question of a cardinal reorganization of the cargo and passenger flows in the region and the coordination of the activities of national railroads. Sumitomo proposed to create "centers of integrated logistics" in all the main cities of Central Asia to manage the entire Central Asian transportation infrastructure.[62]

The Japanese government also offered to extend huge credits for the reconstruction of airports in Bukhara, Urgenche, and Samarkand (all in Uzbekistan). The Japanese corporations Mitsubishi, Mitsui, and Shemize will carry out the reconstruction.[63] Japanese credits will also be used to modernize the Kyrgyz airport Manas in Bishkek and the Kazakh airport in Astana.[64] After the modernization, the airports will be capable of handling the Airbus A-310 and Boeing planes. Among other things, this means that the air connections between Europe and Asia will gradually shift to the south of the Eurasian continent, and Central Asia will be transformed into an important transit point on this route. Accordingly, China has already offered to give Kazakhstan several air corridors to South Korea and Japan.[65] It is hardly surprising that the world's largest airlines are gradually planning new flights to take these new circumstances into account.

The United Nations has also supported these multilateral efforts to develop mutually interfaced global, regional, and national transportation infrastructures for purposes of promoting cooperation between Europe and Asia. In December 1998, the UN General Assembly adopted a special resolution on the transit system in Central Asia. The resolution explicitly urges donor countries and international organizations to increase financial and technical assistance to the region in order to improve transit in the region. The goal is to overcome the isolation of that area from world markets. UNCTAD is the coordinator of international efforts in this sphere.[66]

The inclusion of Central Asia into the global telecommunications network is proceeding at a still faster pace.

Telecommunications Highway

Because of its geographic position, Central Asia has been assigned an important place in the global project for a Trans-Asian and Trans-European optic fiber line. Approximately twenty major telecommunications corporations, headed by the Siemens firm, are creating a single telecommunications superhighway that will link Shanghai and Frankfurt/Main. This line, which unites all of Europe and Asia into a single telecommunications and information system, will traverse the territories of thirteen states, including Kazakhstan, Uzbekistan, and Turkmenistan. In December 1997, the first test experiments were conducted on the Kazakh section of this line (with a length of 1,750 km).[67] In the beginning of 1998, construction was completed on 700 kilometers of the segment of the optic fiber line in Turkmenistan; that segment was built through credits from the Export-Import Bank of Japan in accordance with a project by the Japanese corporation Nichimen.[68] In the fall of 1998, the Trans-Asian and Trans-European line began to operate.[69]

The global telecommunications project gives life to a multitude of local and regional initiatives. As in the case of oil and gas resources, Asian capital has played a most active role in the development of modern telecommunications in the region. In May 1997, the South Korean chaebol Daewoo acquired—through a privatization tender—40 percent of the stock in Kazakhtelekom, which replaced the former Ministry of Communications; for this reason alone, Daewoo finds itself involved in virtually every telecommunications project in Kazakhstan.[70] A tandem of Daewoo and Korean Telecom triumphed in a tender to reconstruct and manage the telephone system of Tashkent.[71] The Uzbek-South Korean joint-venture enterprise "Aloka-Daewoo" won a contract to provide transit connections for the governments of Central Asia with other states in the CIS, and also to deliver equipment and machinery to the new Kazakh capital in Astana.[72] The Indonesian state telecommunications company Indosat intends, together with the Kazakh enterprise Zharyk, to finance the creation of a satellite network in Kazakhstan.[73] The Indonesian Bakrie Group, in partnership with a Malaysian firm, is developing a market for cellular communications in Uzbekistan.[74]

New Strategic Alliances

Asian companies have also been successful in gaining entry to other spheres of the economies of the Central Asian states. Thus, the transnational LNM Group (which has roots in India), in the course of a privatization tender, bought the Karaganda metallurgical complex—the largest industrial enterprise in Kazakhstan and all of Central Asia, with a design capacity of 6.3 million tons of steel per year.[75] A German branch of the South Korean chaebol Samsung established control over the Zhezkazgan and Balkhash copper plants in Kazakhstan, with an aggregate output of 400,000 tons per year.[76]

The Japanese companies Mitsui and Marubeni, which are world leaders in oil refining, are participating in the construction and modernization of the oil refinery complexes in Bukhara and Fergana (Uzbekistan).[77] The Export-Import Bank of Japan and the corporations Chiyoda and Nichimen, as part of a multinational consortium, are reconstructing a petroleum refinery in the city of Turkmenbashi (Turkmenistan), while Itochu, JGC, and Nissho Industry are adding to the same enterprise a plant to produce propylene.[78]

The energetic activities of the South Korean chaebol Daewoo in

Table 7.6

Country Breakdown of Direct Foreign Investment in Kazakhstan
(in percent)

Country	1993–94	1995	1996	1997	1998[a]	1993–98[a]
China	0.5	0.2	0.0	14.9	8.8	5.3
Great Britain	1.3	15.5	28.9	14.8	7.8	13.8
Indonesia	0.0	0.0	0.0	5.9	7.0	2.4
Japan	0.6	3.0	0.0	0.6	14.7	2.3
South Korea	0.0	27.5	26.4	34.2	3.4	19.5
Turkey	6.9	8.1	4.5	3.1	9.8	5.8
United States	71.4	15.6	9.8	9.9	25.9	28.2

Sources: Compiled from *Tendentsii razvitiia ekonimiki Kazakhstana*, TACIS, November 1998, Table 9.7.5.
[a]1998 data is for January–September.

Uzbekistan have inspired journalists to rename the country "Daewoostan." Daewoo has created here from scratch a plant (immense by local standards) to assemble automobiles; it has a productive capacity of 200,000 vehicles per year. Daewoo is also constructing a plant to produce motors; the design capacity at that plant is 300,000 units per year.[79] The same chaebol has opened in Tashkent a plant to assemble televisions.[80]

South Korean and Japanese companies have also entered into the textile industry of Uzbekistan, Turkmenistan, and Kazakhstan, where they have established joint-venture enterprises with local partners.[81] The South Korean company Sindona bought a tea-weighing factory in Almaty, while the chaebol LG opened an assembly plant to produce household electronics.[82]

Private Malaysian capital has purchased several enterprises of light industry in Kazakhstan, and it is also participating as joint ventures in the capital of a number of Kazakh financial institutions.[83]

In sum, the economic growth of Central Asia is increasingly determined by the influx of investments from countries in the Asian-Pacific region. This thesis is graphically illustrated by the country structure of investments in the economy of Kazakhstan, which is devouring the lion's share of all direct foreign investment in Central Asia (see Table 7.6).

In 1995–97, South Korean chaebols were the largest investors in the Kazakh economy. In 1997–98, relatively large direct investments came to Kazakhstan from China, Indonesia, and Japan. Altogether, for the period 1993–98, South Korea provided almost one-fifth of all direct foreign investment and ranked second only to the United States. During the same period, Japan, China, and Indonesia accounted for only one-tenth of this investment. However, in 1998, Japan was the second largest foreign investor in the Kazakh economy (surpassed only by the United States).

The above facts make it possible to say that the economic leaders of the Asian-Pacific region have formed a mutually complementary scheme to open up Central Asia. In this scheme, China plays the role of serving as the leading trade partner of the region; Japan is the principal creditor; South Korean chaebols act as the main investors. Such a plan, to be sure, is purely speculative; it merely reflects the objective comparative advantages held by each of the three leading Asian-Pacific states in the global competitive struggle for resources and markets. With parallel efforts (through export-import flows, credits, development aid, and investments), China, South Korea, and Japan—together with several other countries of the Asian-Pacific region—are drawing the five Central Asian states (but especially Kazakhstan, Kyrgyzstan, and Uzbekistan) into the general system of the division of labor.

Incorporation of Central Asia into the international division of labor and the processes of the world economy are taking place under conditions of globalization. Globalization is giving birth to a new paradigm of competition and cooperation. The competition for Central Asian and Caspian resources can lead to the formation of largely unexpected strategic alliances of transnational corporations and nation-states. As has already been pointed out, the main players in the struggle for oil and natural gas in the region are the largest world corporations.[84] On the whole, those most interested in opening up and the accelerated development of Central Asia are companies in the private sector. Behind this private capital stands the nation-states—or, more precisely, what remains of these in the epoch of globalization and internationalization of economic activities. Sooner or later, these states will be forced to construct their own foreign policy according to the demands of business.

The embryo of the new geo-economic formations (which, in turn, spawn geopolitical relations) are clearly apparent in the Central Asian context. American oil and energy corporations became the pioneers in the creation of new alliances of interests; moreover, they have been active in all possible areas, including Central Asia, Russia, China, and so forth.[85]

This essay has already referred to the construction of the Kazakh-Chinese energy bridge with the participation of American capital. Chevron, which has experienced certain difficulties with the export of Kazakh oil, has exhibited growing involvement in the Chinese area. In January 1998, the first delivery of oil from Tengiz was unloaded in China for a test refining in XUAR.[86] One cannot exclude the possibility that the Kazakhstan-China oil pipeline will combine Karmay with the Tengiz oil fields.[87] The Chinese National Oil Company has invited interested companies to participate in the construction of an oil pipeline from Kazakhstan to China and announced that a number of American oil and gas companies had already responded to these proposals.[88]

The American oil business is widely represented on both sides of the Kazakh and Chinese borders. For example, in February 1996, Texaco received the rights to conduct oil exploration on two large blocks of the Tarim River basin in China.[89] However, the most striking example is the fact that Mobil, while increasing its expansion in the oil sector of Kazakhstan, is cooperating in the closest possible ways with the Chinese National Oil Company.[90]

In general, this reflects the tendency to transform China into a powerful center of economic interest, with its development being of critical importance to transnational corporations. In the coming decade, those companies that do not receive at least one-third of their profit from the Asian-Pacific markets will cease to be global concerns.[91]

If one takes into account the above and other economic alliances, the insistent proposals of a number of leading American political analysts about forming an American-Chinese tandem in Central Asia become more comprehensible. Zbigniew Brzezinski has explicitly and repeatedly presented these ideas; in effect, he proposes to treat the People's Republic of China as an anchor of American policy in eastern Eurasia and to cooperate with China in developing the hydrocarbon resources of the region.[92]

Without doubt, there is competition between the companies of these and all other states. Nevertheless, there is also obviously a growing tendency to expand the dialogue regarding coordination and even unification of efforts to develop a region that is difficult to access.

The most rapid economic opening of the Central Asian region also corresponds to the interests of Japan. That country, moreover, is striving to propose a system of security for all of Asia. According to an idea that was first aired by Taro Nakayama (the prominent functionary of the Liberal-Democratic Party and former minister of foreign affairs), in the first stage China, the United States, North Korea, and South Korea should reach certain agreements. That understanding would then make it possible to create the basis for the expansion of agreements on the entire continent. Nakayama proposes to build the system of Pan-Asian security on the basis of a "single energy space."[93]

In a polished form, the same idea has become an organic component of the concept of "Eurasian diplomacy," as announced by former Prime Minster Ryutaro Hashimoto. For Japan, the basic principles of mutual action among countries in the region of the "silk route" (which will include the states of Central Asia and the Caucasus) consist of the following. First, these relations will be incorporated into the general policy of Eurasia. Second, Japan will endeavor to promote the cooperation of states lying along the silk route for the purposes of creating common transportation, communications, and energy systems, and especially for the development of energy resources. Third, parallel with the intensive economic development of a new silk route, Japanese diplomacy is concentrated on establishing a dialogue among all interested parties so as to secure peace and stability in this part of the world.[94]

Hashimoto's conception has incorporated the main outlines of mutual action by Japan and China in the region of the silk route. One way or another, everything here revolves around the same energy and related ecological problems. These include the necessity to restructure the energy balance of China in favor of ecologically cleaner forms of fuel, and the goal of reducing the proportional energy intensity of production (for which Japan is prepared to offer advanced technologies and financial means). It is clear that the cooperation in resolving energy and ecological problems is creating a good basis for the coordination of actions on world markets for oil and natural gas. And this cooperation includes the Central Asian region that is only now opening up. It is no accident that Japanese companies stand behind all the super-projects for the transportation of Central Asian oil and natural gas to China and onwards to the Asian-Pacific region. Indeed, it is precisely these Japanese companies that plan to participate in the financing and implementation of these projects.

Nor is the United States forgotten in this conception: union with America remains the basis of the security system in the Asian-Pacific region. Moreover, Japan's position is distinguished by a particular flexibility. In the style of economic diplomacy, Japan has formulated special multilateral groups ("Japan-Russia-Central Asia," and "Japan-Turkey-Central Asia"), which include the key representatives of governments, corporations, and banks.[95] The missions are summoned to evaluate the opportunities for compromise and to identify overlapping areas of interests.

The fate of Central Asian resources depends on how the triadic relations among Japan, China, and the United States develop. All three participants in this new strategic triangle have both overlapping and diverging interests. The very political and economic architecture of Central Asia, like its geographic position, categorically requires that the competitors find some kind of common balance for their mutual interests. Moreover, the American, Chinese, and Japanese triumvirate possesses unique opportunities to use the strong sides of the partners and to react effectively to the constantly emerging problems.

These opportunities have appeared, for example, in providing economic assistance to the Central Asian countries. When Turkmenistan in the early 1990s did not know how to reach a consensus with the IMF regarding its economic policy and found itself in effect cut off from foreign credits and loans, the government of Japan (which, unlike other developed countries, is not bound by the ideology of neo-liberalism), promptly offered this assistance.

Japan has also, rather quickly, opened substantial lines of credit for Uzbekistan, which had similarly manifested intractability in its dialogue with the Bretton Woods institutions. Moreover, a significant share of this assistance to Uzbekistan went for the purchase of oil equipment from American firms. The latter circumstance was an important factor in facilitating what was presumably a difficult decision.[96]

The unique Japanese experience in preparing long-term plans of economic growth for developing countries and whole regions can also be useful in the Central Asian region. The Japanese International Cooperation Agency (JICA) has already prepared a general plan for the development of industry in Kyrgyzstan[97] and for machine-building in Kazakhstan.[98] Moreover, in contrast to the programs of the IMF, such plans assign priority to the task of providing development in the production sectors, not financial stabilization.[99]

Prospects

The reorientation of Central Asia toward so powerful a center of economic gravity like the Asian-Pacific region is not a linear process. On the contrary, it must navigate around many obstacles, including some additional new ones, such as the Asian financial-economic crisis that developed in 1997. That crisis, apparently, will curtail the expansion of South Korean capital into Central Asia. Thus, Daewoo has been forced to sell the bloc of stocks in Kazakhtelekom that it acquired in the course of privatization (in tandem with American and Kazakh banks).[100] The government of Kazakhstan believes that difficulties can also arise for the Indonesian owners of Munaigaz.[101]

Japan is also undergoing a serious economic test. It is difficult to say how much the shocks it has experienced will influence the scale of its economic assistance to the countries of Central Asia. In any case, Japan maintains an acute interest in developing a raw-material base in Central Asia. The crisis has affected China less than the other Asian states. Its trade, at any rate its physical volume, with the states of Central Asia is very unlikely to contract in any significant way in the next few years.

The crisis has stimulated a further opening of the economies of the Asian-Pacific and, in particular, has accelerated the internationalization of Japanese and South Korean corporations. By buying up the stocks and other forms of participation in property, West European and especially American capital has become an organic part of the local corporative structures in both the production and financial sectors of the economy. The contrary is also true: the capital of Japan and other Asian countries are becoming part and parcel of Western economic structures at the corporative level. An accelerated internationalization at the level of property is strengthening the bases for multilateral strategic unions to develop the global economic space.

The immediate economic prospects of Central Asia are determined by the development of trends in the world's petroleum industry.

In all of these traditional producers and suppliers of oil, the cost of producing hydrocarbons is substantially lower than in the Caspian region. The investment image of the latter is somewhat undermined by the disappointing results, at least to this point, in the search for major oil deposits in Azerbaijan. In January 1999, the international consortium Caspian International Petroleum Company announced that it would cease its activities in exploring the deposits of Karabakh.[102]

Nevertheless, the leading world corporations have not completely abandoned interest in Central Asia and Azerbaijan. Colossal financial resources allow them to optimize their own development strategies for the long-term perspective. On the eve of the new century, the oil and gas transnational corporations were given a rare opportunity to buy up, at relatively cheap prices, hydrocarbon resources for future development. That is precisely the character of the agreement reached by a group of American and Japanese companies with the government of Kazakhstan in the fall of 1998. According to this deal, the Kazakh government turned over to the Japanese National Oil Company and the American firm Philips Petroleum part of its share in the deposits of the Caspian shelf.[103]

The relative cheapness of access to the Central Asian hydrocarbon resources is due to two factors: (1) the exceedingly intense struggle among the oil and natural gas producers to obtain foreign financial and technological inputs; and (2) the dismal social-economic conditions of post-Soviet transitional states, which are forced to grant foreign capital unprecedented, attractive terms for activity. Moreover, the resource-poor states of the Asian-Pacific region have a special vested interest in securing for themselves a part of the future production from the Caspian deposits. Agreement to share the output insures them against future price fluctuations, which are impossible to forecast. Apparently, this explains the tendency for the more active involvement of Japanese corporations in the activity of international consortia in the Caspian region, which was already perceptible in 1996 when American companies surrendered some of their shares to Japanese participants.

However events might unfold, the prospects of the Central Asian states depend, to a critical degree, on the situation in the Asian-Pacific region. Central Asia can embark upon a trajectory of stable development only through an intensification of economic cooperation with the countries of the Asian-Pacific region.

The Central Asian states can overcome their geographic isolation only if they find a niche in the global economic architecture. Potentially, as noted above, such a niche could mean its inclusion in the energy, transportation, and information flows along the Great Silk Route. Moreover, the Central Asian states should adopt the standard rules of the game and attach themselves to projects initiated by the developed economic centers. Their strategy should be aimed at the maximum utilization of interests in development that come to the region from without.

The first official signal of the readiness of Central Asia to act in such a constructive way was the "diplomacy of the silk route," advanced in early 1999 by the president of Kyrgyzstan, Askar Akaev.[104] That conception of "silk route diplomacy" is an elaborate justification for the economic, political, and cultural integration of Kyrgyzstan into the world, essentially via the renaissance of the Great Silk Route. The fact is that Central Asia has no other option if it wants to ignite economic development and to achieve an acceptable rate of development. The only alternative to this development is the continuation and intensification of the all-encompassing economic and social degradation.

Notes

1. Calculated from World Bank, *Statistical Handbook, 1996. States of the Former USSR* (Washington, DC, 1996), pp. 210–11, 248–49, 423–24, 453–54, 520–21.

2. Data kindly provided by B. Rumer.

3. G.D. Bessarabov, "Dvustoronnie ekonomicheskie sviazi Kitaia so stranami SNG i problemy obespecheniia interesov Rossii," in *Strategicheskie faktory riska dlia Rossii*, no. 3 (Moscow, 1996), p. 7.

4. R.H. Munro, "Central Asia and China," in *Central Asia and the World*, ed. M. Mandelbaum (Washington, DC, 1994), p. 232.

5. A. Saliyev, "A Way to China," *Central Asian Post* (Bishkek), no. 12 (27 March 1997), p. 5.

6. *Narody Rossii. Entsiklopediia* (Moscow, 1994), p. 203.

7. See J.P. Dorian, D. Wigdortz, and D. Gladney, "Central Asia and Xinjiang, China: Emerging Energy, Economic, and Ethnic Relations," *Central Asian Survey* 16 (1997): 477.

8. V. Telegin, "Resursy uglevodov mira i potentsial'nye vozmozhnosti Kazakhstana v ikh razvitii," *Panorama* (Almaty), no. 8 (27 February 1998), p. 9.

9. *Panorama*, no. 24 (6 June 1997), p. 9; O. Reznikova, "Central Asia in the World System," in *Transition to a Market Economy in Central Asia. Lessons from the East Asian Experience* (Tokyo, 1996), p. 156.

10. See, for example, J. Kemp, *Energy Superbowl: Strategic Politics and the Persian Gulf and Caspian Basin* (Washington, DC, 1997).

11. *Panorama*, no. 25 (28 June 1996), p. 4.

12. A. Konoplianik (with the participation of A. Lobzhanidze), *Kaspiiskaia neft' na Evraziiskom perekrestke. Predvaritel'nyi analiz ekonomicheskikh perspektiv* (Moscow, 1998).

13. M.G. Salameh, "The Geopolitics of Oil in the Asia-Pacific Region and Its Strategic Implications," *OPEC Review* (Oxford) 21 (1997): 128.

14. *Panorama*, 1997, no. 37 (26 September), p. 2.

15. *Panorama*, 1996, no. 40 (18 October), p. 10.

16. *Panorama*, 1997, no. 7 (21 February), p. 13.

17. T. Abramenko, "V Pekine prokhodit sessiia Vsekitaiskogo sobraniia narodnykh predstavitelei," *Panorama*, 1998, no. 10 (13 March), p. 5.

18. C. Clover, "The Game Gets Under Way in Central Asia," *Financial Times*, 8–9 November 1997, p. 2.

19. *Panorama*, 1997, no. 40 (17 October), p. 7.

20. See H.G. Broadman and X. Sun, "Distribution of Foreign Direct Investment in China" (World Bank, Working Paper 1720, February 1997).

21. *Panorama*, 1997, no. 41 (24 October), p. 9.

22. *Panorama*, 1997, no. 46 (28 November), p. 9.

23. *Panorama*, 1996, no. 40 (18 October), p. 10.

24. Ibid.

25. *Panorama*, 1997, no. 46 (28 November), p. 9.

26. *Panorama*, 1997, no. 7 (21 February), p. 13.

27. "Ekonomika KNR: uspekhi i perspektivy," *Biulleten' inostrannoi kommercheskoi informatsii* (Moscow), 1998, no. 34 (24 March), p. 3.

28. Salameh, "The Geopolitics of Oil in the Asia-Pacific Region," p. 130.

29. "Central Asian Survey. A Caspian Gamble," *The Economist*, 7 February 1998, p. 11.

30. Revealingly, the Almaty newspaper *Panorama* confirms the absence of complete clarity in the question as to what the Indonesian company that has entered the Kazakh market represents. According to some information, this is a multinational corporation that includes several participants, including states from Southeast Asia. See *Panorama*, 1998, no. 2 (16 January), p. 8.

31. On the close ties of the leading Indonesian groups with Japanese corporations and banks, see H. Vriens, "The Grandson Also Rises," *Asia Inc.* (Hong Kong) 4, no. 3 (March 1995): 46–51.

32. Gosudarstvennaia komissiia Kirgizskoi Respubliki po inostrannym investitsiiam i ekonomicheskoi pomoshchi, *Vneshniaia pomoshch' Kirgizskoi Respublike. Ezhegodnyi otchet 1996 goda* (Bishkek, 1997), pp. 22, 24, 85.

33. *Tendentsii razvitiia ekonomiki Kazakhstana*, TACIS, November 1998, Table 9.7.3.

34. *Izvestiia* (Moscow), 30 August 1995, p. 3.

35. *Panorama*, 1997, no. 14 (11 April), p. 6.

36. *Rossiiskaia gazeta* (Moscow), 26 October 1996.

37. *Kazakhstanskaia pravda*, 3 December 1997, p. 3.

38. *Panorama*, 1998, no. 12 (27 March), p. 4.

39. P. Vlasov, "Piaterka i dva tuza. SShA i Kitai nachali bor'bu za 'rossiiskoe nasledstvo SNG," *Ekspert*, 1998, no. 2 (19 January), p. 57.

40. "China Fears for Its Wild West," *The Economist*, 15 November 1997, p. 64.

41. *Commonwealth of Independent States in 1998 (Digest of Provisional Statistical Results)* (Moscow, 1999), p. 55.

42. S. Gorbunov, "Energograd raspravliaet kryl'ia," *Kazakhstanskaia pravda*, 11 December 1998, p. 2.

43. Ibid.

44. "AES v Kazakhstane: prodvizhenie proektov i navedenie energomostov prodolzhaetsia," *Kazakhstanskaia pravda*, 30 October 1997, no. 4.

45. *Aziia. Ekonomika i zhizn'* (Almaty), no. 41 (October 1996), p. 23.

46. *Kazakhstanskaia pravda*, 15 May 1996, p. 1; 27 May 1997, p. 2.

47. D. Artykov, "TASIS-TRASEKA: perspektivy razvitiia," *Ekonomika i statistika* (Tashkent), no. 2, 1996: 47.

48. Ibid., p. 48.

49. V. Zhuravlev, "Konkurenty khotiat otniat' u BAMa zvanie magistrali veka," *Delovoi mir* (Moscow), no. 28 (25–28 July 1997), p. 6.

50. Ibid.; I. Shul'ga, " 'Transsib': v poiskakh utrachennogo vremeni," *Kommersant-Weekly* (Moscow), 1997, no. 26 (22 July): 46.

51. Zhuravlev, "Konkurenty," p. 1.

52. Shul'ga, " 'Transsib,' " p. 45.

53. *Biznes-MN* (Moscow), 1995, no. 34 (20 September): 18.

54. *Panorama*, no. 42 (11 November 1996), p. 2; no. 31 (August 1996), p. 4.

55. *Pravda Vostoka* (Tashkent), 29 April 1997, p. 1; *Aziia. Ekonomika i zhizn'*, no. 8 (February 1997), p. 24.

56. M. Apyshev, "Economic Problems at Crucial Moment of History," *Central Asian Post*, no. 5 (8 February 1999), p. 2.

57. E. Kotova, "Iaponiia vybiraet Turkmenistan v strategicheskie partnery," *Delovoi mir*, no. 38 (2–6 October 1997), p. 3; *Kazakhstanskaia pravda*, 1 May 1997, p. 3.

58. *Kazakhstanskaia pravda*, 5 February 1998, p. 2; 28 December 1996, p. 1.

59. Ibid.; *Panorama*, no. 5 (6 February 1998), p. 1.

60. *Aziia. Ekonomika i zhizn'* no. 50 (December 1997), p. 3.

61. *Panorama*, no. 20 (23 May 1997), p. 3.

62. M. Nurpeisov, "Forum v Tokio," *Panorama*, 20 March 1998, p. 9.

63. *Central Asian Post*, no. 12 (27 March 1997), p. 3.

64. *Panorama*, no. 17 (1 May 1997), p. 4.

65. *Kazakhstanskaia pravda*, 25 September 1997, p. 1.

66. *Kazakhstanskaia pravda*, 9 December 1998, p. 12.

67. T. Izdibaev, "'Kazakhtelekom' pristupaet k realizatsii programmy modernizatsii telekommunikatsii na 1998–2001 gody," *Panorama*, no. 8 (27 February 1998), p. 10.

68. *Aziia. Ekonomika i zhizn'* no. 5 (February 1998), p. 24.

69. *Panorama*, no. 40 (16 October 1998), p. 9.

70. *Panorama*, no. 22 (6 June 1997), p. 8; no. 17 (1 May 1997), p. 6.

71. *Aziia. Ekonomika i zhizn'* no. 2 (January 1997), p. 2.

72. *Panorama*, no. 28 (18 July 1997), p. 9.

73. *Panorama*, no. 43 (7 November 1997), p. 9.

74. *Russkii telegraf* (Moscow), 26 September 1997, p. 7.

75. "The Carnegie from Calcutta," *The Economist*, 10 January 1998, p. 53; *Kazakhstanskaia pravda*, 9 December 1997, p. 2.

76. *Panorama*, no. 34 (6 September 1996), p. 8.

77. *Delovoi mir*, 1997, no. 32 (22–25 August), p. 4; 26 August 1997, p. 3.

78. I. Sasan, "V Turkmeni-'iaponskii desant,'" *Aziia. Ekonomika i zhizn'*, no. 29 (July 1997), p. 13.

79. Ministerstvo inostrannykh del Respubliki Uzbekistan, *Diplomaticheskaia panorama (spetsal'nyi vypusk)*, no. 5/6 (June–July 1996), p. 63; *Kommersant-Daily* (Moscow), 18 March 1997, p. 11.

80. Ministerstvo inostrannykh del Respubliki Uzbekistan, *Diplomaticheskaia panorama*, p. 64.

81. *Delovoi mir*, 1 July 1997, p. 5; P. Fredenburg, "The Kazakhstan Connection," *Asia Inc.* 4, no. 10 (October 1995): 16.

82. *Panorama*, no. 46 (27 November 1998), p. 5.

83. *Panorama*, no. 39 (10 October 1997), p. 7; no. 20 (22 May 1998), p. 6; no. 47 (4 December 1998), p. 5.

84. See O. Reznikova, "Transnational Corporations in Central Asia," in *Central Asia in Transition. Dilemmas of Political and Economic Development*, ed. B. Rumer (Armonk, NY, 1996), pp. 67–105.

85. On the formation of alliances with American and Russian corporations, as well as the expansion of contacts on the Iranian front, see ibid., pp. 95–97; S. Dukhanov, "Vashington ishchet primireniia s Tegeranom (interv'iu s Dzh. Kempom)," *Delovoi mir*, no. 25 (27 December 1996–2 January 1997), p. 2.

86. *Kazakhstanskaia pravda*, 12 February 1998, p. 2.

87. "Ekonomika KNR—uspekhi i perspektivy," *Biulleten' inostrannoi kommercheskoi informatsii*, no. 34 (24 March 1998), p. 3.

88. N. Abulkhairov, "My stali uchastnikami Bol'shoi Igry," *Kazakhstanskaia pravda*, 14 October 1997, p. 2.

89. F.K. Chang, "China's Central Asian Power and Problems," *Orbis* 41 (1997): 493.

90. G. Smyslov, "Tainy 'Bora,' " *Kommersant-Weekly*, no. 35 (30 September 1997), p. 27.

91. K. Courtis, "The New Agenda and Its Four Forces," *Asia Inc.* 4, no. 3 (March 1995): 55.

92. Z. Brzezinski, "A Geostrategy for Eurasia," *Foreign Affairs* 76, no. 5 (1997): 50–64.

93. *Obshchaia gazeta* (Moscow), no. 40 (10–16 October 1996), p. 4.

94. P. Khasimoto, "Evraziiskaia diplomatiia (neofitsial'nyi perevod)," *Nezavisimaia gazeta*, 12 August 1997, p. 5.

95. *Panorama*, no. 27 (11 July 1997), p. 4; no. 34 (5 September 1997), p. 9.

96. U. Magosaki, "The Japanese Aid Policy to CIS Countries" (Sasakawa Peace Foundation, Issyk-Kul' Forum, Tokyo, 2–3 October 1996), pp. 5–6.

97. Japan International Cooperation Agency, "The Study on the Master Plan of Industrial Development in the Kyrgyz Republic. An Interim Report" (Tokyo, February 1996).

98. *Panorama*, no. 8 (26 February 1999), p. 5.

99. K. Ohno, "Creating a Market Economy: The Japanese View of Economic Development and Systemic Transition" (paper presented for the World Bank World Development Report. 1997 Project, 7 August 1996).

100. *Panorama*, no. 23 (12 June 1998), p. 7.

101. *Panorama*, no. 6 (13 February 1998), p. 2.

102. M. Klasson, "Mestorozhdenie Karabakh zakryvaetsia," *Vremia-MN*, 26 January 1999, p. 4.

103. "Eshche odin kontrakt veka," *Kazakhstanskaia pravda*, 15 September 1998, p. 1.

104. A. Akaev, "Diplomatiia shelkovogo puti," *Nezavisimaia gazeta*, 10 March 1999, p. 15.

8

Central Asia:
Midterm Economic Prospects

Stanislav Zhukov

The complex analysis of economic and social development offered in the preceding chapters demonstrates that, at the turn of the century, the level of uncertainty about the future prospects of Central Asia is increasing. Moreover, this mounting uncertainty is due both to domestic and to international factors.

On the one hand, the ideology of economic and state construction that the ruling circles of Central Asia have maintained since the breakup of the USSR is becoming increasingly inadequate for dealing with the new and quickly changing conditions of development. It is also becoming ever more difficult to ascribe the failures of economic policy to the onerous legacy of a "colonial" past. The idea of asserting national sovereignty at any price has lost its mobilizing power even for elites, not to mention the overwhelming mass of the impoverished population.

In addition, conflicts within elites have sharply escalated. The first wave of privatization of the limited number of efficient economic assets has been completed. Now the new owners (for the most part consisting of the *nomenklatura*, that is, representatives of the old Soviet political elite) must repulse attacks from those elites who feel themselves to have been either excluded or cheated by the initial phase of privatization.

On the other hand, the external environment of development has also changed radically. The decline in world prices of raw material commodities has seriously undermined the economic position of those Central Asian countries that were drawn into the international division of labor as exporters of oil, gas, and metals (ferrous, nonferrous, and precious), as well as cotton fiber.

Serious changes have also transpired in the attitude of the world community. In the 1990s, developed countries quite generously assisted the new states to strengthen their independence and to lay the foundations for independent development; they often paid no attention to the results of the economic policy pursued in these states. Toward the end of the decade, however, foreign donors and sponsors had no choice but to become more demanding. That change was promoted by the financial crisis that began to appear in the so-called emerging markets. This shift in approach resulted also from the fact that the foreign assistance and credits (which were relatively large given the scale of the local economies) did not put the Central Asian countries on a regime of stable, self-sustained growth.

Under a palpable deterioration in domestic and foreign conditions of development that threaten to persist for at least the next several years, it is useful to make a dispassionate, objective assessment of the midterm prospects for the Central Asian region.

An Economic Portrait of Central Asia in the Year 2015

Demographic forecasts provide a reliable orientation for determining the midterm prospects of all the states of Central Asia. The demographic system of any society is distinguished by sufficient harshness and inertia; therefore, the reproduction of the population is only partially susceptible to shocks coming from outside the system. In Central Asia, this general rule is clearly confirmed by the experience of Tajikistan. A catastrophic contraction of economic activity, massive involvement of the population in military conflicts, and the large-scale migration from the country—all this has had only an insignificant influence on the reproduction of the population. Tajikistan has preserved the highest rates of demographic growth in the region.

Table 8.1 presents the midterm rates of population growth as anticipated for the period 1995–2015. For all five countries, we have demographic projections by the State Statistical Committee of the former USSR, which have been corrected to take into account the changes of the first half of the 1990s. In addition, there are also demographic fore-

Table 8.1

Scenarios of Development in Central Asia, 1995–2015
(in percent)

| | | Hypothetical rates of growth, 1995–2015 | | |
| | | GDP | | |
Country	Population	Scenario I: Growth rate needed to maintain per capita GDP at 1995 levels	Scenario II: Growth rate necessary to restore per capita GDP at 1990 levels	GDP rate of growth, 1995–98
Kazakhstan	0.3–1.35	0.3–1.35	4.35–5.40	0.0
Kyrgyzstan	1.5–1.95	1.5–1.95	5.35–5.80	6.2
Tajikistan	2.45	2.45	8.10	–3.7
Turkmenistan	1.75	1.75	4.75	–8.15
Uzbekistan	2.25	2.25	3.90	3.75

Sources: Calculated from the following: Iu. Shokamanov, "Skol'ko kazakhstantsev mozhet byt' v 2030 godu?" *Al'Pari*, no. 4 (1998): 56; A.B. Abdurekhmenova, M. Kaizer, E.Sh. Kasybekov, et al., "Sokrashchenie bednosti v Kyrgyzskoi respublike metodami politiki zaniatosti i sotsial'noi zashchity," in *Strategiia sotsial'noi politiki: rynok truda, zaniatost' i sotsial'naia zashchita naseleniia* (Bishkek, 1998), p. 65; "O prognoze chislennosti naseleniia SSSR," *Vestnik statistiki*, no. 10 (1990): 42; sources cited above in chapter 2, Table 2.1.

casts for Kazakhstan and Kyrgyzstan prepared by the respective national statistical services. According to these national predictions, the demographic dynamics in Kazakhstan and Kyrgyzstan are expected to be less intensive. In Kazakhstan, for example, the population will increase at an annual rate of just 0.3 percent during the period of 1995–2015; this is four times lower than the rates taken as the basis of projections by the State Statistical Committee of the former Soviet Union.

This table also presents two hypothetical scenarios of economic development in the countries of Central Asia. In scenario I, the rates of growth for the GDP correspond to the rate of population growth, which thereby allows them to sustain the per capita GDP as it stood in the mid-1990s. In other words, this first scenario provides for the minimal rate of economic growth necessary to avert a catastrophic variant in the development of events. Such rates do not lead to a restoration of stable economic growth, but merely freeze the current state of semi-syncope, whereby the Central Asian economies are stuck at a low level of economic activity.

Scenario II provides for a rate of growth that must be sustained if, by the year 2015, each state is to recover the per capita GDP that it had reached at the beginning of the 1990s. To reach that target, it is necessary for Kazakhstan to have an average growth rate of 4.35 to 5.4 percent, Kyrgyzstan 5.35 to 5.8 percent, Turkmenistan 4.75 percent, Uzbekistan 3.90 percent, and Turkmenistan more than 8 percent. However, during the most recent years of 1995–98, only Kyrgyzstan and (in part) Uzbekistan demonstrated some potential for the practical realization of scenario II. In Kazakhstan, the GDP remained at the level of the mid-1990s, while in Tajikistan it continued to contract at the rate of 3.7 percent per annum. In Turkmenistan the decline was steepest of all— 8.15 percent.

The high rate of growth for production in Kyrgyzstan in 1996–97 was due not only to the extremely low starting point, but also to the more than tenfold increase in gold output. Apparently, it will not be possible to sustain an intensive economic dynamic for any extended period of time. Thus, in 1998, the rate of growth in the GDP decreased to just 1.8 percent, and in 1999 the growth rate may shift from a positive to a negative figure. To be sure, a forecast by the IMF for 1999–2000 holds that the rate of growth in Kyrgyzstan's GDP will stabilize at the level of 4.5 to 4.6 percent.[1] Nevertheless, even these rates of growth, which are high for the country, fall short of those that are needed to realize scenario II.

As noted in Chapter Three, the economic dynamics of Kyrgyzstan are determined exclusively by the level of extraction of gold. Beginning in January 1996, the world prices on this precious metal demonstrated a distinct tendency to fall. The decision of the banks of Great Britain and Switzerland, as well as the IMF, to review the structure of gold and hard-currency reserves and to sell a total of 1,815 tons of gold can propel a further decline in gold prices.[2] However, even if the most optimistic forecast of experts by the London gold exchange comes true (whereby gold prices rise to 320 dollars per troy ounce), in this case the Kumtor gold fields will yield a negligible profit. The point is that the cost of production for one ounce of gold, according to some estimates, runs at approximately the same 320 dollars.[3] In our judgment, by the year 2015 Kyrgyzstan will not succeed in regaining the level of general development that it had achieved by the beginning of the 1990s.

The chances for Tajikistan to restore the level of development that existed in 1990 are still slimmer. To do so, this country must sustain—

for two whole decades—a phenomenal per annum growth rate in the GDP of 8.1 percent.

In principle, Kazakhstan can count on recovering its 1990 level of development only in the event that it substantially increases its extraction and export of oil. The rather rapid progress in the project for a Caspian pipeline consortium does increase the likelihood that scenario II will be realized. The transportation of oil through that pipeline is expected to begin in 2001. In the initial phase, the capacity of the oil pipeline will amount to 28 million tons of crude oil per year. The Kazakh government holds 19 percent of the stock in the consortium; "Kazakhoil," the national oil company, holds another 1.75 percent.[4] The other participants in the consortium include Chevron (USA), Mobil (USA), Orix (USA), British Gas (UK), Shell (USA), LUKoil (Russia), Rosneft' (Russia), and Agip (Italy). The participants of the consortium have not yet determined whose oil, and according to what schedule, will be pumped through the pipeline. However, in the first stage, Kazakhstan can apparently already count on a quota of 5 to 6 million tons. In addition, Kazakhstan will receive additional income as payment for shipping oil across its territory. In the years after 2010, the capacity of the oil pipeline is planned to grow to 67 million tons of crude oil per year.[5]

Nevertheless, Kazakhstan apparently cannot rise above a growth rate of 5 to 6 percent per year. Of course, during periods of rapid increases in world oil prices (as in the 1970s) and high rates of growth in oil production, the large producers of oil have recorded impressive economic gains. However, given the persistence of a relative surplus in the supply of oil on world markets and the rather low prices, Kazakhstan will have to make extraordinary efforts if it is to attain a 5 percent growth rate.

To judge from the growth dynamics of 1995–98, Uzbekistan is experiencing the least difficulties for realizing scenario II. First, if one extrapolates from the social and political limitations, a possible shortage of energy resources could become a serious barrier to economic growth here. Notwithstanding the massive investments and the involvement of the leading world corporations in the oil and gas sector, oil production in Uzbekistan in 1995–98 has remained at the level of 7.6–8.1 million tons per year.[6] Moreover, in 1998 Uzbekistan found itself unable to fulfill its plan to increase the production of oil; it fell short of the planned target by 0.7 million tons (almost 10 percent). Second, the country also faces a physical limitation on such important productive factors as arable land and water. Third, Uzbekistan also must cope with the negative consequences from spontaneous processes in the employment sphere.

In Turkmenistan, the GDP decreased at an annual rate of 8.15 percent in 1995–98. However, in the event this country gains access to export markets for its natural gas, it indeed is in a position to realize scenario II, not to mention scenario I.

From the beginning of the 1990s, virtually every year Turkmenistan has made grandiose announcements about plans to construct pipelines to export natural gas. And every time each successive plan has proved a failure—principally for financial and economic reasons. Given these circumstances, it is simply impossible to make any rational assessments about the likelihood that this country will succeed in realizing its various projects to develop and export its natural gas.

The demographic forecasts make it possible to evaluate, in a substantive way, the prospective changes in the labor market. In the 1990s, not a single post-Soviet state (including those in Central Asia) conducted any kind of coherent, considered policy with respect to employment. In the best case, governments made decisions that were spontaneous and uncoordinated; such measures were essentially a reaction to the momentary development of events.

Table 8.2 presents two scenarios for the growth of employment in the Central Asian countries to the year 2015. The first scenario presupposes that by 2015 the ratio of jobs to aggregate population will remain in each country just as it was in 1995. The second scenario assumes that the ratio of employment to aggregate population will be at a level of 30 percent.

It is well known that in the Soviet era the official economic doctrine provided for total employment of the entire adult population. Therefore, the proportion of those employed to the total population of the former Soviet republics was significantly higher than in other countries of the world. In other words, all the transition states have major "reserves" for reducing absolute and relative employment that would be less socially explosive than in market-based societies. Namely, they can remove from the workforce, in massive numbers, such categories as housewives, pensioners, and the like.

Rough calculations show that employment pressures on economic growth will vary from one country in Central Asia to the next. In both scenarios, authorities in Turkmenistan will have to deal with the least serious problems. Thus, in 1995–2015, employment in this country will

Table 8.2

Forecast of Growth of Economically Active Population (EAP) in Central Asia (in millions of people)

| | Annual Rate of Growth of EAP, 1995–2015 | | |
Country	Scenario I	Scenario II	Jobs created in 1990–1995
Kazakhstan[a]	0.379 (1.959)	−1.274 (−0.071)	−1.012
Kyrgyzstan[a]	0.625 (0.831)	0.201 (0.369)	−0.107
Tajikistan	1.234	1.006	−0.009
Turkmenistan	0.758	0.277	0.131
Uzbekistan	4.801	2.552	0.217

Sources: World Bank, *Statistical Handbook 1996. States of the Former USSR* (Washington, DC, 1996), pp. 197, 231, 413, 441; World Bank, *Statistical Handbook. 1995* (Washington, 1996), p. 233; World Bank, *Gosudarstva byvshego Sovetskogo Soiuza. Statisticheskii sbornik. 1993 god.* (Washington DC, 1994), pp. 315, 555, 603, 699; sources cited in Table 8.1.

[a]The main figure is obtained through the forecast of the size of the population as prepared by the national statistical services and research institutes. The figure in parentheses is based on the forecasts about the size of the population as calculated by the State Statistical Committee of the former USSR.

increase by 277,000–758,000 jobs. In other words, if one excludes the variant of an explosive increase in unemployment, Turkmenistan must create between 14,000 and 38,000 new jobs each year. Given the fact that in 1990–95 employment here has been growing by an average of 26,000 per year, the Turkmen economy is entirely capable of coping with this goal. In addition, our calculations of prospects are based on the official demographic statistics, which are inclined to exaggerate the size of the population in the country.[7]

More serious problems lie in wait for Kyrgyzstan, where the increase in jobs over the coming twenty-year period will amount to 201,000–831,000 jobs. In other words, it will be necessary for this country to create 10,000–40,000 jobs per year. Moreover, from 1990 to 1995, the absolute number of jobs in this country fell by more than 21,000 per year.

Tajikistan and especially Uzbekistan will encounter problems that defy easy solution. The former must create 1.0–1.2 million jobs, the latter 2.5–4.8 million jobs.

Interestingly, in the event the second scenario is realized, the employment pressure on economic growth in Kazakhstan will even decrease.

It is worth remembering that in all five countries the economy is already burdened with a surplus labor force. Chapter Two presented calculations showing that, in 1998, Kazakhstan—without any loss—could in principle release 20 percent of those employed in the economy. The corresponding figure is 37 percent in Kyrgyzstan and 18 percent in Uzbekistan. Tajikistan and Turkmenistan are similarly burdened, in the same massive character, with a surplus, inefficient work force.

Apart from the population, there is one more economic parameter that one can, rather confidently, predict for the midterm perspective: the amount of arable land. During the years of Soviet rule, all the Central Asian countries, which are located in the zone of an arid climate, reached a maximum in the utilization of land resources. If one takes into account investments and other limitations, in the next decades—according to the best-case scenario—the states of the region will succeed in sustaining a tolerable condition whereby the arable land won from nature during the years of earlier development will remain under cultivation. However, in the case of Kazakhstan, even that scenario is unrealistic. In 1991–98, it already lost almost 27 percent of the cultivable land area, a process that is still under way.[8]

Taking into account the demographic forecasts, the present author has estimated the per capita availability of cultivable land in the Central Asian countries by the year 2015 (see Table 8.3). The greatest pressure on land will be in Tajikistan. By 2015, in terms of the per capita arable land, this country will be on the same level as China in the mid-1990s. Uzbekistan will be on the level of contemporary Tajikistan. In this respect, the situation will be relatively better in Kyrgyzstan and Turkmenistan. Only in Kazakhstan, because of its enormous territorial expanse and the relatively modest size of its population, will the relative deficiency of arable land not be threatening, even if things develop in the worst possible way.

An analysis of the prospective scenarios for the development of the Central Asian states makes it possible to draw several general conclusions. First, if one excludes the unlikely prospect of an oil and gas boom in Kazakhstan and Turkmenistan, then all five countries will have to make extraordinary economic efforts in order to restore the level of development that they had already attained at the time when the USSR was disbanded. One would like to be wrong here, but unfortunately there is no reason to expect that Central Asia will experience an "economic miracle" like that of East Asia.

Second, the conditions for economic (hence social and political) development in the region will become substantially more complicated in

Table 8.3

Arable Land Resources
(hectares per capita)

Country	1995	2015[a]
Kazakhstan[b]	1.91	1.31 (1.46)[c]
		1.07 (1.19)[d]
Kyrgyzstan	0.28	0.21[c]
		0.19[d]
Tajikistan	0.15	0.07[d]
Turkmenistan	0.31	0.22[d]
Uzbekistan	0.19	0.13[d]
Algeria	0.29	
Afghanistan	0.42	
China	0.08	
Morocco	0.33	
Pakistan	0.15	
Tunisia	0.34	

Sources: Confederation of Independent States in 1998; *FAO Production Yearbook. 1995* 49 (Rome, 1996):19, 21, 23, 27–28, 30, 65–66; sources cited in Table 8.1.

[a]It is assumed that in 2015 the total amount of arable land in the Central Asian states will remain the same as in the mid-1990s.

[b]In 1990–1995, the total amount of arable land in Kazakhstan fell by 10 percent; therefore, the calculations for this country in 2015 are given in two variants. The first figure assumes that Kazakhstan does not succeed in stopping the decline of arable land, which will fall another 10 percent; the second figure (in parentheses) assumes that the country is able to stop the decrease.

[c]Forecast prepared by the national statistical services or research institutes.

[d]Calculations based on prognoses prepared by the State Statistical Committee of the former USSR.

the next decades. The local economies (primarily those in Kyrgyzstan, Tajikistan, and Uzbekistan) will obviously be incapable of coping with the stresses generated by demographic pressures. Indeed, surplus employment had already reached enormous proportions by the end of the 1980s. In the following decade, the employment situation became still more acute. The capacity of agriculture and the service sphere, which are already overburdened with a surplus workforce, to absorb additional labor is finite. Until the present time, neither Uzbekistan, Kyrgyzstan, nor especially Tajikistan has demonstrated any kind of coherent approach to the problem of employment. To a large degree, that failure is due to the lack of resources at the disposal of the national governments. Nor will those resources to deal with this problem be augmented any time in the foreseeable future.

Third, the high rates of growth in the population and workforce will be aggravated by a shortage of arable land. It is well known that one of the main causes of the disintegration of Tajikistan in 1991–94 was the extremely acute competition for land as the main factor of production. By the year 2015, in terms of per capita areas of available arable land, Uzbekistan will be on approximately the same plane as Tajikistan in the mid-1990s. With corresponding intensity, therefore, Uzbekistan will face the probability of instability because of this struggle for land. Just as quickly there will appear a relative shortage of land in the southern areas of Kyrgyzstan. In characterizing the numerous interethnic conflicts in the Osh oblast of the country, Bekut Beshimov (a deputy of the Kyrgyz parliament) describes them as "a rapidly growing population struggling over scarce land resources in a multiethnic environment."[9] An analogous situation is taking shape all across the overpopulated Fergana valley.

Fourth, the relative shortage of land is aggravated by the low productivity of agrarian complexes in the countries of Central Asia. Thus, in the first half of the 1990s, the yield of cereals in Uzbekistan was only 64 percent of that in China, while in Tajikistan it was only 36 percent of the Chinese level.[10]

These and many other factors argue quite persuasively that, in the period under review here, the economic structure of the Central Asian countries will undergo a process of "primitivization." The further drift of Kyrgyzstan, Tajikistan, and Uzbekistan toward the ranks of least developed countries is due not only to the failures of the current economic policy, but also to structural problems beyond the control of national governments.

These estimates suggest that the economic burden on agriculture in Central Asia, with the exception of Kazakhstan and to some degree Turkmenistan, will continue to intensify. That alone demands a more detailed analysis of the situation in the agrarian sector.

Agriculture

The oil and gas issue dominates discussion about the problem of development in Central Asia. However, with the exception of Kazakhstan, the economies of the Central Asian states are primarily agrarian. Thus, agriculture's share of the GDP was 44 percent in Kyrgyzstan (1998), 31 percent in Uzbekistan (1997), and 38 percent in Tajikistan (1995).[11] Moreover, in these same three countries, the contribution from agriculture to the production of added value exceeded that from the industrial branches and construction.

Still more salient is the dominant role of agriculture in the employment structure. In 1998, the agrarian sector accounted for 64 percent of the aggregate labor force in Tajikistan, 48 percent in Kyrgyzstan, 46 percent in Turkmenistan, 40 percent in Uzbekistan, and 24 percent in Kazakhstan.[12] In Tajikistan, Kyrgyzstan, and Turkmenistan agriculture is the dominant sphere of employment. In Uzbekistan, this sector is equal to the service sphere in generating jobs.

In all five Central Asian countries, agriculture provides more jobs than the secondary sector of industry and construction. Thus, in Tajikistan agriculture provides 5.6 times more jobs than the other sectors; the corresponding figure is 3.6 times in Kyrgyzstan, 2.5 times in Turkmenistan, 2.2 times in Uzbekistan, and 1.4 times in Kazakhstan.[13] Moreover, the role of agriculture in creating jobs is increasing. In other words, throughout the 1990s (and, in some cases, already in the 1980s) Central Asia underwent a process of re-agrarianization. This phenomenon is extremely complex and finds reflection in the growing proportion of the rural population, but also in the increasing contribution of agriculture in absorbing surplus labor.

It is important to make two basic principles explicit. First, re-agrarianization is an objective process in the transitional period. It occurs when the national economy and society as a whole pulverize and eliminate the structural proportions that existed within the framework of a single Soviet economic space, and when this emerging new society and economy acquire new structural parameters. Second, in all currently developed and successfully developing countries, agriculture acted (and acts) as a motor of development. It does so in the sense that agriculture does not simply provide an accelerated development of industry, but itself brings economic growth. It suffices only to look at the recent experience of Vietnam and China. Agriculture is not some secondary, insignificant element in the economic structure; it is, rather, the most important sector, which under certain conditions can function as a motor of development for the entire national economy.

What are the prevailing tendencies in the agrarian sector of the Central Asian states? Here it should be emphasized once again that the quality of post-Soviet statistics, which was already abysmal, has degraded to an unacceptable level during the last two years. Nevertheless, it is possible to use this mass of available statistical material by applying the appropriate cross-checking; by employing that approach, in most cases one can overcome specific deficiencies and difficulties.

In the 1990s, the Central Asian countries—both in the literal and figurative sense—"devoured" the fixed productive capital that had been accumulated in the agrarian sector (see Table 8.4).

The picture that has emerged in Kazakhstan is particularly dismal. In less than a decade, this country lost more than one-quarter of its arable land. If one also considers the low efficiency of Kazakhstan's crop cultivation, the loss of arable land was largely predetermined. However, there are no grounds to consider that this process represents an optimization and jettisoning of the worst lands received from the former Soviet Union.

With respect to animal husbandry, the rate of contraction in the head of livestock was still higher. In just eight years, the number of cattle decreased by half and the number of sheep and goats fell to one quarter of their earlier number. The decrease in the number of sheep and goats was almost as great in Kyrgyzstan.

Taken by themselves, these facts cannot be evaluated either positively or negatively. In Vietnam, for example, especially in the first years of economic reform, the number of hogs decreased because the government ceased to subsidize the grain that had been used as livestock feed. On the other hand, the export of cereals became extremely profitable for the producers, since the government deregulated prices and decentralized foreign trade. However, Central Asia has not witnessed any significant positive changes in the agrarian sector. Animal husbandry, especially in Kazakhstan and Kyrgyzstan, continues to decline. In Kazakhstan, cereal production is also quickly going to ruin.

In the next few years, Kazakhstan must expect a massive new collapse in animal husbandry as a consequence of the record-low harvest of cereals in the 1997–98 agricultural year. Kyrgyzstan, in the second half of the 1990s, succeeded in slowing the process whereby arable land went out of production; indeed, it even managed to increase slightly the number of cattle. However, the head of sheep and goats continued to decline, although not as quickly as in the first half of the decade.

Tajikistan is also continuing to "devour" its fixed productive assets in crop cultivation and animal husbandry. It is revealing that the scale of losses in the agrarian sector of this country (which has still not recovered from the ruin of chaos and war) is hardly much more than in Kyrgyzstan. Chapter Two drew attention to the fact that, despite the

Table 8.4

Characteristics of the Agrarian Sector in Central Asia, 1991–1998[a]
(Base year 1991 = 100)

Country	Year	Cultivated land area	Number of cattle	Number of sheep and cattle
Kazakhstan	1991	100	100	100
	1995	90	71	57
	1998	73	42	30
Kyrgyzstan	1991	100	100	100
	1995	93	73	45
	1998	93	77	40
Tajikistan	1991	100	100	100
	1995	100	82	74
	1998	78	75	66
Turkmenistan	1991	100	100	100
	1995	100	82	74
	1998	123		
Uzbekistan	1991	100	100	100
	1995	102	102	92
	1998		102	85

Sources: Commonwealth of Independent States in 1998, pp. 206, 221, 266, 281, 296.
[a]Some indicators are calculated for earlier periods.

fundamental differences in ideology of reform and economic policy, the interim macroeconomic results of the market transition in these two countries are quite similar. A detailed analysis of the agrarian sector confirms that proposition.

Only Uzbekistan succeeded in increasing, if slightly, the amount of arable land and also to mitigate somewhat the impact of destructive processes on animal husbandry. To be sure, it is difficult to rid oneself of the impression that from the mid-1990s the Uzbek statistics have become still less reliable than before. The fact that the key economic indicators of this country have been subjected to statistical manipulation is becoming ever more obvious.

Such considerations, along with skepticism about official statistics, are still more apropos of Turkmenistan. Were one to believe the official statistics, the agrarian sector in that country has achieved impressive successes.

It is clear that the "devouring" of cattle became an organic element in the adaptation to new social-economic conditions for the dominant part of the population in Central Asia. Put quite simply, they were deprived of any other way to sustain their physical survival.

In general, various tendencies have been gaining momentum in the agrarian sector, and these will substantially complicate economic growth in the Central Asian states in the mid- and long-term perspective. It would actually be more accurate to say that certain earlier tendencies (which had already emerged in the Soviet era) still continue to operate. Indeed, they have merely acquired their maximum intensity during the post-Soviet era.

First, the absolute number of people employed in agriculture has increased in all the countries of Central Asia (see Table 8.5). In Kyrgyzstan and Turkmenistan, the agrarian sector remains the principal reservoir for the accumulation of jobs. Even in Kazakhstan, after the substantial contraction in 1990–1995, thereafter agrarian jobs again began to increase at a rather fast pace.

Second, the productivity of labor continues to decrease in the agrarian sector, a dynamic that in turn affects the stability of the entire process of economic growth. In Kyrgyzstan and Uzbekistan, this decline was already apparent in the 1980s. In 1990–95, the productivity of agrarian labor fell an additional 57 percent in Kyrgyzstan, 21 percent in Kazakhstan, and 18 percent in Uzbekistan. In the second half of the 1990s, Uzbekistan succeeded in slowing somewhat this fall in the productivity of labor in agriculture, while Kyrgyzstan even managed to demonstrate a certain growth. In Kazakhstan, however, labor productivity in agriculture fell another 23 percentage points.

Third, in the 1990s, the fall in labor productivity in the agrarian sector was apparent both with regard to the economy as a whole, but especially in the secondary sector.

All these tendencies developed against a background where any kind of fundamental institutional improvement in agriculture was lacking (with the exception of Kyrgyzstan). The key institutional improvement, which is acutely needed in transition countries, is the development of private farms. However, private farmers cultivate only 9.9 percent of the arable land in Uzbekistan, 3.2 percent in Tajikistan, and 0.9 percent in Turkmenistan (see Table 8.6).

Why should all these tendencies be unqualifiedly treated as negative phenomena? The first pattern—the collapse of animal husbandry with-

Table 8.5

Employment and Productivity in the Agricultural Sector

Country	Year	Employment (1990 = 100)	Output per worker (1990 = 100)	Relative productivity in agriculture	
				Total economy = 1	Industry and construction = 1
Kazakhstan	1980	90	99		
	1990	100	100	0.54	0.30
	1995	84	79	0.60	0.42
	1998	90	56	0.45	0.24
Kyrgyzstan	1980	80	106		
	1990	100	100	1.18	1.23
	1995	120	43	0.95	0.81
	1998	129	55	1.03	0.62
Uzbekistan	1980	71	131		
	1990	100	100	0.75	0.65
	1995	120	82	0.80	0.56
	1998	124	80	0.73	0.46

Sources: See Tables 2.1 and 2.3.

Table 8.6

Economic Significance of Private Farms in Central Asia

Country	Year	Number of private farmers	Population per private farmer	Rural population per private farmer	Percent of arable land assigned to farmer
Kazakhstan	1998	65,000	239	110	20[a]
Kyrgyzstan	1998	45,100	104	70	22[b]
Tajikistan	1998	9,300	658	493	3.2[a]
Turkmenistan	1997	1,800	2,646	1,508	0.9
Uzbekistan	1997	24,000	1,002	631	9.9

Source: Commonwealth of Independent States in 1998, pp. 201, 206, 216, 221, 261, 266, 276, 281, 291, 296.
[a]Data for the year 1997.
[b]Data for the year 1996.

out any positive parallel improvements in other sectors—is manifestly negative and requires no explanation. The decline of labor productivity in the agrarian sector and the disturbing lack of institutional improvements attest to the serious violations of the "iron laws" of development.

Reference here is to those unalterable conditions that determine the prospects not only of the agrarian sector, but the entire course of economic growth as a whole. Research on economic growth, drawing upon centuries of experience, has identified these "iron laws," which empirically presuppose at least four main elements:

- The productivity of labor in the agrarian sector must steadily increase.
- Parallel to the above, independent private farms should increase their share of the aggregate output of agricultural production.
- Stable industrial growth is possible only in those countries that have observed the first two conditions (in particular, the increase in labor productivity).[14]
- The direct ties and feedback between agriculture and the manufacturing industry should develop and be strengthened. In other words, industrial branches should have a demand for agricultural products, while the rural population and agricultural sector should become an important market for the industrial goods produced in the country.

To be sure, the developed international division of labor has seriously modified the "iron laws of development," as extrapolated from the experience of today's developed countries. This is especially true of the interaction between agriculture and manufacturing. However, unless these conditions are observed and adapted to the imperatives of globalization, economic growth is doomed to a painful breakdown, with grave social consequences.

As indicated above, Central Asia has not observed a single one of these categorical imperatives. This means that the region has, in an accelerated fashion, accumulated the potential for a powerful crisis, which sooner or later will inevitably explode into destructive social turmoil. The Russian Empire experienced that kind of disintegration in 1917. That collapse had been preceded by two decades of attempts to compartmentalize the agrarian crisis and the failed reform of P.A. Stolypin, who tried unsuccessfully to create a strong new class of private farmers.

However, economic policy conducted in the region until recently discriminates against the agrarian sector. The latter has been transformed into a resource donor for import-substitution in industry (as in Uzbekistan), or is used in the interests of trading intermediaries (as in Kazakhstan and Kyrgyzstan). The proportion of budgetary, credit, and investment resources channeled to the agrarian sector does not correspond to its role and significance in the economy of these countries. Forced to rely upon the role of donor to other sectors of the economy, agriculture itself is amassing—at an accelerated rate—the potential for a fundamental crisis.

Until now, only Kyrgyzstan has shown some weak signs of a shift in government policy so as to give more attention to agriculture. It proclaimed 1998 a year for the struggle against poverty. However, practical realization of this anti-poverty program imperatively presumes a reorientation of financial and material resources toward the agrarian sector, but not a single Central Asian state is independently prepared to do that. Foreign donors must encourage and push the local governments to make this change in policy. This is all the more true given the fact, as already demonstrated, that the resources for development in the region come principally from abroad.

The present policy, if maintained, will promote the preservation of a dual economic structure and increase the gap between the export (global) and nonexport (local) sectors. However, the Central Asian states themselves as well as the largest foreign donors are coming, increasingly, to understand the danger of continuing this policy. One of the difficulties blocking the needed change in policy is the fact that the process of development in Kazakhstan, Kyrgyzstan, and Uzbekistan has acquired its own inertia; it is no simple matter to overcome this. Moreover, changes in the macroeconomic policy must be precisely geared to the specific conditions prevailing in these countries. Notwithstanding the presence of some common and typical features, the development of the Central Asian countries is distinguished by considerable uniqueness.

It is interesting to evaluate the experience of Uzbekistan in the light of what has just been said. Here the government has deliberately frozen the economic situation in agriculture; moreover, it assumes that accelerated industrialization will allow the country, in the future, to begin resolving problems in other sectors of the economy. The agrarian sector remains a donor for industry and the urban social sphere, while the characteristics of efficiency in agriculture itself are falling. Moreover, this situation first appeared after the country became independent, but actually dates back to the late 1970s.

In this writer's view, the government's approach was in general justified during 1990–94, when an independent state was first emerging. However, once Uzbekistan consolidated its independence, this policy became counterproductive. The industrial and investment policy pursued in this country discriminates against the agrarian sector, light industry, and textiles. Whereas the proportion of agriculture in the GDP of Uzbekistan amounted to 31 percent in 1997, and whereas this sector accounted for 41 percent of all jobs, the share of aggregate capital investment amounted to just 6.9 percent in agriculture and 4.0 percent in the light and textile industry.[15]

Thus a paradoxical situation has taken shape. Uzbekistan has a comparative advantage precisely in the agrarian sphere, but does not even attempt to rely upon these advantages. This pattern was also a symptomatic deficiency in the earlier Soviet system of economic management. Thus, in 1997, after six years of independent development, Uzbekistan processes just 15 percent of the cotton fiber produced in the country.

Uzbekistan is losing time as it defers the large-scale institutional reform needed in the agrarian sector. Of all Central Asia, only the Uzbeks and Tajiks have a centuries-old experience of working the land; only Uzbekistan has the objective basis for developing grassroots capitalism (that is, small and medium-sized entrepreneurship). Nevertheless, one does not see any serious institutional reform in the agrarian sector, or in the sphere of small-scale industry. All this is clearly apparent from the data presented in Table 8.7.

Finally, and perhaps most important, the policy currently being pursued does not contribute to resolving the problem of employment. Agriculture is already overburdened with excess employment; indeed, in recent years, the situation here has been stretched to the extreme limits. Industrial production created with the assistance of foreign investment and credits, by contrast, is very capital-intensive and has a limited demand for labor. In this author's view, the Uzbek economy will—in the very near future—find itself being squeezed by demographic pressures and the negative balance of payments.

The most glaring indicator of the declining efficiency of the agrarian sector is the absolute and relative decrease in the use of modern machinery and equipment. Whereas in 1992–93 machines were used to harvest approximately 40 percent of the raw cotton, this indicator had fallen to 6 percent in 1996 and then to 4 percent in 1997. In the main producer oblasts (Bukhara and Fergana), manual labor was used to harvest the entire cotton crop in 1997.[16]

Therefore, Uzbekistan has conducted a Soviet type of industrial policy

Table 8.7

Development of Private Farmers *(Dekhkane)* **in Uzbekistan**

Year	Number of private farms	Land cultivated (thousands of hectares)	Share of total arable land	Average size of private farms (hectares)
1990	1,358	9.1	0.2	6.7
1991	1,868	13.7	0.3	7.3
1992	5,492	45.1	1.1	7.6
1993	7,538	70.6	1.7	9.4
1994	14,236	193.1		13.6
1995	18,085	264.6		14.6
1996	19,828	308.2		15.1

Sources: Timur Nizayev, "State Supports Private Entrepreneurship," *Central Asian Post*, no. 11 (20 March 1997), p. 3; *Osnovnye pokazateli sotsial' no-ekonomicheskogo razvitiia Respubliki Uzbekistan za 1996 god* (Tashkent, 1997), p. 135; Statisticheskii komitet SNG, *Statisticheskii biulleten' SNG*, no. 11 (Moscow 1996), p. 106; *Narodnoe khoziaistvo Respubliki Uzbekistan v 1993 g. Statisticheskii ezhegodnik* (Tashkent, 1994), pp. 308, 421; *Uzbekistan za gody nezavisimosti* (Tashkent, 1994), pp. 4, 13–14.

parallel to the progressive de-industrialization of agriculture. To be sure, in the short term, the massive utilization of cheap labor has made it possible to mitigate the acute problem of finding jobs for the population. However, in the long-term perspective, this is preventing the formation and development of viable and efficient structures in the agrarian sector.

Despite its unfavorable condition, agriculture continues to be used as the "milk cow" for other sectors of the economy. Suffice it to say that in 1996 the state procurement prices on cotton were 26.6 percent below the actual costs of production. In 1997, for each ton of cotton that producers sold to the government, they lost 22.7 percent of the funds spent to produce it.[17] In the final analysis, the government covered these losses, since it regularly writes off the accumulated debts owned by agricultural producers to their suppliers and to the banking sector. However, this artificially maintained "unprofitability" does not simply deflate the pompous official rhetoric about the supposedly profound transformations in the agrarian sphere. The producers are forced to operate within the framework of some kind of general abstract plan of development— regardless of the level of their own production costs. There is absolutely no point in talking about any kind of positive prospects for these producers. They cannot independently plan even their own production process, construct a financial plan of work, or purchase intermediate goods and equipment.

Agriculture, like virtually all other sectors of the economy in Uzbekistan, is incorporated into the general state plan of development. This is analogous to the situation that prevailed in the Soviet Union. Predictably, the results of economic development in that kind of state-factory are also similar.

How is the profit, created by cotton growing and in certain branches of the extractive industry, being expended? The majority goes to realize the state's industrial policy (see further details in Chapter Four). A smaller part is used to reconstruct the agrarian sector itself.

The main limit to the expansion of agricultural production in Uzbekistan is the shortage of land and water. The area of arable land here has stabilized since the mid-1990s at the level of 4.1 million hectares; water consumption has similarly remained at the level of 45 to 46 billion cubic meters.[18] Even if one imagines that by some miracle Uzbekistan succeeds in overcoming the water shortage, it would lack the equipment for new irrigated land because of the lack of investments. The area of irrigated land, which increased more than threefold during the years of Soviet rule, was possible only because of the nonmarket character of Soviet economics, which simply did not pay any attention to costs.[19]

Under these conditions, it is possible to ensure the growth of production only by internal shifts within the agriculture sector itself. In 1990–97, the sown area here was partly redistributed from cotton to cereals. As a result, the area used to raise cotton decreased from 1.83 to 1.54 million hectares; hence cotton's share of the total area under cultivation fell from 44 to 37 percent. The area used to grow cereals, by contrast, increased by 814,000 hectares; its share of total crop land rose from 24 to 44 percent.[20]

As a result of this reallocation of land use, the gross harvest of cereals rose from an average of 2.05 million tons in 1990–93 to an average of 3.24 million tons in 1994–97. The average annual cotton harvest during these same two periods fell from 4.52 to 3.72 million tons.[21] No kind of substantial gains in the efficiency of production were to be observed with respect to cotton. Although the average annual yield of cereals did increase by 9 percent, the average yield of cotton in this period fell by 5 percent.[22]

To be sure, by increasing the production of grain, Uzbekistan has an opportunity to reduce imports of this commodity and thereby close a serious, regular gap in its balance of payments. At the same time, given the contraction of losses from the export of cotton, the balance of pluses and minuses is far from transparent. However, the calculations of Eskender Trushin and the estimates by experts of the World Bank show that each hectare of cotton produces 1.2 to 4.5 times more added value than does a hectare used to raise cereals.[23]

This restructuring of the agricultural sector in Uzbekistan is mandated not by economic expediency, but by considerations of a falsely understood "national security." The Soviet experience, however, amply demonstrated the total futility of this goal if pursued without regard to the laws of the marketplace.

* * *

Even if the largest Central Asian states develop at the maximum possible rates and in accordance with the most favorable scenario (which is anything but certain), then by the year 2015 Kazakhstan and Uzbekistan will only have succeeded in restoring the level of development that they achieved by the beginning of the 1990s. In other words, they will have required a quarter century to overcome the regression spawned by the transition and transformation. Moreover, reference here is only to a single indicator of economic activity—the gross domestic product. The per capita volume of goods and services available to the population in 2015 will be substantially less than it was in 1990.

The capital-intensive and labor-saving character of development, which all the Central Asian countries are largely forced to follow, does not correspond to their basic demographic and social profiles. The experience of many developing countries that have a massive agrarian periphery and that at one time adhered to the policy of an accelerated and imbalanced industrialization has shown that the positive spillover effects of this model are negligible.[24] In contrast to the agrarian and service-oriented variants of development, the industrially obsessed model of development absolutely cannot contribute to the liquidation of zones of poverty and destitution.

By 1997, signs were already clearly apparent that the models of development chosen by the Central Asian governments in the first years of independence were in serious need of correction. The imperative for a responsible economic strategy is to find some kind of balance so as to promote the development of a capital-intensive and internationalized export sector and yet provide support for local productive forces. One of the main priorities of economic policy, at any event in Kyrgyzstan, Tajikistan, Uzbekistan, and to a significant degree in Turkmenistan, should be agriculture.

The real needs of these countries consist in an agrarian reform that is austere and maximally egalitarian (in the initial phases). It must also include the formation of a system of micro-credits for small and petty producers in the real productive sectors, as well as the organization of massive public works to reduce the gravity of such problems as poverty and destitution.

Moreover, the "global" and "local" economic sectors should not be regarded as mutually exclusive. Rather, the art of economic policymaking should be to create opportunities for the parallel development of both sectors. If this new direction is not taken, then spontaneous regulators will take charge. Social protest movements by the lower classes will periodically demolish the accumulated economic potential and, for a short time, ensure the flow of resources to the agrarian sector by sheer force. Moreover, however cynical this might sound, a special demographic adjustment will commence in Central Asia. Through mass starvation and epidemics, the population of countries in the region will contract to a level that corresponds to its fragile economic potential.

In the developing world, there are many countries that for decades remain in a condition of depressed or semi-depressed stability. As an analogue to Uzbekistan, for example, one could cite the case of Algeria, where the average annual rate of growth in the GDP amounted to just 2.1 percent during the period 1980–97.[25] An analogue for Kyrgyzstan is Mongolia, which, in the course of the last seventy years, has developed at an annual average rate of 2.6 percent.[26]

The entire sum of economic, social, and political information on contemporary Central Asia forces one to assume that a "controlled degradation" or a "depressed stabilization" is the most likely scenario for further development. In the twentieth century, Central Asia has survived two revolutionary cataclysms. In the 1920s, an economic system of the Soviet type was forcibly superimposed on this region; that new system demolished the nomadic and semi-nomadic economies of Kazakhstan, Kyrgyzstan, and Turkmenistan, and it seriously deformed agriculture in Tajikistan and Uzbekistan. In the late 1980s, the Soviet economic system began to disintegrate, once again exposing Central Asia to destructive impulses from without.

The question of whether the countries and peoples who traversed the Soviet experiment can offer something more than a "controlled degradation" remains unanswered. Of course, even that path does not exclude various economic successes and even breakthroughs in certain branches. However, the foregoing analysis has demonstrated that the Central Asian countries themselves lack the preconditions to make a transition from the trajectory of "controlled degradation" to a trajectory of stable, rapid, economic growth.

It is possible to ensure this transition only by relying upon outside factors. The formation of a long-term strategy of development, which makes it possible to incorporate the national economy organically into the global economy, and to activate local productive forces to the maximum degree possible—this is the chief intellectual and political challenge that confronts the ruling elites in the Central Asian countries at the start of the twenty-first century.

Notes

1. International Monetary Fund, *World Economic Outlook. Spring, 1999* (Washington, DC, 1999), p. 15.

2. N. Mikhailov, "Grozit li miru zolotaia likhoradka," *Finansovaia Rossiia* (Moscow), no. 19 (20–26 May 1999), p. 7.

3. Ibid.; A. Karetnikov, "Zapovedi predkov i legenda kirgizskikh reform," *Obshchaia gazeta* (Moscow), no. 12 (25–31 March 1999), p. 5.

4. I. Kriviakina, "Rossiia zarabotaet na tranzite kaspiiskoi nefti," *Finansovaia Rossiia*, no. 19 (20–26 May 1999), p. 2.

5. *Panorama*, no. 43 (6 November 1998), p. 9.

6. See *Commonwealth of Independent States in 1998*, p. 56; *National Corporation Uzbekneftegaz* (Tashkent, 1998), p. 50.

7. For details, see Chapter Two in this volume.

8. Interstate Statistical Committee, *Commonwealth of Independent States in 1998* (Moscow, 1999), p. 206; Natsstatagentstvo Respubliki Kazakhstan, *Sotsial'no-ekonomicheskoe polozhenie Respubliki Kazakhstan, ianvar'-dekabr' 1998*, no. 12 (Almaty, 1999), p. 24.

9. V. Cheterian, "Pressure-Cooking in the Ferghana Valley," *Transitions* (Budapest) 6 (1999): 52.

10. Calculated from the sources cited in Table 8.3.

11. See *Commonwealth of Independent States in 1998*, p. 17, and Table 2.3.

12. Calculated from data in *Commonwealth of Independent States in 1998*, pp. 201, 216, 261, 276, 291.

13. Ibid.

14. J. Waelbroek and I. Adelman, "Agricultural Development Led Industrialization in a Global Perspective" (paper presented to the Eighth World Economic Congress, New Delhi, December 1986).

15. *Osnovnye pokazateli sotsial' no-ekonomicheskogo razvitiia Respubliki Uzbekistan za 1996 god* (Tashkent, 1997), p. 137; and Chapter Two, Table 2.3.

16. I. Karimov, "Razvitie sel'skogo khoziaistva—istochnik blagosostoianiia naroda," *Ekonomika i statistika* (Tashkent, 1998), no. 2: 8.

17. M. Iusupov, "Sposoby finansovogo ozdorovleniia sel'skogo khoziaistva," *Rynok, den' gi i kredit* (Tashkent, 1998), no. 7 (July): 21.

18. Statisticheskii komitet SNG, *SNG v 1997 g. Statisticheskii ezhegodnik* (Moscow, 1998), p. 606; *Narodnoe khoziaistvo Respubliki Uzbekistan v 1993 g.* (Tashkent, 1994), p. 283.

19. For details, see B. Rumer and S. Zhukov, "Economic Integration in Central Asia: Problems and Prospects," in *Central Asia. The Challenges of Independence*, ed. B. Rumer and S. Zhukov (Armonk, NY, 1998), pp. 131–33, 136; E. Trushin, "Uzbekistan: Problems of Development and Reform in the Agrarian Sector," in ibid., p. 263.

20. Calculated from data in *SNG v 1997g.*, p. 584.

21. Calculated from data in ibid., p. 587.

22. Calculated from data in ibid., pp. 584, 587.

23. Trushin, "Uzbekistan," p. 273.

24. For an example of the detailed econometric research on this problem, see: M. Ravallion and G. Datt, "How Important to India's Poor Is the Sectoral Composition of Economic Growth," *World Bank Economic Review* 10 (1996): 1–23.

25. World Bank, *World Development Report, 1998/99* (Washington, DC, 1998), p. 280.

26. Ibid., p. 281.

Index

About the Editor and Contributors

Oksana Reznikova is a senior research associate at the Institute of World Economy and International Relations (IMEMO), Russian Academy of Sciences.

Boris Rumer is an associate at the Davis Center at Harvard University.

Eskender Trushin and Eshref Trushin are economists conducting research in Tashkent, Uzbekistan.

Stanislav Zhukov is a senior research associate at the Institute of World Economy and International Relations (IMEMO), Russian Academy of Sciences.